THEOLOGICAL FOR⌐

If theological formation is a journey, then this work will serve as an indispensable guide to the major contours of Christian thought. With vast erudition of great thinkers and traditions, penetrating analyses of different perspectives, and exceptionally useful learning tools, Mark Ellingsen not only accompanies the readers but also empowers them to develop their own capacities as theologian-pastors.

—Daniel D. Shin, associate professor of Theology
and World Christianity, Drew University

Mark Ellingsen's *Theological Formation* is an introduction to theology that combines old and new in a way at once down-to-earth and scholarly. His fourteen chapters take up classic topics related to the Nicene creed, leading the reader through major traditional and modern options, concluding each chapter with even-handed advice on how readers can shape these options into their own theology. Ellingsen also helpfully includes outlines summarizing the options for students. The result is a book that will be helpful to Orthodox and Catholic, Lutheran and Reformed, Radical Reformation and Pentecostals, Fundamentalists and Liberals, and Nondenominationals in different countries—whether they be students in theology and religion departments or divinity schools and seminaries, or those in adult education programs in Christian congregations, or intelligent inquirers seeking theological formation for any number of reasons. There is nothing quite like it, and one can only hope it forms many in the next generation of theologians.

—James Buckley, professor of Theology emeritus,
Loyola University Maryland

In an age where the art of doing theology is irrelevant to some or too academic, complicated, and unintelligible to others, here is a volume that makes theology come alive for beginners, pastors, and those who teach it. A unique feature of the book is the classification of theological thought into models/typologies, with respectful treatment of diverse theological or denominational traditions under each *loci*, supported by extensive biblical and historical references. The depth and riches of theological thought is brilliantly presented in a succinct and easy to understand manner. A valuable tool for all students of theology.

—J. Paul Rajashekar, Luther D. Reed Professor of Systematic
Theology, United Lutheran Seminary, Philadelphia

MERCER UNIVERSITY PRESS

Endowed by

TOM WATSON BROWN
and
THE WATSON-BROWN FOUNDATION, INC.

THEOLOGICAL FORMATION

Making Theology Your Own

Mark Ellingsen

MERCER UNIVERSITY PRESS
Macon, Georgia
MMXX

MUP—P602

25 24 23 22 21 20   5 4 3 2 1

Books published by Mercer University Press are printed on acid-free paper that meets the
requirements of the American National Standard for Information Sciences—Permanence
of Paper for Printed Library Materials.

Printed and bound in the United States.

This book is set in Adobe Caslon Pro.

Cover/jacket design by Burt&Burt.

Library of Congress Cataloging-in-Publication Data

Names: Ellingsen, Mark, 1949- author.
Title: Theological formation : making theology your own / Mark Ellingsen.
Description: 1st. | Macon : Mercer University Press, 2020. | Includes
bibliographical references and index. |
Identifiers: LCCN 2020027590 | ISBN 9780881467475 (paperback)
Subjects: LCSH: Theology, Doctrinal. | Theology, Doctrinal—History.
Classification: LCC BT75.3 .E45 2020 | DDC 230.07—dc23
LC record available at https://lccn.loc.gov/2020027590

For

KATE

JACK

ADDIE

and any other Ellingsens or Santoses who might join them

ACKNOWLEDGMENTS

To write a book that might help get readers excited about Theology and the History of Christian Thought, to start doing Theology themselves, has been a real treat, a dialogue with the future. Of course I've spent more than 40 years doing that in the classroom and in congregations, undertaking this labor of love. But the fact that this work might be of some use to somebody after I'm not around makes it even better. It was studying and engaging in these disciplines that first made Christian faith come alive for me. Actually doing theology has formed my faith, given me tools and outlooks to deal with life—both the good and the bad. And so I hand this book over to you in hopes that it gets you thinking about yourself, your faith, and your life, that it contributes not just to your theological formation but your faith formation too.

Yes, this book is about the future, dedicated to helping readers become their own theologians, to further formation in the faith. But it's also a book of the present, a book written at a tough time for the American churches, as pews empty and the number of Religiously Unaffiliated grow. I didn't write it alone, for I was drawing on the giants of the faith for all the insights in this book. And then I've learned a lot from my students (especially those of the Interdenominational Theological Center) and parishioners over the years, not to mention my teachers at Yale and my colleagues in all my academic positions. Putting finishing touches on this book was facilitated by the work of the best copyeditor I've had for all twenty-two of my books. Thanks for your great work Patrick Jolley! Also thanks to the man who supervises everything at Mercer University Press, Marc Jolley, who has been a great supporter and advisor throughout the process. The best and most important of my present and past collaborators has been Betsey Shaw Ellingsen with whom I've shared nearly half a century of friendship, love, and collaboration (on this book too).

But a book about the future, about formation and faith, naturally leads me to think about the next generation of Ellingsens, Betsey's and my grandchildren. Since at my age I can't be sure of how many more book dedications I'll have to write, Betsey and I decided we would dedicate this one to the three we have already (Kate, Jack, and Addie) as well as any others who might appear, so just in case they will have had a book by their grandfather too. Both Betsey and I send this out to them with the same prayer I'm sending to all readers, that you and they will sometime share with me the fun and excitement that thinking about your faith and your life's meaning can provide, to have a life a formed by your worldview and by faith.

CONTENTS

INTRODUCTION

Theology is the Queen of the Sciences, it was said in the Middle Ages. She governs all sciences and other academic disciplines. They are all to be related to Theology or at least to Christian teachings. Theology was to have input on all areas of church life and ministry, to inform our reading of Scripture as well as what pastors do in administering programs and counseling (at least to correct us when we go astray in these undertakings). It is also intended to be a profound and helpful way to deal with questions about the meaning of life.

Alas the Queen has abdicated, retired (or been overthrown). Theology no longer seems to play this significant role in most churches, in the lives of pastors and laity, and certainly not in society. Other academic disciplines have been "liberated" from Theology since the Renaissance. And if any connections with Economics, Psychology, Political Science, Literature, or Science are made it needs to be initiated from Theology's side.

Likewise, Theology has lost its voice in the Church and its academies. You can graduate from some mainline church-related colleges without ever taking a course in Theology (or even Religious Studies). In many denominational seminaries, Theology and History of Christian Thought are not even taught until students first study the Bible and have some sort of Pastoral Care or Interpersonal Dynamics courses (and so students learn how to read the Bible and do Pastoral Care without any Theology). And in the parishes of America, too often you can forget it (as well as Bible study)! In that context as well as in denominational offices Psychology, Management Techniques, or Pop Culture are much more likely to guide community dynamics than theology. No surprise the Western church is facing the problems it is. As the famed modern Swiss theologian Karl Barth once wrote to pastors: If theology is not a joy, you'll probably abandon it on Sunday too, and then you'd better seek another line of work (*Church Dogmatics*, Vol. III/4, p. 68).

We clearly need more and better "Theological Formation": There is a deliberate ambiguity in the title of this book. On one hand theological formation refers to the formation of one's own theological understanding. It can also refer to the formation of a theological position. In addition "theological formation" may refer to the formation of the theological or Christian virtues along with the Christian outlook in one's life. The relevance of the theological discipline, any hope for its making a contribution in modern society and the Church, depends on keeping these dimensions of the phrase together.

This insight shapes the textbook you have in your hands and makes it different from other Introduction to Theology texts on the market. The old way of introducing theology is not working. Typically the textbook used is the authors' systematic or their historical analysis of how the various doctrines came to be formulated. Professors using these texts may add their own particular points of view in lectures. The results are often stimulating, refreshing insights about the Christian faith and the History of Christian Thought. But these classes are experienced by most students as mere *facts* they *have* to learn. Though the professor has likely found theology not just as an exciting intellectual exercise but also the most profound way to deal with questions about the meaning of life, most students enter such courses and even leave them convinced that it is all irrelevant. More often than not the instructor's passion for Theology never really gets communicated to the students. Little wonder that many students continue to find Theology a mere academic exercise with little real relevance.

This book tries to remedy these dynamics. It is a textbook that will teach some things, but its real purpose is not so much to teach Theology or the History of Christian Thought, but to prod students to learn how to do theology for themselves. The aim is to lay out all the historic options on each of the classical doctrines, providing fair and balanced articulation of the strengths, Biblical bases, and weaknesses of each option. Interspersed with these articulations, especially following the articulation of all the options on the issue considered, are questions aiming to get readers to think about what they believe. Corresponding to each chapter you also get Charts, which list all the options considered under each topic. This will be a handy tool in pulling together for yourself all that you have been reading, especially as you circle back from the chapter you are reading to those previously considered. Presenting the different historic options that have appeared on a given issue, with encouragement by the instructor and the study helps in this book, make it more likely that students will begin to stake out their own opinions on these various options. They will begin to assess which options they like, learn with which ones they disagree and why, and in so doing begin to define for themselves what it is they believe.

I hasten to add that with this approach I am not trying to stifle theological creativity, to contend that every theologian conforms to one of the options described. Like any typology, the ones in the Charts fall short. Charting the options on each doctrine is just a map or GPS. And just as really to understand the terrain you actually have to visit what's on the map, so users of the book need to spend time visiting (studying) the options I've sketched in order to discern what the map failed to portray. There may be other options I've missed in my typologies (though in many cases the typology I provide exhausts all the logical options on a given issue). Instructors may feel that they or other theologians have found positions transcending the typologies, found ways to synthesize the options listed. Great; let me and your students know. The point of the Charts is to get students of Theology and their teacher thinking about their own positions in relation to major options, to push them to gain as much specificity in their proposals as the options presented afford.

In short, this is a book to get you to *do* theology for yourself. And as you become clearer on your own position, the viewpoints of others (important historical figures and contemporary theologians) become more intriguing, because you can truly engage these thinkers in a dialogue. At the same time, as this sort of dialogue transpires, students begin to look at their own lives in light of these theological questions. When that happens, you not only begin to formulate your own theological perspective. You begin to see how your life has been or is being formed by these beliefs. (In fact, you probably believed these things all along, but just hadn't articulated this set of beliefs as clearly.) Theology becomes relevant. The Queen of the Sciences is back on the throne. This book aims to give college and seminary professors a tool to make this happen.

THE STRUCTURE OF THE BOOK

Chapters are arranged in accord with a relatively old-fashioned way of organizing Theology, the loci system. Thus with the exception of the first and last chapters, the order of topics considered in the chapters merely follows the order in which they are addressed by The Nicene Creed. But this order is intended to be neutral, not binding. There might be theological or existential reasons for students or instructors to proceed in a different order, consider some doctrine (the one he/she would emphasize) first—like Justification, Sanctification/Holiness, or even Eschatology.

A similar strategy explains why formal questions of Theological Method precede the chapters on the doctrines. My motives here are pedagogical, not prescriptive. It has been my experience in working with students that once theological students have taken a position on the character of the theological task, the nature of Scripture, and the like, they are well on their way to developing their own Theological Method. And once Methodological issues are clarified it becomes easier to organize the various doctrinal themes into a coherent whole, to determine which theological options have the strongest Biblical rationale, and how the construals theologians make of the various doctrines relate to each other.

These pedagogical considerations in no way mandate that the only way to do Theology is to clarify one's Method first before examining the doctrine embedded in the Creed. On the contrary, a number of theological perspectives presented in the first chapter would argue that because Methodological considerations are merely formal questions, one can begin to reflect on the material content of Christian faith prior to taking up questions of Method. In view of these considerations, then, readers should draw no systematic conclusions about how to do Theology from the way the chapters are arranged. In fact, it would be quite appropriate to use the book selectively. One might consider examining first a topic taken up later in the book and moving in reverse order or randomly.

USING THE TEXT

It is true that in writing this volume the principal audience I have in mind has been for Introduction to Theology or History of Christian Thought courses in undergraduate or seminary contexts. However the text could function satisfactorily at later stages of theological education, after students had mastered most of the fundamental concepts or the thought of certain important theologians.

Even outside academic environs, perhaps in parish study groups or pastoral meetings devoted to Continuing Education, this text might have a contribution to make. Wherever people are interested in formulating or refining a theological perspective, have a passion for clarifying what they believe, this text may serve as a partner in conversation. For it is in theological conversation among Christians in community that theological formation really happens.

Back to the academy or to the theologically astute parish pastor: Obviously if instructors are looking for fresh cutting-edge theological insights by the author, this is not the book for them. This is a book for stimulating conversation. And because I am using typologies to characterize the various historic options on the classical doctrines, professors may contend that their own position is more nuanced or richer than the options listed. In that case, dialogue with the typologies may help them better articulate the uniqueness of their own positions in relation to those options.

The book will function well in courses where the instructor assigns students a paper on what they believe early in the term or different papers on each one of the topics in this volume. Having sketched a position on some of these topics, students should then be able to identify in the lists in the appropriate chapter the position that best captures or summarizes their point of view. The brief exposition correlated with the relevant position will provide students and their peers with critical commentary and additional questions concerning their positions, as well as the theologians whom they should consult for more insights and depth. This makes possible dialogue with the great theologians associated/identified with these views, and in so doing makes them and their ideas relevant to students.

Instructors might enter the theological formation process initiated by this book in a variety of ways. They might choose to meet privately with students in order to extrapolate on the brief exposition in the book. They might wish to provide such commentary in the classroom. Likewise there may be flexibility with regard to assignments. A course using this text need not be a writing course (especially if it is used outside the academic environ, such as in the parish).

The volume can work as long as some format is provided which furnishes opportunities for students to articulate or think about their own views on theological subjects. The text might serve at any stage of theological education in a course devoted to almost any theologian or classical subject. As students begin to formulate their reactions to the material being studied, this volume might be consulted and might prod them to refining their initial insights.

Theological formation, both in the sense of developing one's own theological position/s and also in the sense of having one's life formed by one's beliefs is a process, a process that happens best in community and in dialogue. This book is just a companion; the options it presents are just dialogue partners for the journey.

I

THEOLOGICAL METHOD

Theological Method is not properly speaking a doctrine. But it is an essential element in the formation of a Theology. Because of the topic's complexity, this will need to be the longest chapter. And yet the self-conscious importance this issue has for a theologian may vary. Those theologians opting for numerous sources for her/his theology are more likely to make Theological Method a starting point for reflection (Justin Martyr, *First Apology*, xlvi; Friedrich Schleiermacher, *The Christian Faith*, 1–3; John Mbiti, *Christian Century* [27 August–3 September, 1980]). While those with theological commitments just to the authority of Scripture and Tradition or to Scripture Alone often de-emphasize Methodological questions or even make Methodological decisions only in an ad hoc manner. (Clement of Rome [*Epistle To the Corinthians*, XLV], Karl Barth [*Church Dogmatics*, Vol. I/1, #5] and modern Biblical Narrative Theology [George Lindbeck, *The Nature of Doctrine*, 116–117] illustrate this approach.)

Essentially Theological Method is the topic that encourages us to sort out our positions on five related issues: (1) Sources of Authority; (2) One's starting-point for theological reflection; (3) How the authority of Scripture is construed; (4) Hermeneutical Tools employed in interpreting the faith (like the Law-Gospel dialectic, Dispensationalism, etc); and (5) Proofs of God's Existence. We begin by laying out the historic options of the first of these five issues.

SOURCES OF AUTHORITY

Virtually every classical Christian theologian has identified Scripture as a source of authority (2 Timothy 3:16). But there is a history of controversy about the nature of the canon. As a result, in the earliest decades of the Church's history dating back to the Apostolic Fathers like Clement of Rome and Ignatius of Antioch, Scripture and Tradition functioned together as sources of authority. This was of course necessary prior to the actual formation of the Biblical canon.

There is little doubt that during its first decades, the Church relied on oral tradition about Jesus more than written texts about Him. (Even though the Hebrew Bible was available in many churches, most early Christians knew its contexts orally.) By the second century the Church had not only asserted the authority of Hebrew Bible against a heretic named Marcion who had tried to negate the Old Testament, but most of the texts which form the New Testament today were in use.

Though several lists of New Testament Books appeared earlier, the oldest list to include all the Books of our Bible (including the Apocrypha) appeared in AD 367 in the writings of the ancient Alexandrian Bishop, Athanasius (*Epistles*, XXXIX.4–5). Given Athanasius' African roots, it is significant that Councils of the North African church (Hippo in 393 and Carthage in 397) affirmed this list officially.

Having a binding decision on the Books of the Biblical Canon has by no means led the Church catholic to eliminate other sources of authority. The majority of theologians throughout history, especially Roman Catholics and those of the Eastern churches, have continued to affirm the *Authority* of *Scripture and Tradition*. Among these theologians, though, a disagreement emerges regarding how we determine authentic Tradition.

First we need to be clear that for these theologians not everything we encounter that is said to be our tradition at the local level qualifies as binding, authoritative tradition. *Tradition* (with a capital "T") is the living voice of the dead from all over the Church. It refers to what the Church has taught everywhere throughout its history. The doctrines pertaining to the Trinity and Christ are examples. How broadly is Tradition defined, what affirmation belong to it, is largely a function of denominational differences and how each understands Tradition to be established.

The Roman Catholic heritage posits a *Conciliar Model* for Tradition. Based on references to The Jerusalem Council of Acts 15, which addressed the question of admission of the Gentiles to the Church, Roman Catholicism insists that those actions of the Councils of the Church are infallible and binding on the faithful. This is designated as the *Ordinary Magisterium* (*Catechism of the Catholic Church*, 884).

In addition, the Catholic Church also instituted at the First Vatican Council of the nineteenth century the *Extraordinary Magisterium*—the belief that the Pope, as spiritual heir of Peter, speaks as an infallible teacher of the Tradition when he speaks *ex cathedra* (from the Chair). Besides the special authority that seems to have been conferred on Peter by Jesus (Matthew 16:18) there are number of instances reported in Acts (15:7ff.; 10:44ff) when Peter took the role of spokesman for all the Twelve. On only two occasions, when affirming the Immaculate Conception (the belief that Mary was not conceived in Original Sin) in 1854 and The Assumption of Mary into heaven in 1950, has Papal Infallibility been invoked. In each case these affirmations came as a result of long-standing belief in these teachings in Catholic popular piety. In view of how few times Popes have invoked this authority, very carefully and only after careful study of the Church's history, perhaps Protestants and Eastern Christians should rethink their critique of this idea.

There seems to be some significant strengths to appealing to the authority of Tradition alongside Scripture. Besides being the oldest model, dating back to Biblical times, a reliance on Tradition as a check-and-balance to prevent false interpretations of the Bible seems to be as good way to ensure mandating a focus on God's Word. In trying to understand a Biblical text, why not draw on the great minds and traditions of the Church to help us? That can be a good safeguard against the rampant individualism of our day, a reminder of the communal character of Christian faith.

On the other hand, skeptics might argue that to put Tradition on equal footing with Scripture is to confuse the Word of God with human reflections about it. Also problematic with these Roman Catholic models is that they seem hierarchical, not sensitive to a leadership role for the laity. Readers must decide whether the desirability of good order and reliance on authoritative expertise in interpreting the faith outweighs these weaknesses.

Many Eastern churches have a different construal for establishing Tradition, which in part responds to the critiques of the Roman Catholic Model just noted. This approach is also endorsed by certain Protestant theologians like Martin Luther (*The Large Catechism*, IV.49; cf. *The* [United Methodist] *Book of Discipline*, 104). These theological approaches construe authentic tradition as *Consensus Fidelium*. Like proponents of the Ordinary Magisterium, Christians endorsing this way of thinking deem positions taken by Councils as important in determining authoritative Tradition. But on grounds of this option, the decisions of a Council are only considered authoritative when received by the Church as a whole over time (George Florovsky, in *Eastern Orthodox Theology*, p. 118). The success of the reception process understood as the working of the Holy Spirit is what makes an affirmation indefectible and authoritative. Thus the Trinitarian and Christological formulations are not deemed authoritative on these grounds because of decisions of the Council of Constantinople and Council of Chalcedon, but because these affirmation have been received by the Church over the centuries. Acts 15:22 might be cited in support of this vision.

The strengths of this Eastern Model are in line with the strengths of the Roman Catholic Models regarding how it protects a sense of order and community in response to the rampant individualism and relativism of our times. The Eastern Model also affirms a role for the whole community, not just the Bishops, or a single leader (the Pope) in determining authoritative Tradition. But it might be argued in response that most of the other weaknesses of the Roman Catholic Models pertain. Ultimately what worries critics is that human consensus should not be placed in a position of judging the Word of God, it might be argued! And besides, there is a certain unwieldiness in the Eastern model, an imprecision about what teachings have achieved consensus. We can identify more precisely what Tradition is on Roman Catholic grounds. And it could also be contended that there is not that much of a role for laity in determining Tradition in the Eastern model, for laity can easily and have been manipulated by the clergy who exercise authority over the Church in the Eastern traditions.

Many Protestants opt for only one source of authority—*Scripture Alone*. And most Protestant denominations without a liturgical tradition consider only the Old and New Testaments to be authoritative. The Apocrypha is not even included as part of Scripture, though it may be used occasionally in Anglo-Catholic and Lutheran circles. This elimination of the Apocrypha was simply the culmination of skepticism about the authority of the Books which dated back to the time of the famed Latin translation of the Bible by Jerome in the fourth century. The strength of relying only on God's Word, not human opinion, to determine the Church's Ministry, seems apparent with this model. But there also seem to be insufficient safeguards against distorted interpretations of Scripture with this model. Critics from the Catholic and Eastern side see it as individualism gone wild.

Not all Protestants focus exclusively on Scripture as the sole source for theology. Several Protestant traditions, notably the Episcopal, Methodist, and even Lutheran heritages envisage a supporting role for Tradition. It may be deemed authoritative insofar as it agrees with the Biblical witness, or at least insofar as it does not contradict Scripture. Texts in 2 Thessalonians (2:15; 3:6) might be cited in support of this perspective. Perhaps the clearest examples of these theologians' appeals to Tradition might be cited in the Trinity, which is not unambiguously Biblically authorized, and yet seems compatible with the Biblical witness. As we noted above, Martin Luther appealed to Tradition in this way to authorize infant Baptism. Such appeals to Tradition may seem to insulate these theologians from the critiques of a rampant individualism (subjectivizing Christian faith). For now a check-and-balance seems to exist to rule out incorrect interpretations of Scripture. The problem is, however, that Tradition in this model remains subordinate to Scripture in the sense that Biblical insights may still criticize Tradition. This opens the door to the authority of private interpretation once again, as someone (presumably to the interpreter alone) must determine when Tradition is to be corrected by Scripture. But such a point of view in turn has the virtues of the typical Protestant model, a belief that we submit to the authority of the Word of God (in Scripture) over the interpretations of human beings (in Tradition).

Another pair of sources of theology to appear in Christian history has been the duo of *Scripture and Reason*. Enlightenment Rationalists (Philosophers committed to the use of reason to discern the nature of reality) like Immanuel Kant (*Religion within the Limits of Reason Alone*, I.A.C) and G. W. F. Hegel (*The Absolute Religion*, III.c) or Empiricists (those committed to the use of experience to discern reality) like David Hume (*Essay Concerning Human Understanding*, IV.XVIII.5) operate with just these two sources. The Unitarian-Universalist Church is the institutional embodiment of these Enlightenment dispositions. Only if Scripture accords with Reason (as certain readings of John 1 might entail; also see Acts 17:2; 18:4, 19) is it authoritative on these grounds.

It is evident that proponents of this model are typically advocates of Liberal Theology, interpreting the Christian faith in ways that are acceptable to Reason and even present social convention. This can be both a strength or a weakness. On one hand, this entails that the theologian's reading of Scripture is likely to find acceptance among contemporary readers, as the version of Christianity propounded will seem intellectually credible, even up-to-date. But this strength might be deemed as weakness for others, as such an approach will minimize the supernatural, miraculous character of the Biblical witness. This is not an approach that will get its proponents in touch with the ancient ways and thought patterns of the earliest Christians. But if we want to update our faith, that can be a virtue.

Some theological options link *Experience and Scripture* as dual authorities. This approach divides into several sub-groups. The oldest group, dating back to the early centuries, if not in line with New Testament Christianity, posits a strong dependence in the experience of the Holy Spirit as a present experience. Second century church leader Montanus lived at a time of transition when the Church was no longer experiencing revelations of the Holy Spirit like it had in the Biblical era. The Church was just beginning to develop liturgical forms of worship. Outbreaks of prophetic ecstasy including speaking in tongues characterized the movement. Among its supporters included the famed theologian Tertullian (see below) and the late second- century Martyr Perpetua. Adherents of this radical Pentecostal Movement are reported to have spoken of the Holy Spirit in the first person, even speaking in Trinitarian formulations (Didymus the Blind, *On the Trinity*, 3.41). In short this movement granted more authority to present revelations of the Spirit than to the written Word of God in Scripture and Tradition.

The same set of beliefs surfaced among sixteenth-century Reformers like Andreas von Karlstadt and Thomas Muntzer. Black revolutionary Nat Turner also exhibits these commitments to the authority of present experience of the Spirit, a belief that was not unusual among Black slaves.

Another related sub-group is the Society of Friends/Quakers. Originally led by George Fox, Quakers posit the <u>Inner Light</u> as the primary locus of spirituality. Rooted in the testimony of John 1:9 and Revelation 3:20 this reality is a direct personal connection with God and the Holy Spirit. This voice is available to all, having nothing to do with rituals or creeds. Every heart functions as God's altar and shrine.

This entails that though Scriptures are deemed authoritative and inspired they do not exist alone without the Inner Light. The Quaker position clearly aims to restore the authority of Scripture not so evident in the first sub-group (the allies of Montanus). But does this option really preserve the authority of Scripture, insofar as the experience of the Inner Light plays an equal role in establishing church authority?

A third subgroup to consider is found primarily in Africa among African Independent Churches like The Cherubim and Seraphim Church. With this model, in accord with Acts 10:3ff.; 16:9-10; I Corinthians 14, the experience of the Holy Spirit which is authoritative takes the form of dreams and visions which provide revelation and insight alongside Scripture. At least two of these African churches, The Kimbanguist Church and The Brotherhood of the Star and Cross, maintain that the Spirit has disclosed a new revelation regarding the divinity of their founders. There is clearly a freshness, a sense of God's Presence, that comes about when we heed the new revelations and experience given by the Holy Spirit. But as in the case of Montanism, the risk is that such a model may effectively grant more authority to present revelations of the Spirit than to the written Word of God in Scripture and Tradition. And then the cost is that the Gospel and the uniqueness of Jesus Christ may be lost, distorted, or quashed by our new insights of the Spirit.

The Wesleyan-Methodist heritage offers as final alternative on the issue of sources of authority—*The Wesleyan Quadrilateral.* The idea here is that we should use all the sources God gave us in formulating our theologies. And there are 4 sources (thus a *Quad*rilateral): Scripture, Tradition, Reason, and Experience. This model, never actually endorsed by John Wesley, but seeming to be in line with his thought, appears to combine all the strengths of the options just considered (*The* [United Methodist] *Book of Discipline*, 104). We find strength in seeking God in all the various ways in which He reveals Himself. More Liberal theological options endorsing the Method of Correlation (see below) also endorse three if not all four of these sources. And to the extent that they and Methodists endorse the priority of Scripture, it seems that a clear subordination of human ways of seeking truth to God's Word has been posited. For Biblical texts which seem to offer support, see Ecclesiastes 1:16 and Acts 17:22–28. On the other hand, see the critique of alternative sources of knowing God in Colossians 2:8. In addition, we are left with the problem noted in the Scripture Alone and Scripture and Tradition models, that in determining the meaning of Scripture we may be deferring to the authority of the individual interpreter over the wisdom of the Tradition.

The options pertaining to the Sources of Authority for Christianity have been laid out. We are now ready to move to questions of how to actually do theology, determining one's starting-point and the way in which the Scripture's authority is construed. This brings us to as consideration of the various Methodological options which have appeared in the history of the Christian tradition.

METHODOLOGICAL OPTIONS

Before considering the various Options in Theological Method, we need to consider two core intellectual presuppositions that have permeated Western academic theological research for at least two centuries. The options we consider must be in dialogue with these suppositions or reject them, and so in evaluating the strengths and weaknesses of each option we need to ask what each does with these suppositions. Theology today needs to come to terms with *Historical Critical Methods of Biblical Interpretation* as well as widespread agreement that *Interpretation is Subjective.*

Core Intellectual Assumptions for Doing Theology Today

Significant segments of modern seminary faculties (Biblical Scholars) are committed to reading the Bible critically, to an appreciation that the Bible is a human book with a history we can discern and on the basis of which we can criticize many of its supernatural claims. Of course an appreciation among Christians that we ought not to take everything in the Bible literally, that not all the Biblical accounts happened as reported, is an ancient insight, dating back to Origen in the third century (*On First Principles*, IC.II.5; IV.III.5). In the sixteenth century Martin Luther was critical of certain books of the Bible (*Licentiate Examination of Heinrich Schmedenstede*, in *Luther's Works*, Vol. 34, p. 317). But Historical Criticism, as we know it, did not begin until the nineteenth century when several German scholars influenced by the philosopher G. W. F. Hegel and his conviction that historical research can lead to understanding eternal realities (*Lectures On the Philosophy of Religion*, III.C.II.3) began to investigate the Bible's history. The cutting-edge developers of these insights were first eighteenth-century Rationalists like Hermann S. Reimarus and later F. C. Baur and David Friedrich Strauss. Some of the groundwork for this research had been laid in the previous century by the radical Portuguese, Dutch, Jewish philosopher Baruch Spinoza. Note, then, that Historical Criticism is a German Enlightenment intellectual movement rooted in Rationalism, with an original agenda of prying Christian faith loose from theologically conservative suppositions about the authority of the Biblical text as such.

Given the origins of this style of Biblical scholarship, it is obvious why this approach to the Bible is perceived as a threat to theologically conservative approaches, but is widely embraced by more progressive theological options. This insight is especially evident when we consider the implications of historical research as well summarized by late nineteenth –early twentieth century German scholar Ernst Troeltsch (*Gesamelte Schriften*, 2:729–753). His analysis of the three principles of historical research well explains why theologically conservative positions are on the defensive in our intellectual context.

Troeltsch first contends that all historical research operates with a *Principle of Criticism*: This is the commitment never to accept an ancient text as authoritative just because it is ancient. Respect for the authority of the Bible is immediately challenged with this supposition. The second working supposition of historians is identified as the *Principle of Correlation*. On these grounds all events of the past must be analyzed in terms of their contexts, causes, and outcomes. This supposition renders the concept of miracles as untenable, since on its grounds we must be able to understand events in light of their context and causes.

The third working supposition of the historian is the most challenging one for faith. This is the *Principle of Analogy*. On its grounds, an ancient account is unlikely actually to have transpired unless it has an analogy in contemporary experience. Since the Resurrection accounts of Jesus has no such analogies, they are unlikely to be accurate historically. The historical method is predisposed to reject the heart of Christian faith!

In view of historicism's dominance in academic circles, it is little wonder that in most mainline church circles the truth of the Bible's literal sense has been met with suspicion. In recent decades some have challenged the validity of Troeltsch's analysis. And yet his suppositions are pretty much common sense for most of us. For example, the claim that a healthy heterosexual couple who have lived together a number of years were engaged in a purely platonic relationship would likely be met with some skepticism (Principle of Criticism). In evaluating the truth of this claim, we would proceed to assess the circumstances that brought about these living arrangements, taking into account the couple's reputation for truthfulness (Principle of Correlation). But our skepticism about the claim would also no doubt be related to the fact that most of us have little present experience with cohabiting heterosexual couples who are purely platonic (Principle of Analogy). The three principles enunciated by Troeltsch are regularly employed by most citizens of Western society. An effective theology for today needs to take them into account when referring to the truth of the Bible.

The other core assumption of Western society relates to our suspicions about absolute truth, the belief that all truth is relative to the perspective of the interpreter. For this insight, we are all heirs of the German Enlightenment philosopher Immanuel Kant. It is often said that he is *the* philosopher of modern Protestant Theology. (We should perhaps make that an ecumenical claim.)

Kant was attempting to respond to the implications of an earlier Scottish philosopher David Hume who had concluded that the scope of knowledge is limited, that all empirical evidence only provides a series of phenomena and that our views of cause and effect or the substance of things are just human constructs (*Enquiry concerning Human Understanding*, IV.1; XII.1). Kant tried to address this skepticism while taking into account Hume's critique. He did this by distinguishing the *noumenon* (the "thing in itself") and the *phenomenon* (one's perception of the noumenon). We can never perceive the noumenon, but are merely perceiving phenomena that the mind orders under the appropriate fundamental structures of the mind (what he calls "synthetic a priori judgments" such as space and time) (*Critique of Pure Reason*, Int.; I.1; II.III). In short, all we know is a function of our own interpretation. All knowledge is subjective!

We continue to live the relativistic consequences of knowledge that Kant has introduced. Many (even most) of the Methodological Options we shall shortly consider presuppose these assumptions. And these suppositions pose challenges to Christian faith. It is harder to regard Christian faith as absolute truth when absolute truth is not possible to discern. If we construct all that we know, then it seems that God might be nothing more than a concept we construct. This conclusion was drawn by the nineteenth-century German philosopher, Ludwig Feuerbach, a radical follower of G. W. F. Hegel and an ally of Karl Marx (*Essence of Christianity*, II–III). His critique needs to be kept before us as we examine the viability of the Methodological Options to follow.

It is commonly said today that we exist in a Postmodern ethos, that the issues raised by the so-called modern philosophers just considered have been transcended. But it is not altogether clear what is Postmodern about Postmodernity. It is also common to define the difference in terms of Postmodernity as an era in which all knowledge is a cultural artifact, is socially constructed. Nothing is known apart from its cultural setting and that setting constitutes what is known. Kant does not seem to have been overcome by these Postmodern assumptions. We are still the ones who make knowledge; it is a creation of human beings and their communities.

With these two insights—the nature of historical research and the role of the interpreter's contribution to all knowledge—we turn to consider the various Theological Methods that have appeared in Christian history. They can be grouped into two or three genres—the *Method of Correlation*, the *Orthodox Method*, and a third, which may be a genre to the first approach, the *Method of Critical Correlation*. We begin with an overview.

Overview of Methods: Distinct Starting-Points

Earlier we noted that a core issue in Theological Method is the starting point. The families of Methodological options can be distinguished on this basis. All theology attempts to relate the Word of God to our lives and context. But where do you start—with the Word or with your context and experience? The answer given to that question has implications for how you construe Scripture and/or the other sources of your theology.

The oldest Methodological Option, let us call it the *Orthodox Method*, would have us begin with the Word of God, and so usually with a literalistic reading of Scripture (at lease those parts of it whose literary genre typically demand a literal reading—the Gospels, Epistles, and Old Testament narratives). The Word of God interprets us and our context, shapes our experience. Through it we know who we are and the context in which live.

There are obvious strengths with this Method. It is focused on God's Word, not on bringing other intellectual categories to the text, and so seems less likely to distort the Word's meaning. Colossians 2:8 seems to verify this Method. On the other hand, the de-emphasis on contextualizing the Gospel could lead to the conclusion that proponents of this model are less able to present a relevant Gospel. In addition, the bias towards the Bible's literal sense and apparent endorsement of absolute truth seems challenged by the intellectual assumptions of our day regarding historical criticism and the relativity of truth.

Of course the belief that the Bible has a literal sense, that we can come to agreement on theological concepts, is pre-Kantian. But there are some Post-Enlightenment Philosophies and Literary Analytic Theories that allow for literal, descriptive meanings, and so may offer theologies claiming descriptive meaning some intellectual credibility. These include Common Sense Realism, (the philosophy undergirding the U.S. Constitution) (Thomas Reid, *Essays On the Intellectual Powers of Man*, pp. 364–365), the philosophy of Ludwig Wittgenstein who in his later period saw meaning as customary use in a community (*Philosophical Investigations*, 198), and the Pragmatist Richard Rorty who believes that in ordinary discourse like theology, meaning is possible to achieve (*Philosophy and the Mirror of Nature*, pp. 11, 320). A modern Literary Theory called New Criticism also posits the possibility of discerning the descriptive meanings of narrative literature (William Wimsattt, *The Verbal Icon*, pp. 82, 130, 250).

It should be noted that the commitment to a literal reading of Biblical texts does not entail that all Scripture be read literally on grounds of this approach. Sophisticated proponents of this model would not read the Psalms or Revelation literally, any more than it is common to interpret dreams and poetry literally. This model is committed to interpreting Biblical texts in accord with the hermeneutic demanded by their literary genre. Likewise, the Orthodox Method does not necessarily demand that we must interpret the Old Testament Prophecies as historical testimonies to Christ, that their authors had Christ in mind. Here the distinction between *allegorical interpretation* and *figural interpretation* is relevant. Proponents of the Orthodox Method read the Old Testament figurally. The figural interpretation begins with a text's literal sense. It does not abolish the literal sense, like allegory does, in order to get at some deeper, spiritual or more philosophically credible meaning. But when interpreting a text figurally the theologian understands the literal sense to point beyond itself to another reality elsewhere in the text. For example, when God promises that David's house will rule forever (2 Samuel 7:15–16), the promise literally pertains only to the Davidic Monarchy. Yet read figurally by Christians the text points to the eternal reign of Jesus, the son of David. The Servant Song of Isaiah 61 is literally about the Prophet, and yet figurally the prophecy points to Christ.

The alternative to this Orthodox approach may be called the *Method of Correlation*. It is the polar opposite of the first model. Rather than starting with the Word of God, the theologian on these grounds initiates theological reflection from the perspective/context/experience of the theologian. Then in turn, the Word of God is interpreted in light of the conceptuality employed in first analyzing the context. Usually, as we shall observe, it is a philosophical worldview that is employed in providing the initial analysis of the context, so that the Christian themes then get interpreted with those categories. Employ Marxism or Existentialism in your original analysis of the human condition. And then you will construe the Gospel and the classical doctrines in the Marxist or Existentialist categories.

The strengths and weaknesses of the Orthodox Method are inversed with the Method of Correlation. Proponents of the Correlation model are strong in making the Word of God relevant to the contemporary situation. But in order to do that they must reinterpret God's Word in light of the philosophical and social scientific categories used in their prior analysis. This mandates an allegorical approach to the Biblical text, since rarely if ever does the Biblical text appeal directly to philosophical contexts. (Of course it could be argued that philosophy thoroughly permeates the Pauline [Romans 7:5–6; 8:1–9; Galatians 5:16–19] and Johannine [John 1] literature. And Paul himself seemed to employ something like this Method when preaching in Athens [Acts 17:16–34].) Certainly this approach to Scripture helps proponents to argue for the deeper meaning of the Biblical text (the spiritual meaning "hidden" in the literal accounts) without needing to defend its historical or scientific veracity. The Bible and Christian faith can still be deemed true even if its reported miracles and other claims cannot be verified. And in accord with Kantian insistence on the individual's contribution to truth and meaning, the theologian using this Method is contributing to the meaning of the Word of God. Insofar as those using this Method, then, take into account historical skepticism and the subject's contribution to truth, and since most modern people think is the only account for how we know, the version of Christian faith using a Method of Correlation is likely to be regarded as intellectually credible. But is it at the sacrifice of what the Word of God is actually all about?

Critiques of the Method of Correlation have prodded some Liberal Theologians to develop and operate with a *Method of Critical Correlation*. This approach tries to combine the strengths of the first two models. Chastened by the Orthodox critique of Correlation, and in some cases armed with the latest insights of literary analytic theory, these theologians are concerned that the Word of God has a role in critiquing the philosophical assumptions theologians bring to the Biblical text (thus a Method of *Critical* Correlation). This entails, then, that at least on some occasions the theologian employing this Method may like the Orthodox Method initiate theological reflection with the Word of God. The Word would then transform the faithful who would then employ another conceptuality to describe the transformed experience, entailing that this conceptuality is both critiqued by the Word but in turn redefines the meaning of the Word. From this it follows that the starting point of this Method is not that important. One could as easily initiate the theological reflection with Philosophy insofar as the Word is rooted in some metaphysical framework (David Tracy, *Blessed Rage For Order*, pp. 52ff.).

Just as this third Methodological model exhibits strengths of the first two models, it also seems to exhibit their weaknesses, especially that of the Method of Correlation. While its proponents' interest in examining Biblical texts as they stand, not necessarily seeking to allegorize them, suggests that the Critical Correlation Method will be more faithful to the Word of God, from an Orthodox point of view it seems that Critical Correlation is just a distinct version of the Method of Correlation. In both cases meaning is a function of the interpreter's experience. Feuerbach's critique that religion is reduced to human experience, and God is not a transcendent reality who is more than we are as a species seems vindicated when, like these theologians, everything we say about God is a function of our own experience. On the other hand, the dialogue with common human experience in which proponents of this Method engage may render what they have to say about theology and faith more relevant.

Each of these three Methods has strengths and weaknesses. Theologians need to determine which risks are worth taking, which strengths are most important to cultivate. Proponents of each of these Methods also differ on how to construe Scripture and over the worldview used to interpret the Word (in the case of proponents of Correlation). In explaining these different approaches in what follows, we will essentially be providing a survey of the history of Christian Thought regarding Theological Method. We begin with the oldest post-Biblical model.

Orthodox Method

The first Christians (with the possible exception of Paul and the Johannine author) were not engaged in much philosophical speculation. This is also true of the first post-Biblical theologians, the Apostolic Fathers (Clement of Rome and Ignatius of Antioch). Likewise the next generation of early theologians like Tertullian did not engage much with philosophy or other worldviews of popular culture. There was a passion for fidelity to God's word, understood literally and figurally.

Dogmatic Orthodoxy

For Clement of Rome everything in Scripture is a true utterance of the Holy Spirit (*Letter To the Church in Corinth*, XLV). For Tertullian all Scripture is inspired (*Apology*, XX). These early theologians, employing an Orthodox Method, did not articulate a full-blown theory of Biblical inerrancy, but they certainly implied it. In subsequent centuries many theologians employing the Word of God as a starting point for theologizing would more and more begin to develop a theory of divine inspiration and the Bible's infallibility or inerrancy. By the Middle Ages Anselm was claiming that the Bible neither contains nor aids anything false (*De Concordia*, 6). Late Medieval Nominalists like William of Ockham moved the Catholic Church even closer to an outright affirmation of Biblical inerrancy (*Against Pope John XXII*, 15). This was finally affirmed at the Council of Trent (*Decree Concerning Canonical Scriptures*). And then Martin Luther (sometimes, see *Predigten*, in *Weimar Ausgabe*, Vol. 34^I, pp. 347f.; also see John Calvin, at least in *Institutes*, 4.8.6) and Protestant Orthodox theologians of the next century began expressly to assert that the Bible never errs or that it is divinely dictated (John Gerhard, *Loci Theologici*, II.286; John W. Baier, *Compendium Theologiae Positivae*, 80–81). This approach came more visible in the Puritan era (*Westminster Confession*, I.8–9; XXXIV.2; [Baptist] *Second London Confession*, I) and then fully blossomed with the emergence of Fundamentalism early in the twentieth century (*The Fundamentals*, Vol. 1, p. 105; Vol. 3, pp. 12–14, 25; Vol. 8, pp. 75–85).

Several different variants of the Dogmatic Orthodox Method have evolved as a result of the need to come to terms with challenges historical criticism and modern science pose for an inerrant Bible. The theologians thus far considered pre-date these developments, and as a result their endorsement of this vision of Biblical authority was largely just a consequence of believing that a God Who inspired the Bible could not lead us astray (at least not in matters of faith).

One approach to Biblical Inerrancy is *Inductive*. Proponents of this model like the early twentieth-century champion of Fundamentalism B. B. Warfield (at least in his "The Idea of Systematic Theology") and his mentor at Princeton Archibald Alexander ("Inaugural Address") argued that we can verify the truth claims made by Scripture by studying their correspondence to natural phenomena. But one must reject the suppositions of historical criticism to make this claim. Another related approach, maintained by the famous Anglican Evangelical John Stott (*Understanding the Bible*, p. 202) and also by the Pentecostal denomination the Assemblies of God (*The Inerrancy of Scripture*, p. 7), is to establish the inerrancy of the Bible on the basis of the *Authority of Christ* and His appeal to the Inerrancy of the Old Testament (see Matthew 5:17; Mark 12:35–37). Both of these approaches offer admirable testimonies to Biblical authority, to a confidence in the Word rather than in ourselves. Although the Bible itself does not expressly call itself inerrant, in addition to the texts cited above John 10:34-35, Romans 4:23, and Galatians 3:16 might be cited in support. On the other hand, such a position does not readily lend itself to credibility in the mainline academy or in popular culture, in view of our bias towards historical-critical thinking, what we know about Evolution, and our post-Kantian biases towards subjectivity and relativity in interpretation (see the section above). But in defense of this line of thinking, recent Neurobiological research could be cited in defense of the conclusion that when reading the superior parietal lobe responsible for body and spatial awareness has no role (Greg Hickok and David Poeppel, in *National Review of Neuroscience* [2007]: 393–402). In short, it may be possible in interpretation not to have to inject your experience and context into interpretation. And in that case, we may need to reconsider the validity of this and other options employing the Orthodox Method.

Presuppositionalism

Another approach to affirming Biblical Inerrancy is a *Deductive* approach to the affirmation. This model approaches the question of how to assert the Bible's inerrancy with a set of presuppositions. The basic contention of this Method is that all knowledge implies some presuppositions. Thus arguments for Christian truth are valid only if employed in the context of initial presuppositions (or faith) that God/Christ exists, and that He has infallibly revealed Himself in Scripture. From this presupposition all other Christian claims follow. Among Evangelicals holding this position include nineteenth-century Dutch statesman and theologian Abraham Kuyper (*Encyclopedia of Sacred Theology*, including his Dutch-American heirs), Carl Henry (*God, Revelation and Authority*, Vol. 1, p. 215; Vol. 3, pp. 247, 428; Vol. 4, pp. 27, 41), Francis Schaeffer (*The God Who Is There*, pp. 87ff), and even The Lutheran Church-Missouri Synod (*Gospel and Scripture*, p. 15). From the standpoint of the first alternatives, this approach may seem to water-down the call for Biblical inerrancy insofar it merely asserts these commitments, does not seem to prove them but to posit a circular argument. On the other hand this approach seems to have an intellectual credibility, for the idea that we can only truly understand a subject when we share its presuppositions is in line with the suppositions of many academic disciplines, including science. And just like Science, the Presuppositionalists seem open to having their working presuppositions disproven. Consequently, it seems that truth claims by theologians using the Presuppositionalist Method are in principle on as firm ground as a scientific claim.

Limited Inerrancy/Infallibility

In much the same spirit some theologians who recognize that Historical Criticism and Science make sweeping statements of the Bible's infallibility problematic suggest a more limited version of this assertion. But they are unwilling to part with the concept. And so these theologians refer to the Bible's infallibility in a limited way. It is said to be infallible on matters of faith and conduct, but not necessarily in all its statements (especially those pertaining to history and science). A certain reading of 2 Timothy 3:15–16 could be used to verify this conclusion. This view is most famously articulated by the Statement of Faith of the premier Evangelical school of theology, Fuller Seminary (3). A statement of the Catholic Second Vatican Council seems to affirm something like it (*Dei Verbum*, 11). Even famed Evangelical theologian Carl Henry (*God, Revelation and Authority*, Vol. 4, pp. 201–202; Vol. 5, pp. 406–407) and the widely accepted *Chicago Statement on Biblical Inerrancy* (Exp.) side with this position to a point, insofar as they claim that the Bible may not report with precision every detail, but that the accounts do express the truth aimed for by their authors. They also express an openness to recognizing that the Biblical authors' use of Pre-Newtonian idioms of the day does not entail that they are teaching ontology, that the lack of scientific accuracy in such texts does not imply that scripture errs.

There are certainly attractive features to this limiting of claims to Biblical infallibility (as opposed to the inerrancy of Scripture in its details). The Bible's authority seems protected while we take seriously the common-sense awareness that the Bible is not scientifically accurate and even seems to contradict itself. The question for theological conservatives is why claim infallibility for the Bible on this limited bases, whether proponents of this view have merely surrendered the Bible's authority to the onslaughts of science and historical criticism.

Bible As Culture-Creating Literature

A very similar mainline version of Presuppositionalism has emerged since the late twentieth century. These theologians insulate the Bible from criticisms by historians and scientists by claiming that the Bible is not a book of science and history, but more like a piece of realistic narrative literature which creates a world/culture in which interpreters inhabit. As such it cannot be discredited on scientific or historical grounds. Good literature has value even when it is fictional, just as Shakespeare's *Macbeth* is a great work of art though not rooted in fact.

The later writings of Austrian philosopher Ludwig Wittgenstein provide support for this approach. He speaks of the distinct uses of language (religious uses, scientific uses, historical uses, etc.) called "language-games." Within a language-game, meaning and truth can be discerned, but one cannot use one language-game to discredit another (*Philosophical Investigations*, 3, 567).

Though it might not seem so at first glance, this model is theologically conservative in a way that might appeal to Evangelicals. Its proponents may use the insights of historical criticism, but not to devalue the truth of the Biblical text or the authority of that text. Trading on literary analytic techniques of New Criticism, proponents of this model will not allow speculations about the intention or context of the Biblical authors to function as insights for criticizing what is actually written in the canonical text, like proponents of the next model do.

Another related matter that could be a strength or weakness of this approach relates to the rich diversity of the Bible, how New Testament scholars have discerned so much diversity in the Biblical text so that most of the options studied in this book have a Biblical basis. Construing the Bible as a realistic narrative allows for an appreciation of this diversity, since characters in a narrative always have rough edges just like any of us can be loving and obnoxious in different contexts.

If this model can help us address and represent Biblical diversity, then that can also be a regarded as a negative. It seems harder, then, to develop a consistent, Systematic Theology with hermeneutic, since on its grounds it is difficult to criticize Biblical texts which seem to contradict a theologian's overall emphases. On grounds of this method all Scripture is canonical.

Proponents of this approach include modern Biblical Narrative and Canonical theologians like Hans Frei (*The Eclipse of Biblical Narrative*, pp. 11–13), Stanley Hauerwas (*A Community of Character*, pp. 63–64), to some extent George

Lindbeck (*The Nature of Doctrine*, pp. 17–18, 64–65, 120–122), and Brevard Childs in Biblical Studies (*Introduction to the Old Testament as Scripture*, pp. 16, 298–299). On some occasions Martin Luther seems to operate with this model (*Sermons on the Gospel of John*, in *Luther's Works*, Vol. 22, p. 218), and it might be compatible with certain strands of Black homiletics (Henry Mitchell, as quoted in Frederick Burnham, ed., *Postmodern Theology*, pp. 42–43). Another group of theologians who take a similar position are twentieth-century theologians of the Lundensian School (Anders Nygren, *Meaning and Method*, pp. 157–159, 227–228, 340–342) who, while not appealing so much to the literary narrative character of Scripture, share a reliance with the Narrative theologians just noted on Ludwig Wittgenstein's idea that that there are distinct language games (of which the language of faith is one) that cannot be evaluated by each other's criteria, and that Christian assertions are such a language-game. In relating religion and science, two scientists, Francis Collins (*The Language of Science and Faith*, pp. 82ff.) and John Polkinghorne (*Reason and Reality*, pp. 11ff.) seem to opt for this model.

For Wittgenstein (*Philosophical* Investigations, 23) and so for these theologians, the language of Scripture leads to the nurturing of a form of life, a culture that the faithful inhabit. The faithful become characters in the Biblical text and so actually encounter God, Christ, and other Biblical characters (Hans Frei, *The Identity of Jesus Christ*, pp. 23ff.; George Lindbeck, in *Postmodern Theology*, pp. 38ff.; Martin Luther, *Sermons On John*, in *Luther's Works*, Vol. 24, p. 67; Martin Luther King, Jr., "I See the Promised Land"). We receive a whole new perspective on life; our life-stories are changed by the Word. The implications of this benefit for nurturing the Christian life are immediately obvious.

We have already noted that modern research on the brain suggests that there might be some validity to these theologians suggesting that at least with narrative Biblical texts it is possible to discern narrative meaning. One option for these theologians is to embrace the literary analytic theory of New Criticism which allows for the possibility of identifying a text's normative, descriptive meaning, not giving into the insistence of popular culture and most of the academy that all meaning is a function of the interpreter's experience or context (Anders Nygren, *Meaning and Method*, pp. 376–378; Hans Frei, *The Eclipse of Biblical Narrative*, pp. 320, 323; George Lindbeck, *The Nature of Doctrine*, pp. 119, 101–102).

Later in his career Frei appealed to the Anthropological concept of "thick description," the idea that the literal sense of a Biblical text is the meaning that finds the greatest degree of agreement in the Church (*Types of Christian Theology*, pp. 11–12, 15–16). This represents another mode for avoiding relativism in interpretation. It suggests a third model for talking about a Biblical text's normative meaning. In line with the preceding model, a theologian could speak to how science claims objectivity for its theories on grounds of consensus in the scientific community about its prevailing paradigms (Atomic Theory, Theory of Evolution, etc.), and their utility in dealing with data, their ability to make sense of reality, so we could understand exegetical findings in relation to their consensus in the Christian community and their effectiveness in dealing with new data. (Pragmatism as articulated by Richard Rorty also allows for the possibility of a community arriving at a text's normative meaning [*Philosophy and the Mirror of Nature*, p. 320].)

Many proponents of literary models of biblical interpretation align with the more popular position, preferring to speak of biblical interpretation and theology as a linking or fusion of the Bible's stories with our own. We will consider that model in more detail when dealing further with the Method of Critical Correlation below. We have already noted the strengths and weaknesses associated with contending that finding descriptive meaning of texts is possible.

Another critique typically raised of this identification of Christian faith with a distinct language-game is that these theologians have segregated Christianity into a ghetto of its own with no real connections to everyday life. Indeed, it is claimed by some critics that this theological approach suspends the idea that the Bible stories refer to anything real. These critiques need to be considered carefully.

It is clearly not the intention of these theologians to fall prey to this critique. Hans Frei (*The Identity of Jesus Christ*, p. 138) claims that there is a family resemblance between the Biblical text and historical reality at the point of the Resurrection accounts, such that facts challenging the Resurrection would count against the truth of Christ and faith. Facts demonstrating the failure of Christianity to aid living well would also count against the veracity of Christian faith in the view of Lindbeck (*The Nature of Doctrine*, pp. 64–65). This is an argument that proponents of Presuppositionalism could employ (Luther Lee, *Elements of Theology*, p. 62). As with any scientific paradigm, you do not prove a theory, but data could disprove a claim when that claim is not able to deal with new findings. Whether these conceptual moves are sufficient for establishing truth-claims for theologians operating with the Bible As Literature approach requires more critical evaluation.

Letter/Spirit Distinction

Prior to the development of the previous model the twentieth century saw the birth of the school of Neo-Orthodoxy, a model with roots in the sixteenth and nineteenth centuries dating even back to early African theologians Augustine and Athanasius. Drawing on the Pauline distinction between letter and spirit (Romans 2:27–29; 2 Corinthians 3:6), these theologians, while still contending that the Word of God transforms us, that we find ourselves in the Biblical narratives, take the letter-spirit distinction as an authorization for critiquing the Biblical text. Some portions of Scripture are not Word of God, merely the dead letter, though at times the Bible becomes the Word of God (the spirit). Something like this position had been affirmed in the fourth century by Athanasius who claimed that the Word can only be understood properly by those with a pure mind and who live an honorable life (*On the Incarnation*, 57). Others teaching this idea that the Bible only becomes God's Word when the Spirit enlivens the dead letter include Karl Barth (*Church Dogmatics*, Vol. I/1, pp. 124–125, 127). Roots of this view are also evident sometimes in Augustine, Martin Luther (*First Lectures On Psalms*, in *Luther's Works*, Vol. 10, pp. 4–5, 211–213) and John Calvin (*Institutes of the Christian Religion*, 1.7.4), and some believe that this is the characteristic way of approaching Scripture in the Black Bible-Believing tradition. We can identify some sermons in which Martin Luther King sees to operate in this mode, embodies the preceding Bible As Culture-Creating Literature Model ("The Drum Major Instinct").

There are obviously attractive benefits to this way of thinking. This approach allows proponents to continue to employ the literal sense of Scripture, to believe its stories, and still employ historical criticism and a critical reading of problematic Biblical texts. For on grounds of this approach, not every Biblical text is Word of God. Some texts that seem to negate a theologian's main emphases can be dismissed on grounds of not testifying to the Spirit's witness. In some cases, a Christocentrism (focus on Christ) may be endorsed by this Method, as Karl Barth did. In a sense, then, this approach allows for the embracing of a canon within the Biblical canon.

Another strength of the Letter-Spirit distinction is related to its critical perspective on Scripture. It is easier to systematize one's theology, to focus on some themes rather than others, when one can eliminate a certain degree of Biblical diversity on grounds of the themes of conflicting texts not reflecting the Spirit.

The Spirit's actual Presence in the Word entails in the case of Neo-Orthodoxy and the first Protestant Reformers that Christ is actually encountered in the Biblical text (Karl Barth, *Church Dogmatics*, Vol. I/1, pp. 134, 125; Augustine, *City of God*; see the references above to Luther and King, both of whom may have operated with these suppositions sometimes). This strength, which like the preceding option entails an enhanced spirituality as we fellowship with Christ Himself through the Word, is also complemented in the case of Neo-Orthodoxy and a nineteenth-century version called *Erlangen Theology* by introducing the concept of *salvation history* [*Heilsgeschichte*] (Karl Barth, *Church Dogmatics*, Vol. I/1, pp. 373–378; J. C. K. von Hofmann, *Interpreting the Bible*, p. 128).

Salvation-history is a concept that is said to be distinct from verifiable historical events. It is said to be only accessible to faith. The argument is that because God is active in history and His Presence is unverifiable, known only in faith, so the events associated with His actions in history are unverifiable. For proponents of this view this is a way of continuing to assert many of the Bible's miracles, despite the fact that, as we have observed, historical criticism seems to rule them out in principle. Many of the challenges to faith that are posed by historical criticism to theological conservatives seem addressed by this concept of salvation-history. But is it intellectually honest to claim historicity for events that cannot be verified as historical according to the canons of the academy and the ordinary understandings of history? This is a matter for those forming a theological position to decide.

Method of Indirect Communication   Theology of the Cross

Every option thus far considered has not been unalterably opposed to the use of philosophy in theology. In fact all of the options thus far allow for its use (or the use of other conceptualities), as long as it is not done in a systematic way in which philosophy sets the agenda for interpretation. In short philosophy or the social sciences may be used in theology according to these options as long as they are "baptized," not in contradiction with the Word of God (Irenaeus, *Against Heresies*, I.X.1; Athanasius, *Against the Heathen*, 33; Anselm, *De Grammatico*,

4.72; Karl Barth, *Church Dogmatics*, Vol. III/2, pp. 74ff.). But not so with some proponents of an Orthodox Method, those espousing the Method of Indirect Communication and the Theology of the Cross. These theologians, notably nineteenth-century Danish thinker Søren Kierkegaard (*The Point of View for My Work As An Author*), Martin Luther (*Against Latomus*, in *Luther's Works*, Vol. 32, p. 258), the anonymous *Letter To Diognetus* of the early Church, and even Tertullian (*Prescriptions Against Heretics*, 7), argue that reason and faith are in dialectical tension, that statements of faith are more likely correct when they are paradoxes or seem contradictory to reason.

At first glance there seems to be some validity to the claims of these theologians. The very nature of the Christian faith is an absurd paradox—the affirmation that Jesus Christ is Two and yet One, that through death (on The Cross) He gave life, that God is both Three and yet One.

Likewise God may be said to operate in ways offensive to reason (Martin Luther, *Heidelberg Disputation*, in *Luther's Works*, Vol. 31, p. 39). Even the Christian life is said to be hidden (*Letter To Diognetus*, 5). And Kierkegaard even claimed that becoming Christian is an absurd "leap of faith," one that cannot be explained rationally (*Concluding Unscientific Postscript*, pp. 261ff.).

There is a lot that is attractive in this vision of Christianity and Theology. Because of the intensity of the leap of faith, the subjective involvement of the Christian in making this leap, it follows on both Kierkegaard's and Luther's grounds that Christ is Present to us in faith, that we are no longer disciples-at-second hand (*Philosophical Fragments*, pp. 135–137; for Luther, see above). There is Biblical support for this vision (John 15:18–19; 17:14–17; 1 Corinthians 1:20–21, 27; 3:19). But whether it makes sense to so alienate faith from the world, whether this will ultimately cut off Christians from the world and impede the Christian witness, is a set of questions we must pose to this approach. To some extent, these are challenges and questions that need to be posed to all the Orthodox Methodological options considered. In the worst-case scenario, could the Theology of the Cross lead to Fideism, so that Christian claims are only self-referential, never pointing to realities existing outside Christian discourse? The theological commitments of twentieth-century Welsh Philosopher D. Z. Phillips (*Faith and Philosophical Enquiry*, especially p. 4) and perhaps of the twentieth-century Swedish movement Lundensian Theology (Anders Nygren, *Meaning and Method*, especially. pp. 376–378, but also see p. 253) seem to embody these commitments. Or is such Fideism a desirable alternative?

Method of Correlation

Not long after the era of the Apostolic Fathers, theologians of the Church, many influenced by Philo, a Hellenized Jewish rabbi in Alexandria, sought to relate the faith to the Hellenized culture and the philosophy that dominated in the region. These theologians, called Apologists, were the first proponents of the Method of Correlation. Although these thinkers, Clement of Alexandria, Tatian, and even Origen, were committed to interpreting faith in light of Greek philosophy, their heirs have employed other philosophical or social scientific frameworks as the conceptuality into which faith was interpreted. This model has probably become the dominant one in the academy since the Enlightenment. In order to outline the various options, what follows must also effectively provide a brief survey of the history of philosophy in the West, as readers need at least in the broadest sense an overview of what it is that the various philosophies used by theologians offer us in helping us understand the human condition and God.

Greek Philosophy

The favorite Greek philosopher of the first Christian Apologists was Plato (428–348 BC), not Aristotle (384–322 BC). This follows from the fact that New Testament use of Greek philosophy (see for example Matthew 10:28–29; John 1; James 5:20; 1 Peter 2:11) tends to be more Platonic (see Plato, *The Republic*, IV.442c; *Phaedo*, VI, XIV. A review of the basics of Plato's philosophy is advisable.

Plato believed that the physical world was comprised of fleeting things, and so it is not eternal. True reality is to be found in the universal forms that individual entities share in common. Forms are the substances that similar individual entities share in common. Beautiful objects and events, a lovely work of art and a pretty sunset, share the substance/form of beauty. Readers of this book share the common universal form of humanness. We can discern correct data and observations contained in this book because these particular truths participate in the universal form of "Truth." As essentially spiritual in nature such forms are rational and eternal (*Phaedo*, VI.XIV). Plato then also spoke of human beings as comprised of a body and an eternal soul. Likewise he referred to Logos as the collective reality of all knowledge (see references in the previous paragraph).

Obviously these commitments are evident not just in the New Testament, but in the theologies of a host of the early Apologists. Clement of Alexandria

(*Stromta*, O.XX; VI.V; VI.VIII), Origen (*On First Principles*, I.Pref.3ff.; I.VII.4; IV.III.4–5), and Gregory of Nyssa (*Address on Religious Instruction*, 2) also employed Plato (or Neo-Platonism) in their theologies, translating Christian teachings into Platonic categories. Augustine also at least sometimes employed this Method of Correlation (*On the Usefulness of Believing*, iii.5). Although most pre-Medieval theologians employed an Orthodox Method, they tended to employ Platonic insights when articulating doctrines from their faith perspective.

Since the Enlightenment, questions have been posed to Platonism and its appropriateness for articulating Christian faith. Questions have been raised about its Western orientation (it is after all still the popular philosophy of many Western cultures) and its positing a body-soul dualism. Individualism has also been associated with it, insofar as on its grounds Truth can be acquired by the individual philosopher relying solely on his or her own reason.

In the Middle Ages, especially thanks to Thomas Aquinas and his teacher Albertus Magnus, a number of theologians, notably Roman Catholicism since that time, turned to Aristotle as the Philosopher into whose categories the Word of God is translated (*Summa Theologica*, I.I.10; *Summa Contra Gentiles*, I.I.1.). Essentially the second great Greek philosopher has a lot in common with Plato, his teacher. Both were dualists, endorsed the concept of universal forms, and the role of reason in understanding the forms. But Aristotle was less of a pure rationalist; he had certain empiricist concerns. We see this first in their differences on where to find universal forms. While as we have noted for Plato, the form is an ideal to which the changing material world merely approximates, accessible to reason, and so existing only in Reason (*Timaeus*, 1.51-52), for Aristotle the form is *in* each individual entity, making it what it is (*Metaphysics*, 1.9). This is the sense in which he is more drawn to observation than Plato.

The other difference is that Aristotelian ethics is on a practical plane, rather than the more theoretical one espoused by Socrates and Plato. For Aristotle, achieving virtue was not automatic, requiring effort and practice. Virtues need to become habits (*Nicomachean Ethics*, II.1). Aristotle also believed that virtue was necessary for happiness, but insufficient by itself, needing adequate social constructs like politics to help a virtuous person feel satisfaction and contentment, in this differing from Plato's idealism (*Nicomachean Ethics*, X.9).

The strengths of the Aristotelian vision will be evident when we examine subsequently Aquinas' proof for the existence of God as well as when considering the historic Roman Catholic views on Justification, Sanctification, and the Eucharist. There is a realism here about the role of political institutions that resonates with modern social scientific thinking. The more empirical, causal visions of the created order that Aristotle provides is also a strength. But the same challenges noted regarding the use of Plato and the dualism of Greek philosophy pertain to the theological use of Aristotle as well.

Romantic Philosophy

Romanticism was a movement that developed in the Enlightenment in reaction to its emphasis on Empiricism and Rationalism. This was a time when focus had been on uniformity, on regarding what is universal as the ideal (all vestiges of the West's dependence on ancient Greek philosophy). A reaction, a perceived need to celebrate diversity, followed. The fullness of existence, these rebels affirmed, was to be found in every individual existing entity, which in its own unique way is a small but essential ingredient of existence. Nothing in that connection was deemed more unique than feelings, for in an examination of individual feelings the richness of diversity becomes apparent in its sharpness. Only then do we encounter the richness of being in its fullness. The movement then emphasized intense emotion and the personality of the artist as an authentic source of experience.

Nineteenth-century German theologian Friedrich Schleiermacher is the most prominent representative of deploying Romantic philosophy for purposes of correlation with the Word. He systematically undertook the project of interpreting theological concepts in terms of feeling—specifically in terms of the feeling of absolute dependence, which he identified with faith (*The Christian Faith*, 4, 15–16). For example, in his view the divine attributes of eternality, omnipresence, and the like are not something in God Himself, but merely descriptions of the faithful's experience of the feeling of absolute dependence (18).

Like all the proponents of the Method of Correlation, Schleiermacher's approach seems to guarantee the proclamation of a relevant, intellectually respectable version of the Gospel, since his model negates the importance of history. Consequently, those portions of the Bible that are not historically accurate and scientifically respectable do not impact Christianity's credibility. On his grounds the real meaning of the Bible is not what it says literally, but its deeper experiential meaning, or the experience and feelings of the Biblical authors (103, 130). However, if all we can say about the content of faith is to describe it in terms of human feelings, then Schleiermacher seems unwittingly to support Feuerbach's thesis that religion is nothing more than the best ideas of human beings. Or can a credible defense of Schleiermacher and the Method of Correlation be offered?

Existentialism

Early in the twentieth century another revolution against the academic canons of the era began in Europe. While Western society since the Greeks and through the Enlightenment had focused attention philosophically on essence/ontology, on the thinking subject, Existentialists would have us focus on existence, on how what we do and think creates essence, makes us who we are. The focus of philosophy is said to be on how we exist, not our essence. This led its advocates to insist that we (as solitary individuals) are totally free and responsible for making ourselves who we are, and that this responsibility is a source of dread and anguish in face of the finite meaninglessness in which we exist (Jean-Paul Sartre, *Being and Nothingness*, I. I. 1; II. I. 1, ff.; IV. I. 1, ff.).

German scholar Martin Heidegger was probably the philosopher with the most influence on theologians interested in using Existentialism as a tool for interpreting faith. He framed the Existentialist philosophical commitments with the call to live authentically, to have one's existence to be in harmony with one's essence (who one is) (*Being and Time*, I. 2, 4, 6; II. 1, 2).

As a New Testament scholar, fairly well convinced that little found in the New Testament was historically verifiable, Rudolf Bultmann called for the Demythologization of the Bible. Because of our modern scientific worldview, the mythical worldview is obsolete. Only if the *kerygma* (the proclamation of the Gospel) is stripped from its New Testament mythological framework (demythologized) would it seem tenable (*Kerygma und Myth*, p. 1–11).

Much like Schleiermacher Bultmann regarded the New Testament and its myths as not aiming to present an objective picture of the world, but to express a person's understanding of oneself in the world. Thus myths are to be interpreted anthropologically. Faith claims that the understanding of existence enshrined by New Testament mythology is true (pp. 10–11). Bultmann turned to the Existentialist elements in Heidegger's thought first to provide an analysis of the human condition, understanding sin in terms of our alienation from our essence. And then he used this philosophy to portray the kerygma as the proclamation which frees us from our alienated past so we can live authentically in accord with our essence (pp. 26–31). Christ only functions in this scheme as Savior when He meets us in proclamation. The historical Jesus is the presupposition for this theology, but is not essential for faith (*Theology of the New Testament*, Vol.1, p. 3).

Bultmann liberates theology from challenges raised by the modern worldview and seems to make faith relevant in bold, courageous vision of Christian life. But it is not clear whether his view of the historical Jesus as having no value is in line with historic thinking. And once the otherness of Jesus is removed, the question must be raised if all you are left with is human experience, not God's Word.

There are other models for the use of Existentialist philosophy in modern theology, not as tied to Heidegger's philosophy as Bultmann was. One of these other models has been to construe Søren Kierkegaard as an Existentialist, to understand the whole of his thought as an example of interpreting Christian faith in light of Existentialism. But as we have already noted, Kierkegaard himself did not initiate his theology with a philosophical analysis of human experience (except to call for subjectivity and to criticize German Idealist philosopher G. W. F. Hegel [*Concluding Unscientific Postscript*, pp. 73–74, 103–104, 106–108]). And his criticism of reason and its incompatibility with faith seems out of line with a Method of Correlation.

German-American theologian Paul Tillich represents another effort by a Correlationist theologian to deploy Existentialism as a resource for understanding the human condition. But Tillich was much more of a philosopher, concerned about ontology (the essence of what exists). Although he ultimately criticizes Hegel, like Kierkegaard did, there are some points at which he embraces the German Idealist. For example, though identifying with Existentialism and its appreciation of how we are estranged from our essence, Tillich conceded that Hegel speaks of the human condition in that way too (*Systematic Theology*, Vol. I, pp. 59–68; Vol. II, pp. 24–26, 45).

In fact he objects to Hegel's Essentialism for teaching that existence derives from essence (Vol. I, p. 165; Vol. II, p. 25). However, he not only concedes agreement with Hegel in understanding the human condition. He is willing to understand history in relation to Hegel's idea of a Dialectic (that History and Reason proceed from conflicting Theses leading to a Synthesis [Vol. III, p. 329]) and to construe God like Hegel as Being-Itself (Vol. II, pp. 10, 134-135; cf. Hegel, *Lectures on The Proofs of the Existence of God*, 10).

Another aspect of Tillich's theology that warrants attention is his openness to other religions. To some extent he embraces the trailblazer in these ventures, the early twentieth-century German scholar Rudolf Otto, who had claimed that all religions involve the experience of the *numinous* (the holy) (*Idea of the Holy*, pp. 1–7, 12, 28). It is a universal experience and so all religions are similar. Tillich invokes Otto to embrace this point, even finding links between Christianity and Eastern religions, drawing on the idea of God as ultimate concern (*Systematic Theology*, Vol, I, pp. 211, 215–216, 219ff.). Tillich's use of Existentialism may run afoul of some of the same weaknesses as Bultmann, but to Bultmann's strengths Tillich offers a majestic vision of reality that is all-inclusive.

Process Philosophy

Responding to the Cartesian idea that reality is fundamentally constructed of bits of matter that exist totally independently of one another, mathematician (and then-budding philosopher) Alfred North Whitehead proposed an alternative metaphysic, the idea that reality is an event-based, or "process" ontology in which events are primary and are fundamentally interrelated and dependent on one another. This became the core to his Process Philosophy. Because in his view nature was always in process, it follows for him that God must also be "becoming," that God's Nature is always in process, having His nature determined by what happens in reality (*Process and Reality* pp. 28, 406). On the other hand, though, it is noted that God is said to be unlimited and transcendent in the sense of being primordial. Although not an imperial ruler in his view, God is said to be the creator in the sense of being the presupposed actuality of every creative act, "the absolute wealth of potentiality." As such, the deity exemplifies and establishes the conditions of creation in a process that experience derived from Him motivates. In that sense, God is truly *with* all creation, but not responsible for all that happens (405–407).

Early twentieth- century theologian Daniel Day Williams is the best example of a theologian using Process thought as a framework for interpreting Christian faith (*God's Grace and Man's Hope*). More recent Process Theologians include John Cobb and David Ray Griffin (*Process Theology*, pp. 43, 96–97) who employ a Method of Critical Correlation (see the description below). Given the nature of the relationship posited between God and the world, that God is in and part of the world, while transcending it—*Panentheism*, Process theologians tend to have a difficult time accounting for the world's creation out of nothing. On the other hand, their vision of God as in the world yet transcendent to it, and viewing the created order as in process entails that Creation and Providence are presented by these theologians, as we shall note, in a way most compatible with modern science. Also the emphasis on God's work of creative transformation opens them to endorse socially progressive positions (*Process Theology*, pp. 128ff.)

Besides having problems affirming creation out of nothing, the rooting of faith in an ontology and so in human experience creates the same problems we have identified with all of the different types of the Method of Correlation—rooting God in human experience. But the concept of God being *in* the created order is most compatible with a lot of modern physics (the so-called "God Particle" [Higgs Boson], which holds matter together). And the belief that God's Nature is determined by what happens in reality, that He is not in control of all that happens, is a promising, comforting way of talking about divine Providence.

Psychology or Experience

The use of experience or psychology as a starting point for theological reflection has assumed several distinct strands, depending especially on how experience and psychology are understood. Certainly Schleiermacher's correlating the Word of God with feelings (Romantic philosophy) is an example of relating faith and experience. Liberal interpretations of Pietism and John Wesley in particular might be associated with this approach. An especially good example of this is evident if the Wesleyan prioritization of Scripture (note previously) is not emphasized, and instead we focus on his claim that the inward evidence of Christianity (inward assurance of its truth) outweighs all other testimonies (Letter to the Rev. Dr. Middleton, II.12–III.1). For this claim suggests the Method of Correlation approach with experience functioning as the framework form which Christian doctrine is to be interpreted.

In our Postmodern setting, many faculty claiming to do Pastoral Theology, but not all (as some use psychology only in an ad hoc manner in accord with the Orthodox Method) employ this Correlation Method. To elaborate on this point, let's start with Sigmund Freud, the father of psychoanalysis. The product of a first-rate education in the humanities, Freud's interests in the human mind led him to conclude that the psyche (energies and processes of the mind) is moved by factors that now consciously emerge. The foundational source of psychic energy (the *id*) is chaotic and must be ordered by the ego, which is rooted at the subconscious level by the socialization process that represses these impulses (*Outline of Psychoanalysis*). A sense of powerlessness and victimization is implicit in this view of human nature. An early twentieth-century scholar of Pastoral Care, David Roberts (*Psychotherapy and A Christian View of Man*) embodies this effort to correlate such insights with the Word of God.

A more optimistic view of the human condition has been provided by Carl Rogers, whose non-directive counseling techniques (*Client-Centered Therapy*) have probably had a greater impact on Christian pastoral care than Freud's realism. The ultimate aim of counseling for Rogers is to help the individual "to become himself" (*On Becoming A Person*, pp. 108, 166). The optimism about human nature is readily apparent, for the core of the self is said to move toward self-actualization and socialization (*On Becoming A Person*, pp. 26, 27, 103). A well-known effort to correlate this approach with Christian commitments was offered by twentieth-century Pastoral Theologian Ruel Howe (*Man's Need & God's Action*).

Boston Personalism is a philosophy that underscores the centrality of the person as the primary focus of investigation for philosophical, theological, and humanistic studies. It systematically rejects understanding these fields in terms of impersonal forces, like social dynamics or history. Of course, then, God must be understood personally. We see this commitment to reading Scripture in light of an appreciation of the need to respect the sacredness of every person in two of the movement's founders, Edgar Brightman (*The Future of Christianity*, p. 80) and Albert Knudson (*Methodist Review* [Nov. 1911]: 907).

Another theologian with links to Boston University sometimes associated with Boston Personalism is one of the earliest Feminist theologians of the modern era, Georgia Harkness. Clearly employing a Method of Correlation in her insistence that faith must be presented as intellectually respectable, she described faith in relation to human experience. Methodist that she was, and sounding very Pietistic (a Protestant movement stressing Christian spirituality), she claimed that faith is a life of surrender. It is a "joyful adventure," which feels like it is more than we are." (*Understanding the Christian Faith*, pp. 16–23, 114–120) This is a most compelling vision of Christian life.

The strengths of all these models for relating Christian faith to everyday life are apparent. They also speak to our society's therapeutic orientation, the sense that what Christianity can really contribute is in the spheres of mental well-being and happiness. But the identification of the Word of God with human experience raises again the scepter of whether these options lose the transcendent character of the Word of God, makes it nothing more than human experience.

Indigenous Cultures

All the worldviews this far considered have Western origins. What about relating faith to worldviews of other cultures?

As early as the sixteenth century, Catholic missionaries to Asia began considering these matters. Two of them, Matteo Ricci and Roberto de Nobili, came to be known as Accommodationists. Their basic approach was to correlate the Word of God with the cultures of China and India.

Thus in China, the reverence for ancestors was interpreted as a social, not a religious act, and then reinterpreted as something like Catholic prayers for the dead. Ricci took a lead in this regard in learning other aspects of the culture. In India, the caste system was respected, not forcing upper caste converts to the faith to socialize or worship with those of lower castes. De Nobili took the lead by taking up a vegetarian diet typical of Indian culture, permitting converts to continue participating in Hindu feasts, indigenizing worship, and having priests take up the title of the Indian religious leader "Brahman."

In Africa, the modern era has seen the development of such indigenization efforts. Catholics and Protestant churches celebrating the lives of saints have had some advantage in evangelizing tribes practicing veneration of ancestors. Among Haitian Christians, Voodoo leader Papa Limba is identified with St. Peter. Spiritual Baptist churches in the Caribbean thoroughly indigenize their worship services with African worship styles. The Baptist practice of immersion in baptism links nicely with water cults in Nigeria. In Trinidad such Baptisms must be accompanied by the convert's experiencing a dream or vision, typical of West African cults.

African Instituted Churches like The Cherubim and Seraphim Church, the Celestial Church of Christ, The Kimbanguist Church, and The African Church of the Holy Spirit clearly institutionalize these commitments. Drawing on indigenous tribal religions, these churches, established in response to the Western missionaries' unwillingness to indigenize the faith, largely maintain the practices of ancient African religions such as healing, venerating ancestors, not allowing shoes to be worn in church (it's bad manners to wear shoes in African homes), and maintain traditional village rites and festivals as well as belief in a spirit-filled leadership.

Several modern African theologians have also employed the Method of Correlation to support this integration of African customs and spirituality with the Word of God. John Mbiti offers a critique of the difference between special revelation and natural revelation (*The Christian Century* [27 August–3 September, 1980]). This entails not just that we rely on Scripture, but also on God's revelation to other African religions as norms for our theology. Kwame Bediako does not quite go that far. But invoking Justin Martyr of the early Church (a Correlationist), Bediako argues that traditional African religions show that the Gospel has been anticipated in these religions in their response to the Transcendent (*Christianity in Africa: the Renewal of a Non-Western Religion*).

In fact Justin Martyr was more an ally of Mbiti. The ancient Apologist taught that all rational human beings know the truths of Christianity (for Christians have the *logos* in faith, the same *logos* that all rational human being can access) (*First Apology*, 5, 26). In the modern era, an openness to finding links between Christian teachings and those of other religions and conceptual schemes seems an attractive option. See the discussion of Anonymous Christianity that will follow.

These proposals are certainly commendable in seeking to make Christianity multi-cultural. What needs to be asked is whether the openness to finding revelation in non-Christian faiths undercuts the authority of the Revelation in Christ.

Morality

The obvious relationship between religion and ethics has led many apologists to identify faith with morality, especially dating back to the Enlightenment and the dawn of historical criticism. Since the Bible's miracles seemed unable to stand up to academic rigor, in order to find something valuable in Christianity it needed to be reinterpreted in terms of morality. Among such apologists for the faith include Immanuel Kant (*Religion within the Limits of Reason Alone*), John Locke (*Reasonableness of Christianity*, pp. 234ff., especially p. 252), Albrecht Ritschl (*Christian Doctrine of Justification and Reconciliation*), and Adolf von Harnack (*What Is Christianity?*, pp. 6ff.)

There is much that is attractive to this vision, making faith more intellectually tenable and of more social use (nurturing good citizens), and it may help create links between Christianity and other religions (they share a common moral essence). But questions may be raised about how this vision of the Christian life can relate to the stress on salvation by grace in the Pauline literature (Galatians 3:10ff.) and language of election in the Old Testament (Genesis 15; Isaiah 45:4). Correspondingly Jesus seems reduced to nothing more than a teacher of morality. A version of this model proposed by nineteenth-century German theologian Wilhelm Hermann may be worth considering in response. He does insist that the vision of God is only realized in connection with moral principles (*The Communion of the Christian With God*, I.7; cf. III.2). This seems like a commitment to translating the Christian faith into moral categories. And yet Hermann also claims that the chief end of all religion is communion with God (II.31). This stress on piety and communion with God is not found in the others noted above who use a Method of Correlation to relate the Word to moral categories. But Hermann proceeds to assert that faith is just the power necessary for moral conduct (III.23). Consequently the reference to communion with God is in the service of morality for Hermann.

Hermann also claims that the events in the story of Jesus are a matter of indifference to faith (p. 230; cf. p. 232). This and his stress on the inner life (especially p. 110) suggest Subjectivism dominates in Hermann no less than other proponents of Method of Correlation.

Marxism

The philosophy of Karl Marx cannot be understood apart from that of his teacher G. W. F. Hegel, whose views we elaborate below. Essentially what Marx did was to take Hegel's famed Dialectic (a description of the rational process of how reality works) and purged it of all spiritual content. When we do that we realize that history is driven by economic dynamics, and that history is moving in dialectical fashion (from a Thesis, to its opposite [the Antithesis] to some Synthesis of the two) towards the eventual abolition of all private property, overcoming the alienation the worker experiences towards her/his products ("Private Property and Communism").

Latin American Liberation Theologians are the best example of theologians employing Marxism as their framework for correlating the Word to a relevant philosophy of the day. Among its most famous voices include Gustavo Gutiérrez, Leonardo Boff, and Oscar Romero. (Rubem Alves is another Liberation Theologian, but he employs a Method more like the Method of Critical Correlation [*Theology of Human Hope*, pp. 4–5, 72–74].) Gutierrez affirms something like a "preferential option for the poor," which is the belief in a divine propensity to advocate the interests of the poor, necessitating a similar ethic for Christians ("Liberation Praxis and Christian Faith," in *Frontiers of Theology in Latin America*, pp. 8–9). Elsewhere he and like-minded colleagues speak of collective evil, that is, social sin by which those in control of the system and those profiting from it oppress the poor. A revolutionary struggle is thus necessary, and private ownership will need to be eliminated (see Acts 2:44ff.; Amos 8:4ff.) (*Frontiers of Theology in Latin America*, p. 1). A Socialist agenda is quite evident in such theologizing. Once again, as with all those advocating the Method of Correlation, we must question if a theology created by the interpreter's input forfeits a Word of God that stands over against us and can criticize our perspectives.

Black Power

In the waning stages of the Civil Rights Movement in the United States, radical members of the Movement began speaking of the need for African Americans not just to settle for an end to segregation but to seek real power, including exercising economic power in order to influence events. Associated with the Movement was separatism, at least a sense that African Americans must do for themselves with their own businesses and separate organizations. Martin Luther King's nonviolent approach was challenged with a "liberation by any means" ideology. With Malcom X's and Black Muslim involvement, Christianity was under fire as a "white man's religion." In this context, James Cone, founder of Black Theology, emerged.

At least early in his career, if not throughout, Cone used the Black Power commitments as the dialogue partner for developing his theology, correlating it with the Word of God (*Black Theology and Black Power*, *Journal of the American Academy of Religion* [Dec. 1985]: 768–769). This contributes to his understanding of the Gospel as about Black liberation, the liberation of the oppressed (pp. 755–756, 768–769). In line with the model of correlating the Word with Indigenous Cultures, he also spoke relating Christian faith as practiced by the African-American to African religion, but not in a "precise correlation" (pp. 755–756).

There are indications that as his career progressed, Cone became less wedded to the systematic use of Black Power as a hermeneutical tool and more inclined to turn to the broader Black Christian experience as the norm and source for theology, so that he began to operate in a manner more in line with the Method of Critical Correlation (see below) (*God of the Oppressed*, pp. 16–31, 34; *A Black Theology of Liberation*, pp. 23–35). The focus on the broader Black Christian experience entails that Cone can embrace all the great theologians of the African-American tradition like Martin Luther King, Jr. and Malcom X as allies, construing all as employing he Black experience as correlated with their religious commitments. (But King, as noted, has been interpreted by some as operating with a more Orthodox Method.)

The strengths of Black Theology's vision, how it has sparked an unapologetic Black pride and confidence in the Christian faith to aid in the liberation cause, are unmistakable. This is a theological perspective that is all about overcoming the walls between academics and activism. Its strengths are most compatible, then, with the preceding option—a Method of Correlation employing Marxist categories. But this approach also seems plagued by that model's weaknesses noted above. In addition, charges might be raised that Black Theology is too ethnic particularistic, not truly catholic. In fact Cone was sensitive to avoiding reducing the Gospel to a subjectivism. He claims that his aim is to ensure that the apprehension of truth is to avoid imprisonment to subjectivity (*Black Theology: A Documentary History, 1966–1979*, p. 78). Whether one can succeed in that aim with a Method of Correlation is a question that all theologians must answer.

Feminist Ideology

Though Feminism has much older roots, after World War II a movement of women who had engaged the world began to develop, gaining media and cultural attention. The movement sought to achieve political, economic, personal, and social equality of sexes, including seeking to establish educational and professional opportunities for women that are equal to those for men. Feminist Theology is a movement dedicated to lobbying for women's leadership in ordained positions and respecting the female experience into theology. This is characteristically executed by a Method of Correlation which interprets Christian faith into categories of Feminism.

Most of these theologians are concerned to represent God in a female manner. Mary Daly was an early advocate of this affirmation (*Beyond God the Father*). Typical of other Feminists, Rosemary Radford Ruether notes that the history of the domination of women is related to a world-negating dualism that Christianity has endorsed. Women, she argues, need to be spokespersons for a new humanity that reconciles spirit and body, which will overcome the dualisms with a positive doctrine of creation and incarnation. In this way, she can contribute to reinstating old myths of a virgin-mother goddess (*Christianity and Crisis* 13 [December 1971]: 267–272).

The critical perspective Ruether and most of her colleagues take on Scripture and its patriarchal tenets (1 Corinthians 11:2–16; 1 Timothy 2:9–15) is readily apparent. In addition, she and they also propose a distinct Christian Feminist ethic that nurtures community and shuns male competitiveness and the propensity to manipulate nature technologically.

Feminist Theology shows great promise of liberating women and overcoming male privilege in the Church. But does such a focus on the Feminist agenda unwittingly lead to a preoccupation that would become forgetful of other social agendas? Might its critical perspective on Scripture and insistence on accounting for women's experience fall prey to Feuerbach's critique of Christianity for reducing God-talk to woman-talk?

Womanism

This movement had its origins in response to the needs of women who were racially underrepresented by the Women's Movement and sexually oppressed by the Black Liberation Movement. Members of this Movement, first organized around the work of novelist Alice Walker, assert that African-American women are doubly disadvantaged in the social, economic, and political sphere, because they face discrimination on the basis of both race and gender. Black women's needs have been ignored by both movements, and they struggled to identify with either based on race or gender. African-American women who use the term refer to the Southern folk phrase, "acting womanish." The womanish female exhibits willful, courageous, and outrageous behavior that is considered to be beyond the scope of societal norms.

Several Black women studying Black Theology began using these insights as means of reinterpreting Christian faith, and so Womanist Theology was born. Among the first organizers of the movement have been Delores Williams (*Sisters in the Wilderness*, especially pp. 144–170) and Jacquelyn Grant (*White Woman's Christ and Black Woman's Jesus*, especially p. 209), both of whom use Womanist

Philosophy and experience as a starting point for theological reflection, the conceptuality for critiquing and reformulating the Word of God. Like all Womanist theologians following Alice Walker's model, they do not just focus on women's equality but continue Black Theology's concern about racial injustice and Liberation Theology's concern about uplifting the poor. Not everyone with concern about relating Black women's experience to Christian faith finds Walker helpful. The use of her worldview as an interpretive tool has been rejected by Cheryl Sanders (in *Black Theology: A Documentary History*, Vol. 2, pp. 340–343).

The inclusivity of the Womanist critique of injustice, a concern not just with sexism, but also racism and classism is clearly a strength. But the weaknesses noted above pertaining to Feminist Theology and all proponents of the Method of Correlation seem unaddressed. It is not clear whether when you make the interpreter's experience a necessary ingredient in a theological affirmation you do not forfeit the transcendent, "other" character of the Word of God, ultimately reducing what you have said about the faith to mere human experience.

Deconstruction

This philosophy, indebted to the French scholar Jacques Derrida, is first and foremost engaged in a critique of the relationship between text and meaning. Derrida's approach consists in conducting readings of texts with an eye to what runs counter to the intended meaning or structural unity of that text. The purpose of Deconstruction is to expose the realization that the object of language, and that upon which any text is founded, is irreducibly complex, unstable, or impossible. In short you can never get to the present meaning of a text (*Grammatology*). Consequently, truth and absolute value cannot be known with certainty. But with this apparently nihilistic observation comes freedom.

The guiding insight of Deconstruction is that every structure—be it literary, psychological, social, economic, political or religious—that organizes our experience is constituted and maintained through acts of exclusion. In the process of creating something, something else inevitably gets left out. These exclusive structures can become repressive. These repressive structures, which grew directly out of the Western intellectual and cultural tradition threaten us. We need to deconstruct them, to find ways to overcome patterns that exclude the differences that make life worth living. This does not mean, however, that we must forsake the cognitive categories and moral principles without which we cannot live: equality and justice, generosity and friendship. Rather, it is necessary to recognize the unavoidable limitations and inherent contradictions in the ideas and norms that guide our actions, and do so in a way that keeps them open to constant questioning and continual revision.

Only some Constructive Theologians (a group of modern theologians, most of whom employ a Method of Critical Correlation in order to aid in their commitments to critique the historic doctrines of the faith and construct new definitions faithful both to the doctrine and our context) employ Derrida. These include Peter Hodgson (*God In History*, pp. 162ff.), Serene Jones and Paul Lakeland (*Constructive Theology*, especially 44, 56–57; also see Jason Wyman, *Constructing Constructive Theology*, pp. 167ff.). But use of these insights is even clearer in the literature of Postcolonial Theology (Michael Syrotinski, *Deconstruction and the Postcolonial Africa*). The insights of Deconstruction give these theologians tools to critique the exclusionary character of Western colonial norms. But once again, we must consider the issue Feuerbach raises to all theologians: If we can and must give new definitions to doctrine and the Word of God, then they seem to have no objective meaning on their own, and so cannot transcend human experience.

Evolutionary Science

Exciting insights about the cosmos have been discerned in the last century and a half. Of course we begin with Charles Darwin's development of the Theory of Evolution. Darwin never contended that we have evolved from monkeys as popularly believed. His point about human origins was simply that apes and Homo sapiens had a common ancestor. Research has demonstrated the likelihood that all human beings share a common mother. Our mitochondrial DNA is only transmitted by our mothers, and the similarities are so great among us as to entail the likelihood that human beings share a common African mother. (African, because the greatest variations on this DNA is among peoples of African descent, suggesting that this is the oldest strand.) However, on the other hand, the human species is so genetically diverse that a large ancestral population would be needed to transmit that genetic diversity. Consequently, the minimum population of the community form which our human ancestors spring would have to have been about 7,000 individuals.

Another new theory associated with evolution (and not totally accepted in the guild) is the Theory of Complexity. It posits that as physical systems face disruption they become more structured and organized. Thus when a rock is thrown into water, the pond organizes in ripples, becoming more complex.

The Human Genome Project's findings are also relevant for appreciating the role of environment in our development. It was found that human beings have 70,000 fewer genes than had been estimated. As a result, mathematically there are not enough genetic combinations possible to account for all the different Homo sapiens who have lived. Not just genes, but also environmental influences and differences must be invoked in order to account for all the Homo sapiens who have lived.

The dominant view of the cosmic origins is that it began as a small dense superforce with no form or structure. Then about 13.7 billion years ago, space expanded very quickly (The Big Bang) and continues to expand to this day. Space was comprised of unstable energy. With expansion and the movement of this unstable energy, these dynamics along with cooling of the originally intense heat began the formation of atoms eventually leading with the help of gravity to the formation of stars and galaxies (for Einstein has taught us in his Theory of Relativity that matter is a function of energy and the speed of light). Added to this mix the concept of dark energy, not susceptible to gravity, which provides repulsive gravity so that the universe is not impeded in its expansion by the gravity of matter.

Lately The Big Bang hypothesis is being challenged by the idea of a Big Bounce, that the universe was formed after a retraction of a previous universe. Another set of issues relates to the question of what keeps matter together. Quantum Physics has sought to try to answer this question. An exciting new theory has emerged—String Theory. Its basic supposition is that electrons and quarks (sub-atomic particles that make up protons and neutrons) are not objects, but 1-dimensional oscillating lines (like strings). In matter, these strings oscillate in ways that are akin to how gravity functions, and may indeed create gravity.

The strings wrap together in ways that create the mass of fundamental particles of an atom. But in order to understand how this wrapping works, extra dimensions of reality (beyond space and time) must be posited. Obviously these additional dimensions of reality cannot be perceived. Could these be realms in which God and other spiritual realities dwell?

In trying to explain how matter holds together (how the fundamental particles of atoms create mass) physicists have posited the idea of an invisible field, the so-called Higgs Field. It contains a particle, the Higgs Boson, which has a molasses-like character that brings the various particles and atoms of reality together in order to form mass. String Theory does not entail a Higgs Boson, but the two scientific theories can be reconciled. Since this Higgs Field is invisible, it could be portrayed by Christians as a realm of God, and since it functions like a Theory of Everything explaining all known physical phenomena, this seems like a valid reality with which to identify the divine Presence.

To date not enough hard evidence has been adduced to support String Theory, and so it remains only a viable possibility among physicists. On the other hand, the Higgs Boson has been experimentally discerned.

We can identify an effort to revise Christian concepts in light of the scientific findings noted above in the work of modern American theologian Philip Hefner (*The Human Factor: Evolution, Culture, and Religion*, pp. 132–135), Ian Barbour (*Nature, Human Nature, and God*, pp. 51–53), and Ted Peters (*God—The World's Future*). Wolfhart Pannenberg seems to employ these scientific findings with a Critical Correlation Method (*Toward a Theology of Nature*, especially p. 48; see below for more details).

Proponents of the Intelligent Design seem to use some of the scientific findings to authorize their Biblicist, Evangelical conclusions. Not proponents of a Young Earth Theory, not rejecting Evolution, they employ a heavy emphasis on the Theory of Complexity (described above). Systematically deploying the idea that evolution leading to increasing complexity indicates an Intelligent Designer, Who is God. But they also critique The Theory of Evolution applying to the evolution of new species on grounds that new species could not successfully evolve the antibodies they would need to survive (Phillip Johnson, *Darwin On Trial*; William Dembski, *Intelligent Design*, especially p. 147)

It is not clear that the proponents of Intelligent Design have really used science responsibly, whether Complexity necessarily mandates an Intelligent Designer. As for the other theologians we have noted, like all the other proponents of the Method of Correlation they exhibit commendable strengths in presenting a version of Christian faith which is intellectually appealing, in touch with the latest most up-to-date insights about modern life (in their case, cutting-edge scientific findings). But it is again necessary to ask them whether if you set yourself apart from the Bible's literal sense as they have, letting human activity define the meaning of Christian thinking, then you lose the objective, transcendent character of faith, just relegating Christian claims to expressions of human experience. When you try to root faith, not in the literal sense of its teachings but in the context of another worldview, then you must ground faith in some totally secure universal conceptual system from which you construct all knowledge (a move called "Foundationalism"). And that "universal" conceptual system, as a creation of human beings, reduces everything rooted in it to human experience. All theologians need to ask themselves these questions, whether the Method of Correlation vindicates Feuerbach's claim that Christian theology has ultimately reduced Christianity merely to human experience.

Several of the most famous modern theologians to dialogue with the findings of modern science, recognizing that science does not give absolute truth, have opted for a more Orthodox Method—letting the Word of God stand literally in its own context, simply using scientific insights in an ad hoc way to elaborate on the doctrines of faith when they overlap. But this is to recognize, like the Bible as Literature approach, that theology has its own broad interpretive framework that is not impervious to experience, much like we can say that of science. It is just like geometry and architecture are distinct disciplines but may overlap. Likewise the Christian doctrine of Creation has some real points of contact with Evolution (John Polkinghorne, *Reason and Reality*, pp. 4–5, 12ff.; Francis Collins, *The Language of Science and Faith*, pp. 80ff.). This approach, like the Bible As Literature approach, recognizes that we need some suppositions about reality in order to understand it, but that we must be open to data that negate our suppositions. But then science operates that way too, Stephen Hawking has taught us (*The Grand Design*, pp. 42, 17). Theologians must decide whether they can live with this apparently circular argument or whether it actually provides theology with a certainty no less than science does. For those seeking a middle ground between the Orthodox and Method of Correlation approaches, chastened by the critiques of Correlation but still seeking an ontological rooting for faith, a way to make the Word relevant, the Method of Critical Correlation aims to provide these strengths.

Method of Critical Correlation Reconsidered

We have already reviewed the strengths and weaknesses of this approach. We now need to elaborate further on its various manifestations and the theologians associated with this effort critically to correlate the Word of God and experience. At the outset, it needs to be noted that an important philosopher for almost all proponents of this approach is the twentieth-century German scholar Hans-Georg Gadamer. He argued that the consciousness we have of a situation, our "prejudices," are absolutely essential for understanding and interpretation. This is where historical criticism has gone awry in insisting on objectivity (*Truth and Method*, pp. 269–270). We only understand, then, when our "horizon" (the limited intentionality of text or a person which invites one to advance further) fuses with the text's horizon (pp. 107, 217, 236–237, 263–267). In this sense history is understood as having a legitimate subjective lens.

Gadamer was in dialogue with founder of Phenomenology, Edmund Husserl, who concentrates on the consciousness, on our transcendental subjectivity. That is, his focus is on the pre-reflective structures by which we perceive taken-for-granted objects in the everyday world (*Ideas: General Introduction to Pure Phenomenology*). However, in so doing, while bracketing a concern about the essence of things, whether they in fact exist, Phenomenology does presuppose that there is a subjectivity that extends beyond ourselves, so that our perceptions of phenomena are not just subjective. Husserl makes clear that there is a connection between the world and transcendental subjectivity. In fact, the object of an act of perceiving is structured by the nature of the object in question. There is an ontology in the life-world, and the transcendental consciousness relates to it. But as transcendental, this consciousness that precedes every cognitive act is not empirical or psychological.

In combination, Gadamer and Husserl seem to provide modern theologians using their insights with a framework for claiming that both history and ontology have a legitimate basis in human subjectivity. Just because your own experience is the starting point, this does not reduce what you discern to the self since subjectivity is related to the "stuff" of the world. It is clearer then why proponents of the Method of Critical Correlation, who want to allow for the role of the Word in critiquing our experience and subjectivity (like the Orthodox model) and also ground the Word in an ontology that transcends the subject, or interpreter, might gravitate to these philosophical visions. For Gadamer and Husserl seem collectively to permit affirmations of the objectivity of the Word regardless of whether a subjectivity is the starting point for learning about the Word.

Theologians employing this Method and a Phenomenological philosophical point of view include Bernard Longeran (*Insight: A Study of Human Understanding*), Karl Rahner (*Theological Investigations*, Vol. IX, pp. 28–33), David Tracy (*Blessed Rage For Order*, pp. 207, 45–46, 74–75), Eberhard Jüngel (*God as the Mystery of the World*, pp. xiv, 305, 307–310), Edward Farley (*Ecclesial Man*, pp. 5ff.), Peter Hodgson (*God in History*, especially pp. 7, 89, 135–137, 157, 169–170), and many others identified with Constructive Theology (Sallie McFague TeSelle, *Speaking in Parables*, pp. 125, 138, 139; perhaps Serene Jones, *Feminist Theory and Christian Theology*, pp. viiiff., with her concept of theology and Feminism as maps which may overlap; James Ten Broeke, *A Constructive Basis for Theology*). The question is whether these philosophical commitments and these theologians who embrace them have in fact successfully established the objectivity and transcendence of God's Word while embracing Kant's turn to the subject. Can we really say that Gadamer's understanding of history has avoided an arbitrary relativism? The answer to these questions from an Orthodox perspective is that there is ultimately no difference between the Method of Correlation and Critical Correlation. In both cases, by integrating the Word of God with human subjectivity, either by ontologically embedding the Word in human experience or by making all meanings a function of human experience's input, the Word of God has no objective independent, transcendent reality from which it can stand over-against human experience. Given this Orthodox viewpoint, any theological claim made with a Correlationist Method is a human creation, the result of interpreter's creative construction of meaning.

To be sure, Gadamer himself rejects this conclusion. Things are different in his case, he (and his theological allies) argues. He contends that meaning belongs to a text, is not imposed on it by interpreters (*Truth and Method*, p. 308). And yet if meaning is a fusion of horizons as he contends, then a text's meaning is a function of what the interpreter has brought to the text. There seems to be no escaping the interpreter's subjective contribution to meaning for the Critical Correlationists, and so it seems on their grounds you can never posit a Word of God that shapes our experience. Of course its proponents claim that in rooting the Word of God in an ontology, its objectivity/transcendence is preserved. Is it?

New Quest for the Historical Jesus

Another proponent of this Method has been Gerhard Ebeling and his New Quest for the Historical Jesus. Ebeling and other colleagues were reacting against their teacher Rudolf Bultmann, whose use of Existentialism and a Method of Correlation we have already noted. Ebeling and his colleagues found that Bultmann's supposition that the mere existence of Jesus was enough for faith to be problematic. Drawing on the philosophy of Martin Heidegger like Bultmann had, these theologians found changes Heidegger had made later in his career helpful in aiding their quest to find ways to recover the historical Jesus for theology. Along with the Existential commitments we have already described, Heidegger had begun to speak of the linguistic character of Being. Since reality itself is structured by linguistic patterns, language does not just express the thoughts of the speaker, but in some events actually lets Being be expressed (*Unterwegs zur Sprache*, pp. 255ff.). Theologians appropriating these insights could then proceed to argue that the language-event of the Word of God in Christ brought to expression the very being of the historical Jesus. The faith that comes to expression in the Word is Jesus' faith, for Jesus' Word and Person are one. In that sense the Word, by bringing Jesus' faith to expression, puts us in touch with His Person, with the "historical Jesus" (*Word and Faith*, p. 288ff.).

Note that the Word is the starting point here, but it is a Word understood in the context of Heidegger's presupposition of the linguistic character of reality, and then in turn the Word is transformed and shaped by this insight. A Critical Correlation approach is clearly manifested (*Word and Faith*, pp. 320, 323, 330; *Theology and Proclamation*, pp. 27–28). We have here a commendable effort to recover the historicity of Jesus. But the preceding analysis of the Method of Critical Correlation has already raised the question if whether the contention of the later Heidegger that a history grounded in a metaphysical construct of linguisticality has avoided an arbitrary relativism. This is not the way most people understand history. And with regard to Ebeling and his colleagues' interpreting the Word of God in light of Heidegger's philosophical categories this seems as privy to the charges of relativism in the interpretation that results as their mentor Bultmann and others employing the Method of Critical Correlation (review the critique above).

The Theology of Hope

Primarily embraced by Jürgen Moltmann and Wolfhart Pannenberg, proponents of this Theological Model engage in dialogue with Eschatology (in a realized sense) (Moltmann, *Theology of Hope*, p. 37). Both of these theologians use their eschatological emphasis to address challenges posed by historical criticism without falling prey to the weaknesses associated with the Neo-Orthodox concept of salvation-history. They are able to address the historical-critical demand for an analogy between reported accounts and present experience with regard to Biblical accounts such as the Resurrection by maintaining that such accounts are to be read in light of their future. Those who know the future of these events (the hope that they engender for the future concerning God's ongoing creativity activity in the midst of despair) already have in their experience a predisposition to accept a resurrection from the dead. In accord with the historical critic's demand for an analogy between the historian's contemporary experience and a reported account of the past in order to verify its historicity, the faithful have been provided with and so have an analogy in present experience from which to assess positively the historicity of the Resurrection accounts. Jesus' Resurrection is said to have made history, but we must evaluate it in light of our own subjectivity. To this, Moltmann adds, at least by implication, an argument that Jesus' Resurrection, like all Biblical accounts, pertains to Jesus' future. In that sense His Resurrection cannot be discredited by historical criticism because it is not a past event but a Revelation of what Christ will be in the future (*Theology of Hope*, p. 87).

In starting with the Word (the Resurrection account) and bringing their own understanding of reality to the text, they effectively correlate in a critical way Word and experience (Moltmann, *Theology of Hope*, pp. 180–182, 187–191; Pannenberg, *Jesus—God and Man*, pp. 97–108). The Theologians of Hope clearly have developed an intriguing set of concepts for asserting the historicity of the Biblical witness. But it is less clear that they have preserved the objectivity and transcendence of Christian claims, since the interpreter's perspective impacts the meaning of the biblical accounts.

Moltmann suggests a response to this challenge. With a concern that God's omnipotence not be affirmed at the expense of His loving nature, he posits that God must be transcendent and also this-worldly. The Trinity, he insists, allows us to affirm both (*Crucified God*, pp. 249ff.). But on grounds of a Critical Correlation that he employs, is it not the case that even this assertion is a statement reflecting the interpreter's subjectivity, rendering his God-talk a creation of human nature and experience?

Story Theology

When dealing with the Orthodox Method's model of the Bible as Literature, we noted that several theologians (perhaps a majority identified with Story Theology) employ the Method of Critical Correlation—seeking to correlate the Bible's story with the story of the interpreter to those whom we minister, and also to ground the Biblical story in an ontology (such as the narrative structure of reality). Among these the best known are Paul Ricoeur, who also argues that the Word is more likely true because it embodies structures and conceptions of our experience (*Time and Narrative*, Vol. 2, pp. 29–60, 156–160), John Dominic Crossan (*The Dark Interval: Toward a Theology of Story*, pp. 53–54), Daniel Patte (*What Is Structural Exegesis?*, p. 34), and in the nineteenth century the famed American preacher Horace Bushnell (*Building Eras in Religion*, especially pp. 242ff.; *God in Christ*, pp. 5, 74–75, 86–97). There is evidence that Stanley Hauerwas could be included in this group, though he seems to reject rooting the Biblical accounts in an overall ontology (see *Community of Character*, pp. 68, 144).

In evaluating the strengths and weaknesses of this approach, the strengths and weaknesses of the Orthodox Method equivalent of regarding the Bible as Literature pertain to this approach. In addition, the apologetic strengths and the resources the Story Model provides for making the Word relevant need to be highlighted. The claim can be made that the stories of the Bible are not just a particular genre of literature, but that they embody the truth of existence insofar as reality is narrative. In addition, when we involve our own stories in the dialogue with the Bible, its relevance will more likely be apparent. But on the other side, the same critique of other Critical Correlation approaches pertains. If a text's meaning differs depending on the story of the interpreter, we lose the idea of the Word of God standing over against us and seem to support the idea that God's Word is a human creation.

Other Alternatives

All of the options considered under the Method of Correlation have in principle correlates under the Method of Critical Correlation. For example it might be possible to employ the Method of Critical Correlation in dialogue with treating the Bible as Literature (see above), with Existentialism (as Ebeling does), with evolutionary science, Feminism, Marxism, or Black Power. Two Feminists likely using this Method, Sallie McFague TeSelle and Serene Jones, were already noted. With regard to the use of Marx in Liberation Theology and also regarding Black Power, we have also already observed how Rubem Alves critically correlates the Word and Marxism, and how James Cone as well as and much Black Theology began critically to correlate Black experience with the Gospel, claiming that this has been the Methodological approach of the African-American church. This is evident not just in Cone, but affirmed in a collective statement of a significant number of the first proponents of Black Theology (National Committee of Black Churchmen, *Why Black Theology?*). There is also a movement here away from just focusing on Black Power as the dialogue partner for the Gospel, focusing instead on the "Black condition" and the experience of the Black community in its whole richness. We have already noted James Cone's concern to avoid subjectivism and parochialism. The question is whether the challenges we have noted with all proponents of the Method of Critical Correlation pertain here too: We must ask again whether when you inject a necessary role for the interpreter's experience in determining the meaning of a Biblical text or doctrine you do not run the risk of distorting its meaning and forfeit it and God's reality as an objective reality which can stand over against you, judge you, and change you.

Cone suggests that when the perspective an interpreter brings to the text engages other perspectives, then the aggregate of these perspectives affords a vision of transcendence (*God of the Oppressed*, pp. 102–103). But the concern for Orthodox critics may be that even this aggregate is a collection of human perspectives, and so the meaning of the Gospel it proposes is still a human creation, not a divine Word transcending us. This is a challenge that everyone who would employ a Method of Critical Correlation and try to use Cone's proposal for refuting subjectivism and the critique of Ludwig Feuerbach must address.

Rationalism and Empiricism

This Methodological model is distinct from the Method of Correlation and Critical Correlation approaches noted in that for these Methodological models the Word of God and Scripture are not privileged or prioritized. Indeed, a number of Christian thinkers in history have claimed that reason provides everything faith does with regard to core Christian teachings. Among those to take this stance have been the early Christian apologist Justin Martyr (*First Apology*, xlvi), Enlightenment philosophers René Descartes (*Discourse on Method* V) and John Locke (*Reasonableness of Christianity*, pp. 234ff., 252), as well as more recently African theologian John Mbiti (*Christian Century* [27 August–3 September, 1980]). It is wonderful to think that all have access to the faith, that the common person through Christ has the deepest insights of a philosopher (Romans 1:20–21). The Bible does respond with an exclusivism, that salvation only comes through Christ and not reason (Colossians 2:8; John 14:6). Of course the Rationalist and Empiricist would warn us against taking these texts literally, but urge allegorical readings.

Another example of a modern thinker who embraced the idea that reason reveals God as clearly as Scripture and Tradition was G. W. F. Hegel. We have already caught glimpses of the thought of this famed idealist. Hegel's mission was to take seriously Kant's claim that the mind stamps its seal on all reality (*Phenomenology*, Pref. II.2–3). But he was determined to move beyond Kant in positing an ontology whereby reason is reality itself. Such a belief in the rational character of reality entails that when one thinks, one is in touch with reality itself, with Being-itself. It follows, then, that one best knows the other by becoming subjective, for the other is essentially related to the One (Pref.III.1).

We have already alluded to Hegel's concept of the *Dialectic* (a process, ever moving, from Thesis to Antithesis to Synthesis.) Not only is this the way we think at our best. The Dialectic is also universal Reason (Being or the Spirit). The whole of reality, then, is in process, moving towards ultimate divine-human identity (*Lectures On the History of Philosophy*).

Hegel proceeded to interpret Christian faith in light his philosophical suppositions. He regarded the content of both as the same (*Lectures On the Philosophy of* Religion, III.III.1). Theology turns into philosophy, he claimed. Religion is only necessary due to the variance of the spiritual necessities of men (*Amplification of the Teleological Proof*). Through reason we can understand the claims of Christian faith—that the divine and human in Christ provide a pictorial view of the history of the Divine Idea actualizing the implicit unity of divine and human (*Amplification of the Teleological Proof*; *Lectures On the Philosophy of Religion*, II.II.3). This vision entails that history is to be taken with utmost seriousness, because insofar as it embodies the Dialectic it reveals the substance of Reason and eternal reality. The lesson history teaches, it seems, is that Life is about sacrificing itself in order to become Spirit (III.II.2). The aim of personhood then seems to be, as illustrated in the Trinity, to annihilate itself in the essence of the Godhead (III.I.3). For as we have noted, for Hegel God is Being-Itself (*Lectures On the Proofs of The Existence of God*, 10). Hegel's vision is an inspiring one. But is it faithful to Christian teaching, and does that matter?

Anonymous Christianity

The idea that good people or the faithful of other religions are saved is implied not just by those already considered above, but even officially taught by the Roman Catholic Church (Vatican II, *Lumen Gentium*, 6), without forfeiting the uniqueness of the Revelation in Scripture and Tradition. Others teaching that most religions can lead to eternal life overlap with this option. Texts which could support this position include 1 Timothy 2:4, Romans 11:26, and Mark 9:40. This is certainly an attractive position for those concerned about the fate of good and spiritual people of other cultures and religions. And yet the exclusivism of Mark 16:16 seems to challenge this conclusion.

Secular Christianity

The work of Harvey Cox, his late twentieth-century best-seller *The Secular City*, is probably the best example of an attempt to secularize Christianity. By secularity, Cox meant the deliverance of human beings from religious and metaphysical control over his reason and language. It represents the discovery that we have been left with the world and can no longer blame fortune for what we do with it. With the demise of Christendom and its dominance on Western culture, the Church must respond by finding new meeting grounds with people, engaging in the burning issues of the day. The crucial issue for secular society and the Church, then, must be to become free, responsible agents. Cox's agenda is clearly in line with today's Liberation Theology (though not expressly sharing its Marxist propensities), with all the strengths and weaknesses of that theological vision already noted.

Radical interpreters of German theologian and martyr to Hitler's program Dietrich Bonhoeffer tend to regard him as a proponent of secularizing Christianity, of interpreting it in secular ways. While in prison Bonhoeffer spoke of the need for a "religionless Christianity" in a world come of age. We need to live in the world as if there were no God. These theological commitments entail immersing oneself fully in the world, concerning oneself with the state of creation, not personal salvation (*Letters and Papers From Prison*, p. 144). Such worldliness (forgetting about spiritual matters for the sake of worldly affairs) is a renunciation of religious accomplishments, a throwing of oneself into the arms of a weak God Who wins power and space in the world by His weakness (p. 188).

This interpretation of Bonhoeffer overlooks how strong an ally of Karl Barth he was. It could be that in speaking of a religionless Christianity, Bonhoeffer was simply joining with Karl Barth in the latter's critique of the idea that Christianity is just another religion (consider Rudolf Otto, Tillich, and Mbiti, above). For Barth had regarded religion as a mere human effort with which we undermine God (*Church Dogmatics*, Vol. I/2, pp. 280ff.). If this is what Bonhoeffer had in mind in his remarks, then perhaps it is correct to understand him as implying an Orthodox Method (the Word shaping our personhood, a proponent of regarding the Bible as testifying to salvation-history like his mentor [*Act and Being*, pp. 98–99, 108ff.]).

God Is Dead

In the 1960s the theological world and the media were shaken by several theologians (Thomas Altizer and Paul Van Buren) who proclaimed God's death. They approached their proclamation in different ways. Van Buren on the basis of language analysis concluded that the concept of "god" was meaningless and so needed to be rejected (*Secular Meaning of the Gospel*, especially pp. 64–79). Altizer approached his conclusion through ontology, arguing that God died on the Cross, so that we can be set free from the guilt that comes from having an alien lawgiver in order to be energized enough to give ourselves totally to the world for service (*The Gospel of Christian Atheism*, pp. 145–157).

Both were predated by nineteenth-century German philosopher Friedrich Nietzsche. He was led to proclaim God's death as part of his program to demonstrate the Nihilism he believed was characterizing modern Western culture. In his view the primary means of achieving power for social structures that repress individuals has been to sanctify them by claiming they are instituted by God. Thus in order to be free of all that society tries to suppress us from truly being ourselves, one who is really free needs to transcend religion. We do that by proclaiming that "God is dead!" (*The Gay Science*, 125, 343) Most readers of this book will not be inclined to support this option, for contrary to Nietzsche's intention it can lead to Nihilism. But they will need to keep these positions in mind as they write about God, ever mindful not to fall prey to these critiques.

HERMENEUTICAL TOOLS OF INTERPRETATION

Many theologians find it helpful to develop or rely on certain conceptual schemes that helpfully order the Bible's rich diversity. We examine the two most frequently employed.

Dispensationalism

This approach cites a number of Pauline texts, once but no longer translated as "dispensation" (1 Corinthians 9:17; Ephesians 1:10; 3:2; Colossians 1:25), as the Greek text refers to God's "commission" or "plan." References to different "covenants" in Hebrews 8:4, 6 also are relevant as well as 2 Corinthians 6:9. Dispensationalism seeks to order the Biblical witness by distinguishing within it and the course of history a series of periods or dispensations of God's dealing with humanity. In each dispensation, it is contended, God introduces different tests and responsibilities in each period that apply to the faithful in one period but not in others. Among proponents of this interpretive model have included the Puritan Westminster Confession (VII), Dutch Reformed Pietist Friedrich Lampe (*Geheimnis des Gnadenbunds, dem grossen Gott zu Ehren*, 5:819f.), The Plymouth Brethren, The Scofield Reference Bible, and the Independent Fundamental Churches of America (Constitutions and By-Law, 13, 15).

Different Dispensational theologians differ on the number of periods, anywhere from 3 to 8. The eras may be distinguished in terms of the way God relates to His people, whether offering freedom, grace in another era, or a Zionite (Kingdom of God) dispensation. Others distinguish the eras according the dominant leaders, such as Patriarchal Dispensation, Mosaic Dispensation, and the Zionite Dispensation.

Another related approach, termed *Covenant Theology*, divides the texts into different eras, termed "covenants," usually old and new, like the Old and New Testaments. Again the numeration of these covenants differs, but the primary distinction is between the covenants of works and of grace. This way of interpreting Scripture could be rooted in the early Church theologian Irenaeus (*Against Heresies*, IV.XXV), but most of its proponents claim Reformed church roots in

Orthodox theologian Heinrich Bullinger (*A Brief Exposition of the One and Eternal Testament or Covenant of God*). We've already noted its affirmation in The Westminster Confession (VII, XIX), and then also in late nineteenth- and early twentieth-century Princeton Theology.

These models clearly help us make sense of a lot of the apparent contradictions of the Bible. And the Covenant version of Dispensationalism seems to have solid textual support. But it may be critiqued for undercutting the unity of Scripture or for failing to appreciate Biblical diversity. Another problem may be that Dispensationalism is often associated with speculations about the Millennium, and as we shall observe in Chapter 13, there is a lot of controversy over whether the Bible actually teaches the idea of a 1,000 year reign of Christ, an era of boundless prosperity, prior to or after Christ comes again.

Law and Gospel

The other frequently employed tool is rooted in Pauline literature, his distinction between Law and Gospel (sometimes described as the distinction between the Old and New Covenants) (Galatians 3:10ff.). This model is characteristic of a number of Protestant traditions, notably among Lutherans and the Reformed heritage, playing a central role in the thought of Martin Luther (*Lectures On Galatians*, in *Luther's Works*, Vol. 26, p. 115). Augustine was to some extent a predecessor (*Commentary On Paul's Letter To the Galatians*, Pref. [2]; 57 [4]). This interpretive model teaches that all Scripture and all we say about faith either takes the form of a demand (Law) or is a Word of God's forgiving love (Gospel).

Theologians employing this model differ on how Law and Gospel are to be related. Virtually every theologian prefers to stress the compatibility of the two, just as the two covenants of the Bible form one book. Thus grace does not cancel the demands of God's Law (Matthew 5:17).

The other model, especially typical of Luther and his heritage stresses the distinction of Law and Gospel. Because sin and guilt ever haunt us if Law and Gospel are too closely related we will only hear the message that God condemns our sin if the Gospel is too closely related to the Law. For then the Word of God's love in the Gospel gets heard as a conditional love. Thus Law and Gospel must be distinguished like heaven and earth, Luther says (*Lecture On Galatians*

[1535], in *Luther's Works* Vol. 26, p. 115), with the Law to be regarded as a curse (Galatians 3:10–13).

Another difference in distinguishing Law and Gospel emerges over whether one distinguishes the two solely on grounds of their *grammatical* differences, whether a Christian claim takes the form of an unconditional assertion about God's love and the human condition or if it takes the grammatical form of a conditional statement (if –then). The alternative is to refer to the distinction of Law and Gospel by *affect*, whether God's Word creates fear and despair (Law) in the hearer or confidence in salvation (Gospel). On these grounds the same text can function sometimes as Law and sometimes as Gospel. This latter model allows one to critique problematic Biblical texts, but from the alternative point of view (focusing on the Bible's grammatical meaning) the Affective model seems to reduce the meaning of Biblical texts and Christian concepts to the interpreter's subjectivity.

The strengths and some of the weaknesses noted regarding Dispensationalism seem to pertain to the Law-Gospel distinction. The more you stress Law-Gospel harmony the less likely will you have difficulties in addressing the Bible's unity, but the more problems you may have dealing with the Bible's diversity. Likewise a stress on distinguishing Law and Gospel may challenge the Bible's unity. But the warning about how if you do not you may condemn hearers to believing that the Gospel's Word of love can be conditional.

Uses of the Law

Both visions of the Law-Gospel distinction address the question of how to use the Law if it is subordinate to the Gospel. Virtually all Christian traditions, save Luther and his heritage, claim that there are Three Uses.

Theological Use: This transpires when we use the Law of God to condemn sin. If you assert that "Thou shalt not covet" or "Thou shalt not kill" in order to help people see that they are always coveting or wishing ill for enemies and competitors, then the Law is functioning in its Theological Use. The purpose of condemning sin in this way is to prepare the faithful who have been awakened to their need to hear God's Word of grace and forgiveness. As we'll see when we consider doctrine of Sin, there is some debate about whether the Commandments of God can condemn sin and make you feel guilty own their own or whether you need to accompany the Law with the Gospel in order to get the job done.

Political Use: The Law is used in this way when it is employed in order to provide a norm or to judge the fairness of government laws or rules of procedure in businesses. It is also used in this manner when we are teaching youth to be good citizens, as distinct from living as Christians should (which is the Third Use of the Law, see below). Proponents of this Use of the Law typically endorse the concept of the *Natural Law*. This is the idea that through reason, conscience, or intuition all of us have a common morality, share a moral code that is compatible with those Commandments of The Decalogue. The concept has Biblical roots (Romans 1:14–15) as well as Western legal precedents (see The Declaration of Independence).

Third Use: The Law functions in this way only for Christians, to guide them in how to live the Christian life. If offers guidance on how to live as a Christian. All Biblical exhortations are deemed as giving such guidance. For Martin Luther and his heirs this Use of the Law lapses into a Theological Use, leading us to an awareness of our shortcomings and sin.

Another way in which theologians differ on uses of the Law is which Use they deem the most important. Most theologians and denominational traditions are most likely to opt for the Third Use. Theologians with a strong passion for Social Justice and liberation are likely to focus on the Political Use. And those with dispositions to stress God's forgiveness like Martin Luther would likely focus on the Theological Use of the Law.

PROOFS OF GOD'S EXISTENCE

As noted at the outset, another aspect of Theological Method relates to Proofs of God's Existence. Some theologians find the first one we will consider as unconvincing. Those espousing the first one tend to regard the other three as distorting faith, because when you relate God to human experience you compromise the transcendence of God, run the risk of making God just as projection of human experience, as Ludwig Feuerbach contended. Nevertheless the desire to make the case for God's existence has been strong among Christians and so no theologian can proceed without developing a position on these proofs.

Ontological Argument

Essentially this argument is a deduction, an attempt to trace the logical conclusions drawn from the concept of God. It is so named because it argues for God's existence on grounds of His ontology or essence (in this case the divine essence). Its most notable proponents have been the Medieval Scholastics Anselm (*Proslogion*) and Bonaventure (*Quaestiones disputatae de mysterio Trinitiatis*, Q. 1, Art. I, 3) as well as modern theologian Karl Barth (*Anselm: Fides Quaerens Intellectum*). The argument is that God is greater than all that exists. Consequently God must exist, or there would be something greater than God, since existence is greater than non-existence.

Critics may be quick to discount the circularity of this argument. But proponents of this approach may take this into account by contending that its starting point must be faith, that we can only understand with faith (Pslams 111:10; Proverbs 1:7). Fair enough, but the question remains then if it is really a proof if faith is expected in order for the proof to work. Perhaps it could stand if we adopted a scientific model and allowed the argument to stand unless it be discredited by other publically accessible data.

Moral Argument

With a commitment to inductive reasoning, this argument concludes that given the moral sense that all human beings share, it makes no sense if there is not a Law-Giver, Who is God. Among its proponents include Immanuel Kant (*Critique of Practical Reason*, II.II.V), Anglo-Catholic (later Catholic) theologian John Henry Newman (*An Essay in Aid of a Grammar of Assent*), and famed modern apologist C. S. Lewis (*Mere Christianity*). Essentially this argument contends that the moral law requires a law-giver who is God.

Like the arguments that follow, the Moral Argument will seem at first glance stronger for some than the Ontological Argument because it is inductive. And yet it also could be argued that it and the ones which follow engage in a leap of faith in moving from that data that because there is a Law, because there are causes, that there must be a law-giver or a first cause.

Teleological Argument

This argument proceeds with the assumption that the universe has a purpose or end/*telos*. Isaac Newton (*Principia* Appendix), modern theologian Alvin Plantinga (*God and Other Minds*), and Evangelical proponents of the Intelligent Design point of view have been among its greatest boosters. Newton noted the elegant solar system required a designer. Plantinga suggests that every contingent object we know we assume it was the product of a designer, and so likewise we assume the universe had a designer. One Intelligent Design theorist William Dembski more or less embraces this argument, that we assume that we often infer the prior activity of designing I-minds by the effects left behind, and so that explanatory filter is properly employed when examining the universe—assuming unless it is disproven by hard data that systems of high complexity more likely result from an intelligent cause (God) than from chance or physical-chemical laws (*Design Inference*, pp. 92–223).

Cosmological Argument

This Argument begins like the preceding with an examination of the way things are in the universe, in the cosmos, in a simpler, less presumptuous way than the Teleological Argument. Early theologians Tatian (*Address to the Greeks*, IV.V), Basil (*Homilies on Psalms*, 32.3), and Macrina (*On the Soul and the Resurrection*), along with Medieval Scholastic Thomas Aquinas (*Summa Theologica*, I.2.1) have been its leading proponents. These arguments have been developed from the observation that the cosmos changes, moving from possibility to actuality, is driven by efficient causes, moves from possibility to necessity, and is characterized by gradation.

The chains cannot be infinite. Drawing on the Aristotelian supposition that all realities must have a cause, proponents of this proof may posit like Aquinas did that there must be a first mover, first cause, an absolute necessity, and a highest quality being. And then these theologians equate this first cause, highest qualities, etc. with God.

These are arguments based on observation and more could be developed based on additional cutting-edge scientific observations, such as belief in a being Who possesses the highest complexity growing out of the Complexity Theory previously noted. We have already suggested that the Higgs Boson (the particle which holds atom and so matter together) has been called the God-Particle, and so it could be argued that matter demands a reality that holds it together, and that reality must be God (and ancient theologian Dionysius of Alexandria [*Books Against Sabellius*] taught). Or the appreciation that Creation is a function of energy emanating from the Big Bang could be grounds for arguing that there must be an infinite energy Who is God (Dionysius, *Books Against Sabellius*; Pierre Teilhard de Chardin, *Hymn of the Universe,* especially Pensees, 68ff.).

The Cosmological Argument clearly invites the development of a learned faith that takes science seriously. Once again, though, as in the preceding Arguments, it must be noted that a leap of faith is involved in moving from a First Cause, a highest, necessary Being, etc. to God. In addition, critics of these proofs find it problematic that they effectively found God in human experience, to make humanity the foundation of Theology. And there is no way to get from anthropology to God Himself; you wind up unwittingly endorsing Feuerbach's claim that all religious talk is really about God (Karl Barth, *Church Dogmatics*, Vol. I/1, especially pp. 147–148).

These proofs and the possibility of a *Natural Theology* (the God can be known apart from the Revelation in Jesus Christ) return us to the Methodological question above, about whether we initiate theological reflection with the Word of God or without our own experience.

CLOSING THOUGHTS

For many theologians we must start with the issues raised in this chapter in order to do theology (especially if you are more inclined to the Method of Correlation or Critical Correlation Method). For others, these methodological questions are merely an afterthought to the content of Christian faith (a position typical of an Orthodox Method). But either way you cannot do theology without sometime engaging the issues of this chapter. Especially be sure you are clarifying for yourself precisely how Scripture is authoritative (its literal sense, what the Bible's authors meant to say, some deeper meaning philosophy or one of the social sciences help you discern) and whether some other source (Tradition, reason, experience) orients your thinking. When you clarify these questions and in what order you will consider the sources for your theology, and then you'll really be ready to theologize!

2

GOD AND TRINITY

Because this is a book about the Christian faith, we seem to have authorization from the First Commandment of The Decalogue (Exodus 20:2–3) to consider God at the outset, making God the first and foremost reality we consider. But we need to grant that it is more likely that the concept of God or gods is a later development in religious practice, since the earliest forms of religion were first devoted to discerning and honoring the "sacred order of things," which may or may not have included "powerful beings" like ancestors (Robert Bellah, *Religion in Human Evolution*, especially p. 95).

Other concerns about the decision to begin our consideration of Christian doctrines with God may be raised by those who believe the focus should be first and foremost on Jesus Christ. This is certainly a reasonable position for those who opt for a *Christocentric* theology, claiming that the Person and Work of Jesus Christ is the most important teaching in Christianity. I have already noted the order of doctrines in this book is not in any way prescriptive, but merely a reflection of the logical order of the treatment of most of these doctrines in The Nicene Creed.

Another reservation to what follows is that I seem to be speaking of a distinction between the doctrines of God and Trinity, when in fact for Christians the only God Who exists is Trinitarian. True enough from my perspective. But again we must admit that at least at the earliest stages of the Christian movement the distinction between God and Trinity was made. The first generation of Christians largely accepted the view of God derived from the Hebrews but did not widely endorse the Trinitarian view until the fourth century.

Of course the most basic commitment in the Christian understanding of God is *monotheism*. This is the belief that there is only one Supreme Being (God) in the universe. The early Hebrews were among the first of ancient peoples to adopt this viewpoint. In contrast to the common belief of their time in many gods (polytheism), the Hebrews were rigorously insistent that Yahweh, Whom they worshipped, was one God, the sole object of worship: "Hear, O Israel: The Lord our God is one Lord; and you shall love the Lord your God with all your heart, and with all you soul, and with all your might" (Deuteronomy 6:4–5).

This early creedal confession pertaining to their single object of worship did not in itself constitute the early Hebrews as monotheists. They lived in a polytheistic environment in which God needed to be recognized as one of many gods, though superior to them all (Genesis 31:53; Judges 11:24; 1 Samuel 26:19). Gradually, however, with the rise of the Prophetic Movements in face of foreign domination, Israel began to develop a theoretical monotheism, totally rejecting the existence of other gods. Sixth and even eighth century B.C. prophets came to speak of Yahweh as Creator and God of all peoples (Isaiah 45:12; Amos 9:5–8) in addition to Whom there is no other God (Isaiah 43:10ff.; 45:21). The development of this uncompromising monotheism is an important dimension of the Christian heritage.

This brings us to the question of what is entailed by having a God: What is the Christian God like? In this chapter we will be examining the different theological options that have developed in response to this question. The Biblical witness describes God with accolades. There is no being who exceeds God in any way (Isaiah 44:6). God is eternal, infinite, and self-sustaining, dependent on nothing for existence (Genesis 21:33; Deuteronomy 33:27; Psalms 93:2). The Lord is holy, exalted over all creation (Psalms 99:2, 9; Isaiah 6:3). He is almighty and all-powerful (Revelation 4:8; Exodus 6:3). "In His hand are the depths of the earth; the heights of the mountains are His also. The sea is His, for He made it; for His hands formed the dry land" (Psalms 95:4–5). God is the point of orientation for all creation and holds it together; everything is dependent on Him. All life is found in God, "the Alpha and the Omega, the beginning and the end" (Revelation 21:6).

This God, Who so far exceeds the most magnificent characteristics of the creation, shares something in common with human creatures. He is personal in nature capable of entering into relationship and conversation with human beings. These personal characteristics are reflected throughout Scripture by the way in which God addresses people and the personal way they respond to Him. In the New Testament certain characteristics of God's Personal character are further clarified. In Jesus Christ we learn that God relates to people as a kind of gentle parent; God is "Abba," which is a familiar form of the English equivalent "Father" (Mark 14:36; Romans 8:15). This title appears even in the Old Testament (Psalms 89:26; Isaiah 9:6; 63:16; 64:8).

We will talk about the various ways in which these images have been interpreted shortly. For the present, suffice it to say that the Bible witnesses to God as our point of orientation, Who gives life meaning and protects His people. Before such a Being we can only respond with the Psalmist: "O come, let us worship and bow down, let us kneel before the Lord, our Maker!" (Psalms 95:6).

These Biblical images only provide us with a partial picture of the Christian doctrine of God as portrayed by the earliest Christians and up to the present. The early Church emerged in an intellectual climate, which was heavily dominated by Hellenistic philosophy. Thus it is not surprising that in developing the doctrine of God the Church came to be influenced by Greek ideas, especially those of Plato.

The point of correlation between Plato's philosophy and Biblical insight was the Biblical affirmation of God's sovereign freedom. The Biblical witness is quite clear, as we have seen, in asserting that God is not dependent on creatures as we are on God. The parallels between this insight and Plato's ruminations on the origin of the world in his dialogue *Timaeus* were too inviting to overlook. The Christian concept of God has been unmistakably altered ever since this dialogue with Greek philosophy was initiated for virtually all subsequent theological reflection about God has been heavily influenced by Greek presuppositions.

Plato had taught that the origin of the world was the work of a divine artist or demiurge, which took matter and gave it form by imitating the idea of the Good. This implied a differentiation between the idea of the Good and the creator. Such a move was unthinkable for both Jews and Christians influenced by Judaism. However the Platonic understanding was so ingrained in Hellenistic culture that Christians who had been Hellenized could not but engage with this worldview. The result was that Jews and Christians embedded in Hellenistic thinking came to combine both the demiurge and the Good in their view of God. As a result God came to be regarded as possessing the qualities of both the demiurge and the Good. Likewise the qualities of the Good (which for Plato included incomprehensibility, impassibility, and infinity) were correlated with God's freedom. The end result was the idea of an impassive, unchanging, all-powerful God, Who seems unaffected by human suffering and despair.

The appropriation of such Greek insights by the Church entailed that a sense of God's distance from everyday life was introduced into Christian thought.

The God Who is omniscient, never changes, and cannot be fully known is not impacted by everyday life. To be sure the Hebraic thinking Christians had inherited from its Jewish roots did affirm God's awesome transcendence (see the Biblical references above). And yet the Hebrew God was One intimately involved and identified with His people. The Name of the Hebrew God, Yahweh (translated "Lord" in English), which seems to have been united with other versions of God that the different Hebrew tribes or their predecessors had worshipped, makes that clear.

Yahweh literally translates "He Who is," "I am Who I am," or "I will be Who I will be." The Hebrew also connotes the sense of "being there" (for you) (Exodus 3:14). The emphasis on being or becoming in the name Yahweh provides a fundamental insight into the Hebrew view of God. It means that for the Hebrews God was not a static essence as the use of Greek philosophy predisposes one to think. Rather God was manifested in action. Far from indicating God's aseity, the name of the Hebrew God indicates that God's being is relative, determined by interactions with people. This renders God as more involved and more relevant to the human situation. His very being can be understood through divine interaction with us.

These two strands (the Hebraic and the Greek elements) have engaged each other throughout the history of the Christian tradition. A number of the differences that have emerged in understanding God are related to which of these strands are emphasized (in most cases the Greek strand has dominated). Let's keep this in mind as we review the options that follow.

THE NATURE OF GOD

We have already noted that the New Testament makes clear God's Personal characteristics and how we can relate to God as Abba, a gentle loving Father. All Christian theologians would agree in some sense that God is love (John 3:16; 1 John 3:1; 4:8; 2 Peter 3:9; Psalms 63:3; 92:2). But differences have emerged over whether God is also righteous or just, and how this relates to love.

God As Just

Most Roman Catholic and Eastern theologians as well as Pre-Augustinian theologians opt for a tension between God's love and wrath or righteousness.

The God Who loves us and sent Jesus Christ to save (Deuteronomy 4:37; 7:8; Psalm 102:8) is also a God Who demands righteousness and punishes the sinner (Revelation 6:16–17; Matthew 25:15, 31–45; Numbers 16:41ff.; Psalms 5:1–7; Thomas Aquinas, *Summa Contra Gentiles*, I.96; I.91; Clement of Rome, First Epistle, XXXIV–XXXV; Athanasius, *Contra Gentes*, p. 47). Protestant Orthodox theologians, notably those of the Reformed tradition, also characteristically construe God in this way (Jonathan Edwards, "Sinners in the Hands of Angry God"; [Baptist] Second London Confession, II). James Cone also construes God in this way (*A Black Theology of Liberation*, p. 73). There is certainly Biblical authorization for this viewpoint. This is a God Who demands and will inspire respect. But is this a God Whose scepter of judgment can cause anxiety among the faithful?

God As Love

Most of the advocates of the vision of God that stresses His loving nature, while not denying the reality of His wrath are spiritual heirs of Martin Luther. (Sometimes Augustine teaches about God this way, such as when he talks about God as the very love that links His creatures together [*On the Trinity*, VIII.8.12]. Other times, though, like Luther on some occasions [*Bondage of the Will*, in *Luther's Works*, Vol. 33. pp. 62-63], he will posit a divine-wrath tension [*On Patience*, 19].) In Luther's case we find him on occasion talking about how God gently lifts us out of our doldrums and insecurities, gently putting us in His lap. God's wrath is said to be only His alien, not His proper work (*Lectures On Genesis*, in *Luther's Works*, Vol. 3, p. 139; *Lectures On Galatians* [1535], in *Luther's Works*, Vol. 26, p. 314).

Luther's Christocentrism, his focus on Christ fully revealing God is another factor in this prioritizing grace, for if Christ is loving and He fully reveals God, then God must be loving too (*Lectures On Genesis*, in *Luther's Works*, Vol. 5, p. 46). Another way of subordinating wrath to grace is evident in Luther and his mentor Augustine in the way in which they define the righteousness of God. (Calvin and other Protestants join them in this move.) In a point very important in the treatment of the doctrine of justification, both interpret the righteousness of God in Romans 3:21–26 and elsewhere not as a reference to the wrath and judgment of God, but as something God does—makes us righteous, which happens by grace through faith (Augustine, *On the Spirit and the Letter*, 15; Luther,

Preface To the Latin Edition, in *Luther's Works*, Vol. 34, pp. 336–337). Even the righteousness of God serves His love on these suppositions.

Beside the many texts testifying to God's love cited above, perhaps the strongest Biblical backing for this position is found in 1 Thessalonians 5:9, 1 Timothy 2:3–4, and 1 John 4:16. If you want a portrait of God as accepting and full of love this is clearly an option to explore. The question is whether too much stress on God's love leads to cheap grace.

The difference between these options is obviously a matter of emphasis, and so, perhaps like Luther and Augustine, theologians will work this out on a case by case basis, in which case the problem of conceptually unifying these two portraits of God will require attention. One option could be in theology emanating from the African-American church and Liberation Theology. We find in these theologians (including Martin Luther King) a strong emphasis on God's wrath and judgment against oppressors and oppressive social structures, but more unambiguous love directed toward the oppressed (Rubem Alves, *A Theology of Human Hope*, 114ff; Martin Luther King, Jr., *The Strength To Love*, Ch.1.III). Is this just another example of the God is Just option, with all its strengths and weaknesses, or is it a unique option?

Wrath As a Misperception of God's Love

This alternative stresses God's love so much that wrath is not part of the Godhead, just our sinful misuse or reaction to God's grace. This tends to be a position of more Liberal Theologians like Friedrich Schleiermacher (*The Christian Faith*, 350) and Paul Tillich (*Systematic Theology*, Vol. 2, p. 174) who stress God's passivity in wrath. The Biblical texts cited above for God as love are the best authorizations for this position. The unambiguous affirmation of God's love is certainly an attractive dimension of this option. But it has a harder time coming to terms with a literal reading of the texts noted above regarding God's judgment and wrath.

Yes, God is love, Christian theologians assert. But how love is related to divine judgment is a matter requiring reflection.

GENDER/ETHNICITY OF GOD

Inevitably in our Post-Feminist Movement era, when we talk about God we are led to consider the Lord's ethnicity and gender. Of course the vast majority of theologians throughout history have tended to imply God's maleness, just in virtue of His being our Father. Most have not made much of this point, though Feminists and Womanists would argue that in fact that helps explain male domination in church and society. Some like John Calvin did make God's Fatherhood a justification for prioritizing males, at least claiming that earthly fathers are lit with a spark of God's Fatherly splendor, but not mothers (*Institutes*, 2.8.35). Let's look at alternatives.

God As Mother

Claims about the female nature of God are not just modern. To be sure Feminist and Womanist theologians have made this claim (Mary Daly, *Beyond God the Father*; Delores Williams, *Sisters in the Wilderness*, p. 55). But such claims had been made in the Late Middle Ages by Julian of Norwich (Showings, 58), by Martin Luther (*Sermons On the Gospel of John, Chapters 6–8*, in *Luther's Works*, Vol. 23, p. 325), and in the last century by Martin Luther King, Jr. ("Three Dimensions of a Complete Life," in *Knock at Midnight*," p. 139). All three speak of God as both male and female, as Mother and Father.

Much to the surprise of some critics, there is Biblical precedence for construing God this way: Consider Isaiah 66:13, Psalms 123:2–3, and Proverbs 1:20ff. However, the references to God the Father could be used to stress the Lord's male gender, and it could be argued that God cannot be both male and female. But insofar as God is a Trinity, can be Three in One, could it be that the Christian God can likewise account for dual genders and still be One?

Late Medieval Mystic Julian of Norwich seems to move in this direction by claiming that it is the Son of God Who is female. Jesus' human nature is male in her view, but not His/Her divine nature, because the Second Person of the Trinity is said to be God's sensuality, taking on our human flesh and so is our Mother of Mercy. (Julian is presupposing here that what is sensual must be female.) In addition Julian argues that the Second Person of the Trinity is also our Mother for her role in our substantial creation (*Showings*, 58).

It would likewise be possible to argue that the Second Person of the Trinity is female, insofar as reading Proverbs' references to Wisdom (translated "Sophia") are taken as prophetic references to the Son which confer a female name on Christ. (The Hebrew text of Proverbs [see 4:1–10] also testifies to the female character of Wisdom.) Attention should be given to whether these moves solve questions of divine gender and if not, why not.

God As Spirit

Several good examples of solving the problem of God's gender by rejecting the idea of a Personal God, insisting that Personhood is just a way of symbolic expression of the spiritual nature of the deity, have been endorsed in Church history. The best spokespersons include Origen (*On First Principles*, II/IV.2–3; III.VI.1) and Paul Tillich (*Systematic Theology*, Vol.1, pp. 249ff.). Mary Baker Eddy and Christian Science also assume this position, insofar as God's Personhood is rejected in favor of conceiving of God as Mind. John 4:24 might be cited for Biblical support, and then references to the eyes and ears of the Lord (Psalms 34:15) as well as image of Fatherhood and female traits are to be interpreted symbolically. Theologians must decide if such a liberal and critical approach to Scripture is appropriate, in which case this may be a helpful alternative.

God As Black

This model has been most notable in Black Theology, not just in the thought of James Cone and his colleagues (*A Black Theology of Liberation*, pp. 63–64), but earlier in the work of a nineteenth-century Bishop of the African Methodist Episcopal Church, Henry McNeil Turner (*Voice of Missions* [1898]). In making this point, Cone at least is concerned to proclaim that God is Black in the sense that "Blackness is the primary mode of God's Presence." That is, God always identifies with the oppressed (*Black Theology* [1989 ed.], p.vii). Interpreted in that way, there seems some support insofar as the Old Testament God was the God of slaves (the people of Israel in Egypt) and also insofar as God identifies with Jesus in all His suffering and lowliness. Questions may be raised if such a viewpoint allows God to be a God of the rich, of all people. But Cone responds by claiming that God's truth comes in many colors, revealed in many cultures and unexpected places (*For My People*, p. 206). This model of God raises challenging questions for those of European, Asian, and Native American backgrounds.

Those who reject this model need carefully to consider if their God is more ethnic than they think.

RELATION TO THE WORLD

Once we have clarified what God is like, the inevitable question is God's relation to the universe, to the world. Three logical, historic possibilities present themselves. God is in the world, beyond the world in some other dimension, or a combination of the two options.

Transcendence

This first model finds God to exist in a dimension beyond space and time, not in the world with us. Probably the majority of theologians in history have taken this position. God is radically distinct from the universe. We have already cited a number of Biblical references in support of this position (Psalms 93:4; 95:3–5; 99:2; 145:3; Isaiah 6:3; 44:6). Although there are a variety of emphases on this theme, two theologians who have especially emphasized divine transcendence are John Calvin (*Institutes*, 1.5.4ff.; 1.16.1ff.) and Karl Barth (especially *Church Dogmatics*, Vol. III/2, p. 16). They make this point especially by emphasizing that all that happens in the cosmos is dependent on God, that He (usually a male God is associated with this model) is initiator of all that transpires (a strong doctrine of Providence, see Chapter 5).

When trying to explain Transcendence, this model may lead us to think of God as far off in the heavens. But it might be possible in light of theories in modern physics instead to construe the realm of God as one of the additional dimensions exceeding space and time that physics must now posit in order to account for newer visions like string theory regarding how matter holds together (Stephen Hawking and Leonard Mlodinow, *The Grand Design*, p. 115). And for glimpses of eternity in all its magnificence, we need only remember that while recorded history only extends just over 6000 years, human beings came into existence about 195,000 years ago, dinosaurs reigned on earth 230,000,000 years ago, and it was 505,000,000 years ago until there were finally creatures residing on earth's land. Earth existed in its first 500 million years prior with no life on it. Its age is likely 4.44 billion years. It was not formed until 10 billion years after The

Big Bang. And yet eternity is before that. How big, how ancient is the One Who came before these creations?

The strength of the Transcendence position is not only that it matches popular piety in the pews, but it also entails that the critique we noted in the last chapter by Ludwig Feuerbach regarding God as nothing more than attributing the best of human qualities to an object is more readily refuted. For on grounds of this model, God is nothing (or very little) like human beings. On the negative side, this view runs the risk of rendering God as so different/distant from us that we cannot relate to Him. The next model speaks to this issue.

Immanence/Pantheism

This model finds that God is immersed in the creation, resides here among us. Psalm 139:7-8 is a text that seems to provide authorization for this point of view. Paul Tillich is perhaps the best modern proponent of this view. He speaks of God as Being-Itself, the Ground of Being (*Systematic Theology*, Vol. 1, p. 64; Vol. III, p. 284). Both of these philosophical terms imply that God is *in* or even *is* the stuff of the universe. In claiming that God is All in All as Origen does (*On First Principles*, III.VI.1) we may also be opting for this model (though Origen's own position may also be closer to Panentheism, see below).

A stronger affirmation of God's Immanence is offered by proponents of *Pantheism*—the idea that God is identical with the universe. Although this has not historically been a Christian position, and its strongest advocate has been a Jewish philosopher Benedict Spinoza (*Theologico-Politcal Treatise*, XV) and probably Albert Einstein (*Gelegentliches*, p. 9), it is still a model that Christian theologians might embrace.

This viewpoint, even in its most radical version, seems attractive in its ability to bring God closer to us. Einstein's interest in this way of thinking clearly testifies to how it may be an intellectually satisfactory way of integrating Christianity and science. The problem is that proponents of this vision tend to deny the Personal character of God, and this certainly seems to distance the position from literal interpretations of the Biblical witness. But it could be argued that this model does protect God's transcendence over-against humans when we compare the duration of human beings to the age of the earth and the cosmos.

Panentheism

A middle-ground position seeking the best elements of the preceding options is to assert that God is in and is affected by the world, but still transcends the cosmos. The primary modern representatives of this model have been Process Theologians, whose use of this notion is indebted to the founder of Process Philosophy Alfred N. Whitehead (John Cobb and David R. Griffin, *Process Theology*, pp. 46–47). Others teaching this position include early Church African theologian Caius Marius Victorinus (*Hymns*, IV.II.3.B), at least sometimes Martin Luther (*The Bondage of the Will*, in *Luther's Works*, Vol. 33, p. 45), and Wolfhart Pannenberg (*Toward a Theology of Nature*, especially pp. 154–155). St. Augustine posits a most interesting image in this connection. He claims that God is like a vast ocean and the universe as but a small sponge dropped into that ocean (*Confessions*, VII.V.7). The water of the ocean (God) saturates the universe. A modern view in line with Augustine's image, that the world is in God Who saturates the cosmos, is offered by Jürgen Moltmann (*Trinity and the Kingdom of God*, pp. 90–96).

There seems to be some good Biblical support for the Panentheist position. The preceding texts cited to authorize the Immanence position as well as Colossians 1:15–17, Ephesians 4:6, Jeremiah 23:24, and 2 Chronicles 2:6 are all relevant. The model of Panentheism has a lot of useful strengths, including scientific credibility. We've already noted how quantum physics has hypothesized and seems to have discerned a fundamental field, the Higgs Field, which explains how fundamental particles can stick together and form mass by means of the so-called Higgs Boson, often referred to as the God-Particle. A Panentheistic view could identify God's Presence in the Higgs Field, so that God is in the entire cosmos while insisting that God transcends the field. Of course it is still the case that if we posit this way of describing Panentheism, it follows that insofar as on its grounds and on grounds of other Pantheist options God is immersed in the stuff of creation and so is affected by finite developments, theologians committed to the idea of an All-Powerful God might find this vision problematic. Every theologian, then, must come to terms with the question of whether God is All-Powerful and beyond or outside of reality, or whether the Lord is immersed in the cosmos in some way and impacted by it.

TRINITY

Although the word "Trinity" is not in the Bible, Scripture speaks of a threefold Revelation of God—as Father, Son, and Holy Spirit (Matthew 28:19, as well as the plural character of God as designated by the Hebrews word *Elohim*, attributed to God in the Old Testament). In any case, with language about Father, Son, and Holy Spirit found in Scripture along with the Church's commitment to monotheism inherited from its Jewish roots, early Christians began to find a need to reconcile how God could be Three in One.

What motivated the adoption of the Trinity doctrine was the appearance of several attempts to explain references to Father, Son, and Spirit while affirming one God, which the Church catholic has deemed heresies. But since these options are still around to this day, I present them for your consideration.

Modalism

Sabellius was a third-century Roman who began teaching the idea that God is One, that Father, Son, and Spirit are merely "Modes" or temporary manifestations of the Lord (Epiphanius of Salamis, *Adversus haereses*, lxii.1). Just as I am an author, friend to my peers, spouse to my wife, playing those roles in appropriate context, but still just Mark Ellingsen, so God manifests Himself in different Father, Son, and Spirit roles. Another teaching this position is early twentieth-century African-American Jesus-Only Pentecostal G. T. Haywood and denominations endorsing this position like the Pentecostal Assemblies of the World. These Jesus Only or Black Apostolic denominations hold that Jesus is the entire Godhead, so the Father and Spirit just express ways of relating to or names for God in different dispensations.

The clarity with which the threefold character of God and its unity is articulated by this model is obvious. The Church catholic had condemned it only on the base of implying that if Father and Son are not distinct by nature then when the Son suffers so must the Father, and it is not clear then how the Father could raise the Son. Also this teaching might have problems accounting for Biblical texts like Mark 14:36 and John 14:28, which seem to subordinate the Son to the Father.

With some hesitation about identifying this view with Modalism, we should consider Paul Tillich's Trinitarian vision. For him, Father, Son, and Holy Spirit are symbols. Each symbol expresses a different answer to different questions posed by the human predicament. The Father speaks to concerns about finitude, the Son to questions of human estrangement, and the Spirit a response to question about ambiguities in life (*Systematic Theology*, Vol. 3, pp. 283ff.). This seems like an affirmation of God revealing Himself in three ways or our experiencing God in three distinct ways. But like Modalism, there is no affirmation of God being distinct or communal in the divine essence like the Trinity teaches.

Arianism

Arius was a prominent priest in the third- and early fourth-century Alexandria. His solution to preserving Monotheism was to deem the Son of God, the Logos, as the mediating reality between the impassable God and the world. As we are the creators of our words, so God the Father begets the Word of God. Thus before anything else was made the Word was created, the greatest of all God's creation (Letter To Eusebius).

Although Arius' views were condemned as heretical by the Council of Nicea (see below), the heresy endured for some time in the Roman Empire when eventually the Roman Emperor Constantine and his heirs adopted the view. Something like this option remains taught today by the Jehovah's Witnesses. They also teach the one God (named Jehovah), and that His Son is not God, but begotten of God.

There are commendable strengths with this view. It preserves Monotheism and seems to account for Biblical texts that appear to subordinate Jesus to the Father (texts cited above in discussing Modalism). But the cost is that insofar as Jesus the Son of God is our Savior, if the Son is not God, then God would not be our Savior. This of course is impossible, and accounts for the Church catholic's reaction against this position.

Unitarianism

Proponents of this position of course insist that there is only God, citing The First Commandment in support. Two Spiritualists (those believing in the authority of direct revelation of the Holy Spirit) of the sixteenth and seventeenth centuries respectively, Michael Servetus and Faustus Socinus, were early teachers of this position. Today's Unitarian Universalist Church is a modern proponent. All of them solved the problem of the relation of Son and Spirit to the Father, by denying the divinity of Jesus and insisting that references to the Spirit are just reminders that God is Spirit. Both the strengths and weaknesses associated with Arianism noted above pertain to this view. The question is whether the strengths and weaknesses of the doctrine of the Trinity outweigh these problems.

Development and Rationale for the Trinity Doctrine

The early Church spent more than a century seeking to find a way to maintain the Oneness of God while taking seriously Biblical references to Father, Son, and Holy Spirit. Arianism and Modalism were two alternatives suggested, but the one that was gaining the most support prior to AD 325 was the concept of the Trinity articulated by the North African theologian Tertullian. God is three *hypostases* and one *ousia* (*Against Praxeas*, XII, II–III, XIX)—commonly translated as three Persons and One God.

We need to clarify the original Greek terminology. Both *hypostasis* and *ousia* are properly translated "substance." But ancient Greek thought attributed *hypostasis* to the substance of individual entities like readers of this volume and me. We each have our own distinct *hypostasis.* Likewise the Father, the Son and the Spirit each have a distinct *hypostasis.*

The term *ousia* on the other hand is attributed to the substance that individuals share in common—to the universal forms of Greek philosophy. In that sense all readers of this book and I, as human beings, share a common *ousia.* Likewise Father, Son, and Spirit share the one divine *ousia.* This description of the different terms explains why in English the term *hypostasis* is frequently translated as "Person."

Despite the influence of this viewpoint, the teaching of Arius was dividing the Church until AD 325 when the Roman Emperor Constantine convened a meeting of all the Bishops of the Church in Nicaea. Contrary to much popular contention the Council did not formulate The Nicene Creed as we have it today and did not really authorize the Trinity doctrine. In fact it condemned Arius' teaching and affirmed that Father and Son were of the same substance [*homoouosios*] and then formulated a creed which amounted to a first draft of The Nicene Creed. Reference was also made to the Son being "begotten," but not "made" (not created).

The Council did not take a position on the Holy Spirit's relation to Father and Son (merely confessing faith in the Spirit). But in asserting that the Son and

Father shared a common *ousia* the Council also made clear that if Jesus saves us it is God Who is our Savior. Also significant in explaining the strengths of the Trinity doctrine, the Council of Nicaea made clear that the God Who saved us is the God Who created us. This entails that when you affirm the Nicene formula and the Trinity doctrine (which Nicaea implies) you can never speak of Christ's Work, never speak of salvation, without considering the Father's Work (Creation). The Trinity doctrine effectively assures that we not forget the broader social-ethical implications of Christ's saving Work.

Because of Arianism's rebirth after the Council of Nicaea (largely the result of gaining Constantine's support) the Church's leaders spent more than thirty years struggling with the Nicene formula. Among questions raised was what to make of the status of the Holy Spirit. Finally in AD 362 a famed North African Bishop Athanasius, who had been a champion of the Nicene position against the Arians, convened a Synod of Alexandria involving North African Bishops. They collectively affirmed the divinity of the Holy Spirit, and in so doing effectively endorsed Tertullian's view of the Triune God. This teaching was made official in 381 at the Council of Constantinople, which endorsed the Trinity doctrine and revised the original creed, which had been approved at Nicaea, into the final form it has in today's Nicene Creed.

The strengths of the Trinity doctrine have already been noted. It makes clear that God is our Savior, even though it was Jesus the Son of God Who was instrumental in our salvation. It links salvation (the Work of the Son) to broader Creation concerns (Social Justice and the Work of the Father). The communal character of Father, Son, and Spirit also can account for references in the Old Testament to God's plurality (*Elohim*, as the plural form of "God"). But does the idea of 1+1+1=1 inherent in the doctrine make sense—especially its idea of the Son is begotten, but not created, that the Spirit "proceeds" from the Father (and the Son)? We turn in closing to consider options for clarifying these matters.

Filioque: For and Against

The Creed as adopted by the Council of Constantinople states that the Holy Spirit proceeded from the Father (with no reference to the Son). However, gradually in the churches of Europe and those using Latin in worship added the term filioque (meaning "and the Son") to The Creed, so that it was said that the Spirit proceeds from both Father and Son. So what? Why has this been a problem separating Eastern churches from Catholic and Protestant churches since 1054 to this day, as each side uses a different version of The Nicene Creed?

From a Western standpoint you need the Filioque in order to make clear that Father and Son are equally God. Augustine, one of the early proponents of this affirmation, helps us understand what it means to say that the Spirit "proceeds." He regarded the Trinity as a love affair between Father and Son. Their love is so profound that they love each other into One. The Holy Spirit is said to be the love that makes them One (*On the Trinity*, VI.5.7). Love proceeds from the lover. And yet love is of the person who does the loving. They are the same substance. And if that person is loving it is odd to say he/she creates the love. It is in this sense that the Holy Spirit proceeds from the Father. But it is not just the Father Who does the loving, Augustine claims. The Son also loves the Father back. And so the Spirit (God's love) also proceeds from the Son (Filioque).

Augustine's profound impact on the Catholic Church and later on Protestant churches helps explains their endorsement of the Filioque. The other reasons for affirming it is that it makes clear that Jesus is not adopted Son of God and that the Holy Spirit does not contradict the Revelation in Jesus. If Jesus were adopted Son of God this would happen through the Spirit, and so the Son would be proceeding from the Spirit. That was not ruled out in the original version of The Nicene Creed, and this is why the amendment is necessary. Also if the Spirit proceeds from the Son then the Spirit's Revelations must be consistent with the Son. Consequently, the Holy Spirit never contradicts Christ. Thus it is Christ (the Son) Who promises the Spirit and the Bible speaks of the Spirit of Christ (John 15:26; Galatians 4:6). Is not the Spirit, then, proceeding from the Son? Good arguments.

From an Eastern standpoint these arguments are not persuasive. The Filioque is incorrect because it represents an unauthorized amendment of The Nicene Creed, a revising of a decision of an authoritative Council of the Church. In addition, Eastern Orthodox churches critique the Filioque for effectively chaining the Holy Spirit to the past, rendering the Spirit unable to reveal anything new, save what Christ has already revealed. The West in turn accuses the East of chaining the Church to the past, by not conceding that the Church may gain fresh insights about Conciliar decisions, and that is all that the Filioque intends.

Protestant and Catholic users of this book will need to consider affirming the Filioque in their Trinitarian formulation. The issues at stake in including or excluding it should now be clear. Is it important to ensure continuity between the insights of Christ and the Holy Spirit or is fidelity to the Tradition more important?

We now need to consider how to talk about the Trinity, to try to make sense of the Son being begotten of the Spirit and how 1+1+1=1.

Trinitarian Theology: Options

Of course one option in dealing with the Trinity is to appeal to the concept of Mystery, that the concept defies reason, cannot be explained, and that we distort the faith when we try to make sense of it in concrete images. But if we go that route, do we run the risk of rendering the Trinity irrelevant in practice, if no one understands it? It should be noted that all of the theologians I now consider would share this sentiment somewhat, contending that their images only partially help us understand the Trinity.

Another possibility is to take the route of Friedrich Schleiermacher, contending that the Trinity doctrine does not really express what Christians experience (*The Christian Faith*, 172). New formulations may be necessary in order to capture what was intended. This progressive way of thinking may appeal to Liberal Theologians today. But those who proceed in this way need to consider that perhaps they are effectively embracing Unitarianism with all its strengths and weaknesses noted previously.

Let's turn next to how we can make sense of the idea that the Son is begotten not made. The first theologian to articulate the idea of the Trinity, Tertullian, seems to solve this point for us. He refers to the relation of Father and Son as akin to the *Relationship Between the Sun and Rays* (sun like the Father and its rays like the Son) (*Against Praxeas*, VIII). The sun and its rays are distinct but the sun and its rays are of the same substance. And the rays of the sun have been in existence as long as there has been a sun. The sun *begets* rays, but the rays are not a *creation* of the sun. Others affirming this model include Athanasius (*Four Discourses Against the Arians*, I.VII.24–25; III.XXIII.3–4), Martin Luther (*The Three Symbols or Creeds of the Christian Faith*, in *Luther's Works*, Vol. 34, pp. 219), and Augustine (*On the Trinity*, IV.20.27). Gregory of Nazianzus opted for a similar, distinct image. He spoke of the Trinity as analogous to the common light that might be emitted by three suns (*Fifth Theological Oration*, 32).

Other concrete images for depicting the Trinity:

Readers are encouraged to develop other images for themselves, but what follows is a good overview of most of the images employed by the great theologians of the Church. We have already noted Augustine's idea of understanding the Trinity's union in terms of love: *The Son loves the Father and the Father loves the Son, and the Holy Spirit is the love Who makes them One.* This is certainly a strong statement for theologians wishing to stress that God is love. It was also endorsed by Athengoras (*Supplication for the Christians*, 10), Catherine of Siena (*Prayers*), and Jonathan Edwards (*Discourse On the Trinity*, 30–31). Let's first look at some of Augustine's other images for portraying the Trinity:

—Triadic nature of love, involving subject, loved one, and the relation (*On the Trinity*, VII.10.14).
—Like a tree comprised of root, trunk and branches (*Faith and the Creed*, 27). This position was also taken by Tertullian (*Against Praxeas*, VIII) and Athanasius (*Statement of Faith*, 2).
—Resembles the three-fold structure of the human mind: The mind (akin to the Father) begets self-knowledge (the Son) (*On the Trinity*, IX).
—Father as Mind, Son as Intellect, Spirit as the Will of God; as they are all held together in a human being, so they are held together in the divine being (*Confessions*, XIII.XI.12.). This was also taught by Anselm (*Monologion*, 67) and Martin Luther (*Lectures On Genesis*, in *Luther's Works*, Vol.1, p. 60).
—Like three different forms of water (a river, its source, its ocean outlet) (Faith and the Creed, 17). This was also taught by Athanasius (*Expositio Fidei*) and Tertullian (*Against Praxeas*, XXII.)

Other long-standing theological images for depicting the Trinity include:

—Like a three link chain, each link distinct but indivisible: This was taught by Gregory of Nazinazus' friend Basil (Letter To His Brother Gregory, XXXVIII.4).
—Like a fire passed among three lit torches: Basil's younger brother Gregory of Nyssa employed this image (*Against the Macedonians*, 2.5).

—God is Three for He acts in Three Ways (His actions constitute His essence); yet since these three actions are in harmony, God is One: Gregory of Nazianzus (*Third Theological Oration*, 29.9–13), Gregory of Nyssa (Letters, XVI), and in the modern era Karl Barth depicted the Trinity in this manner (*Church Dogmatics*, Vol. I/1, pp. 340, 426–429) .

—Like an internal conversation: Father the Speaker, Son the Word, and Spirit the Listener (*Sermons on the Gospel of John 14-16*, in *Luther's Works*, Vol. 24, pp. 364–365).

—Father is the Fountain, Son is the Wisdom (Who flows from the fountain), and the Spirit is the Power of God (just as what flows from the fountain comes out with force): This was John Calvin's model (*Institutes*, 1.13.18, 26).

Readers should evaluate each of these options, determining which one/s might best communicate today in our context, and if not, seek other alternatives. It is also interesting to note that some of these images stress One Person of the Trinity a bit more than others. The last image has more emphasis on the Father as source of the Son (who gushes from the Fountain) and the Spirit. The Lutheran heritage and much modern theology tend to put more emphasis on the Second Person of the Trinity, are more Christocentric (Formula of Concord, SD XI.66). And of course the Pentecostal as well as some Pietist theological strands place more emphasis on the Third Person. In formulating one's own way of describing the Trinity, the issue of which Person is most crucial for effective Ministry warrants attention.

CLOSING THOUGHTS

When thinking about God, we have put all the important questions on the table. First there is the issue of what to make of the Trinity, and if affirmed whether and how to clarify the mystery for the community. Other crucial questions: How much should the love of God be emphasized? How about God's gender (or ethnicity)? What is the relationship between God and the universe? Is God transcendent or embedded in the Creation? We turn now to clarify the Incarnational character of God in Jesus Christ.

3

CHRISTOLOGY

This doctrine properly pertains to Who Jesus is, to His Person and not His Work. (The latter belongs to the doctrine of the Atonement.) The New Testament clearly portrays Jesus of Nazareth as human. The accounts of His birth from a woman's womb (Luke 2:7), His bodily needs (Luke 26:42-43), His emotional releases (John 11:35), His suffering (Hebrews 2:18; 1 Peter 2:23; Isaiah 53:3), and His death as punishment for sin (Mark 15:16ff.; Hebrews 2:17; 1 Peter 2:24; Isaiah 53:4–5) certainly indicate that He is not to be regarded merely as some divine being masquerading in human form. Even the affirmation of His birth by a virgin (Luke 1:27; Matthew 1:23) was originally intended to testify to Jesus' humanity, for it clarifies that He had a human mother. But the Virgin Birth, like the Biblical witness as a whole suggests a special kind of relationship between Christ and the Father (John 17:22; Colossians 1:16–17). He is eternally with the Father and exercises divine prerogatives (John 1; Luke 5:21). The numerous times in Johannine literature (6:35; 10:9, 11; 14:6) where Jesus uses the phrase "I am" are likely references to His identifying with Yahweh (Whose Name means "I am Who I am'). Likewise the references identifying Him with the Word (*logos*) (John 1)—a Stoic and Platonic concept signifying that the universe is structured according to universal reason of which our own reason is a part—further suggests identification of Jesus with God or at least with realities that are superhuman.

Another way in which the special relationship with God was made clear was by conferring on Jesus the title Son of God (Matthew 27:54; John 1:34, 49; 3:16–17; 20:31; Acts 9:20; Romans 1:4; 2 Corinthians 1:19; 1 John 4:15; 5:5, 10, 13, 20). Of course there are many other times when this title is not attributed to Jesus, but rather He is identified as Son of Man (Mark 2:28; 9:9, 12, 31; 14:41, 62; Matthew 17:9; 24:30; Luke 17:30; 19:10) or as Messiah, the "Anointed One" (*mashiach* in Hebrew and *Christos* in Greek [Isaiah 45:1; Lamentations 4:20; Matthew 16:16; John 1:41; 20:31; 2 Corinthians 11:4–5]). How one relates these various titles and interprets them says a lot about the theological position taken regarding Who Jesus is.

These Biblical references and the Church catholic have presupposed that the Incarnation is unique to Jesus of Nazareth. But there have been claims to other Incarnations, such as have been made by the twentieth-century African-American religious leader Father Divine as well as African Independent Churches like The Kimbanguist Church and The Brotherhood of The Star and The Cross. Some Feminist theologians along with the Church of Christ, Scientists (Christian Science) have argued that there have been female as well male incarnations, since we are all sons/daughters of God (Rosemary R. Ruether, *Sexism and God-Talk*, pp. 127–130) or that Jesus Himself was androgynous (of neither sex, see Virginia Mollenkott, in *Daughters of Sarah* [March, 1976]: 1ff.). We turn next to the various alternatives committed at least in some way to the Incarnation of God in Jesus Christ that have appeared in the history of Christian thought regarding Who Jesus is.

WHO JESUS IS

There is ecumenical agreement about the divinity and humanity of Jesus. This is a function of The Council of Chalcedon in AD 451. It successfully turned aside several alternatives that we will consider, asserting that Jesus Christ has Two Natures (hypostases—a divine nature and a human nature) but is still One, and yet the distinction of the Natures is not annulled by the union (called the *Hypostatic Union*). Prior to this agreement there had been several alternatives in the early Church, some of which still exist today. Let's examine these alternatives first, before examining the strengths and weaknesses of the ecumenical common sense of Chalcedon and the family/denominational disagreements that still exist.

Monophysite Christology

Concerned to avoid dividing Christ, a fifth-century monk in Constantinople taught that though Christ had Two Natures before the Union that made Him One, this Union created just One Nature. Though condemned as a heretic, he has had colleagues with this viewpoint. Though not all agree, the late second-century African Apologist Clement of Alexandria and a fifth-century colleague Cyril of Alexandria are sometimes thought heartily to endorse Christ's divinity and minimizing His humanity (Clement, *Stromata*, VI.IX; Cyril, To Eulogius). A sixteenth-century Spiritualist Caspar Schwenkfeld spoke of deifying Christ's humanity (the divinity overcoming His humanity).

The heresy remains alive to this day in the teaching of the Oriental Orthodox (Coptic, Ethiopian, Armenian, and Jacobite Orthodox) churches, though they insist that they are **Miaphysite,** not Monophysite in their Christology. That is, they contend that they are not heretics, but insist more firmly that the One Nature of Jesus is comprised of both divinity and humanity.

The strength of this alternative is that it makes clear the Oneness of Jesus. And besides, the New Testament does not explicitly refer to Christ being of Two Natures. But on the other hand, a problem is posed by the fact that it is not made clear most of the time by adherents of this position what the One Nature of Jesus is like. If only divine, then God is not our Savior. (And as we noted when dealing with Arianism, then we are not saved, for only God, not a human can save.) And if the One Nature of Jesus is only divine, then if Jesus is not human how can He bear our sins on the Cross? If the One Nature of Jesus is a mixture of both, then He is neither divine nor human and so the two preceding critiques of this position apply.

Ethiopian Alternatives

In order to address these critiques, two distinct Miaphysite alternatives have emerged in Ethiopia:

Sons of Unction: This alternative teaches that God's decision to become Incarnate in Jesus Christ transpired in eternity (by Unction—anointing). In the One Nature of Jesus His humanity is overcome by His divinity, not unlike what happens in the process of deification (see Chapter Eight) or when water is poured into strong wine and the wine is not diluted.

Sons of Grace: In contrast, this model teaches that God became Incarnate in Jesus through adoption by grace at His Baptism. The One Nature of Jesus that results is a compound of divinity and humanity, just like water is a compound substance of hydrogen and oxygen.

Do either of these options address challenges to the Monophysite view? Historically most denominations have said "no," explaining their estrangement with the Oriental Orthodox churches, though in more recent ecumenical dialogues reconciliation is expected as both sides claim they are saying what the other says, but just in different ways (Joint International Commission for Theological Dialogue Between the Catholic Church and Oriental Orthodox Churches, Nature, Constitution and Mission of the Church"; Joint Commission of The Theological Dialogue Between The Orthodox Church and The Oriental Orthodox Church). Is that the case?

Nestorianism

This exact opposite of the Monophysite position was embodied by a fifth-century Bishop of Constantinople, Nestorius. Concerned to avoid the Monophystie obliteration of the distinction of Jesus' Natures, Nestorius stressed their distinction. For him the union in Christ was like a marriage (two becoming one). But then just like a marriage is comprised of two people he implied that Christ was the marriage of two—two persons. The heresy remains alive today in the official teachings of the Assyrian Church of the East (a small, world-wide body headquartered in Iraq).

The divinity and humanity of Jesus Christ are clearly and well affirmed by this alternative, and its image for depicting their union is attractive. But just as couples remain distinct individuals even in the happiest of marriages, which puts the marriage relationship ahead of their individuality, so the Nestorian model suggests that the divinity and humanity remain separate in a sense. As a result it is not clear on Nestorian grounds that we have a true Incarnation. And if not, if the Son of God is not truly joined to Jesus, then He is not fully involved in saving us. The same problem we had with Arianism and the Monophysite result. Is this a valid criticism ruling out the Nestorian alternative?

Apollinarianism

This mode is the result of the advocacy of a fourth-century Bishop of Laodicea, Apollinarius. He was determined to preserve the unity of Christ, but not at the expense of His divinity. Thus he taught that in Jesus, divinity replaced His human soul. A human body with a divine soul! Again we have an intriguing and concrete way of explaining the union of divinity and humanity. But if Jesus only has a divine soul, He does not have a human soul. On grounds of Greek philosophy and perhaps of the New Testament, if He only has a human body He is only half human. If not fully human He cannot identify with us fully or bear our sins. For these reasons, Apollinarianism has been rejected.

Docetism

An earlier heresy was initiated in the second century. Derived from the Greek word "to seem," this position affirms the unity of Jesus' Personhood by claiming that He is Son of God, not really human. He just *seems* to be human. The same strengths and weaknesses we noted in the Apollinarian option described above pertain. Though Christ's Birth by a Virgin had been articulated earlier (Ignatius of Antioch, Letter To the Smyrneans, 1.1), the doctrine became catholic in responding to the Docetist effort to diminish Jesus' humanity. But the Virgin Birth also fails to receive attention when Jesus' divinity is challenged as in the option which follows. These options illustrate that when theologians flee the Mystery of the Virgin Birth they have ceased to affirm the mystery of the unity of God and the humanity of Jesus, and maybe also abandoned God's grace (Karl Barth, *Dogmatics In Outline*, p. 100).

Monothelitism

Attempting to reconcile the Chalcedonian position and the Monophysites who had been condemned by the Council, seventh-century Patriarch of Constantinople Sergius proposed that while Christ has a divine and human nature they are united in His One Will. That will is divine, taking the place of Jesus' human will. For a time the heresy was endorsed by the Maronite Church based in Antioch, Syria, though it no longer does so officially.

Despite its efforts to find a middle ground between those contending at the Council of Chalcedon, the Monthelite position essentially exhibits the same strengths and weaknesses as the Apollinarian position. Failure to affirm the full humanity of Jesus, since He does not have a human will, entails that we cannot account for how Jesus can bear our sin.

A Great Human Being

Inspired either by new insights of the Spirit or by insights drawn from our modern worldview, several theologians have overcome the dualism of Christ's

Two Natures by asserting his humanity alone. One of the first to make this claim was sixteenth-century Italian Spiritualists Michael Servetus (*On the Faith and the Righteousness of the Kingdom of Christ*, 1.2) and Faustus Socinus. Modern scholars taking this position, that Jesus is primarily a man of perfect morality, include John Locke (*The Reasonableness of Christianity*, 172–174) and probably Immanuel Kant (*Religion Within the Limits of Reason Alone*, especially III.1.VII; II.1.A). It is a position in line with the Unitarian-Universalist Church. Sometimes among Unitarians this Christology has existed side-by-side the affirmation of *Adoptionism*, the belief that Jesus was born as just a human being but was adopted Son of God at some point in his life, perhaps in his Baptism (Mark 1:11). The Jewish-Christian sect of the first centuries, the Ebionites, first held this position and it was maintained by late sixteenth-century Unitarian Faustus Socinus.

A related variety of a stress on Jesus' humanity is found in Liberal Theology. Friedrich Schleiermacher describes Jesus as a man with a perfect God-consciousness (the real meaning of attributing divinity to Him) (*Christian Faith*, 94), and Paul Tillich claimed that Jesus perfectly embodies the New Being (which entails that there is no alienation between His humanity and God) (*Systematic Theology*, Vol. 2, pp. 118ff.). Among U.S. Southern African Americans it was often said that anyone who liberated them was Jesus.

The concept of a God-Man of course defies Reason, and so this Christological proposal is a most rationally attractive one. But is this (especially Schleiermacher's and Tillich's version) just an updated version of Arianism, a failure to recognize that if Jesus is not fully God then God is not our Savior, and only God can save. We turn now to the two Christologies that were dominating in the early Church at the time of the Council of Chalcedon and really influenced the authoritative Christology we have today in catholic Christianity.

Alexandrian Christology

This model is so named for the city in the early Church in which it developed—Alexandria. Its primary organizer was Cyril of Alexandria (Letter To John, Bishop of Antioch, 39; *Five Books of Contradiction against the Blasphemies of Nestorius*, 3.3), but among its earlier proponents were Origen (*On First Principles*, II.VI.3), Athanasius (*On the Incarnation*, 18), and Gregory of Nyssa (*Against Eunomius*, V.5). In the Reformation era, Martin Luther became its primary spokesman, and to this day his theological heirs largely endorse it (*This Is My*

Body, in *Luther's Works*, Vol. 37, pp. 59ff.). Likewise from time to time we find it endorsed in the Roman Catholic, Eastern, and even in Anglican communions (among Anglo-Catholics).

The core commitment of this Christology is to stress the union of the divine and human in Jesus. This in turn leads to the affirmation of *communicatio idiomatum* (communion of idioms, entailing that whatever is said of one of Christ's Natures can be attributed to the other in a derivative sense). On this basis it is appropriate to say that when Jesus wept, God (the Son of God) also wept. Because it is the humanity of Jesus that first suffers and weeps, a solidarity between God and those who suffer is established. Likewise the omnipotence displayed by Jesus the Son of God through performing miracles can be attributed to His humanity. Also on this basis it is appropriate to say that Mary as the mother of Jesus is the Mother of His divinity, the Mother of God (*theotokos*).

This approach certainly makes it clear that Jesus is One. It is essential in traditions that believe that Christ is Really Present in the Communion elements. For those traditions need Christ to be omnipresent, Bodily Present in every Eucharistic celebration happening simultaneously throughout the world at the same time. This can only happen if Christ's humanity is omnipresent. And of course that is true according to the Alexandrian *communicatio idiomatum*.

The problem with this option for some Protestants might be that it has a heavily Roman Catholic/Eastern tradition orientation with its Mariology. But in our Feminist/Womanist ethos, is a greater role for Mary a useful emphasis? Certainly the openness to God suffering when the Man Jesus did is in line with Liberation Theology and a Pastoral Care concern to make people feel that God knows their trials. But is the idea that God suffers or that Jesus' humanity might be said to be omnipresent a diminution of the divine-human distinction?

This is a good point to digress on the doctrine of *Mariology*. Her role is especially significant in the Catholic and Eastern Church piety. In these traditions she is a *Mediatrix*. Like all the saints she may be called on to intervene with God on behalf of the faithful. But the Catholic Church adds that she was *Assumed into Heaven* (did not die) and was *Conceived Immaculately*. She cannot be the offspring of Original Sin, born in sin, or she would not be a worthy bearer of her sinless Son. Though these teachings had Medieval roots they were not established until the Modern Era by papal pronouncements (the only two times the Papacy has spoken infallibly), the Assumption of Mary in 1854 by Pope Pius IX and the Immaculate Conception in 1950 by Pope Pius XII.

Antiochene Christology

The alternative to the Alexandrian position developed in Antioch, and in many ways was a contradiction of the Alexandrian position. The movement was organized by Theodore of Mopsuestia (*Incarnation*, 5, 8, 1), was strongly advocated at an early stage by John Chrysostom, and has been embraced by almost all Protestant denominations, except for those noted above.

Essentially the Antiochene view rejects the Alexandrian emphasis on the unity of Christ's Two Natures. Instead it insists on a distinction of these Natures, and, while not denying their union, is not so inclined to be specific about the nature of their union. The *comunicatio idiomatum* is not employed, and Mary is referred to as "Mother of God" only in the most qualified sense. Consequently, for Antiochenes, Jesus may have suffered, but God did not (though He may have "felt" Jesus' and correspondingly our pain as a loving parent suffers with a child).

The strength of this Christology is that we preserve the integrity of the divinity and humanity of Christ, and for Protestants the avoidance of calling Mary Mother of God is attractive. But all that seems to be said about the Oneness of Jesus is that it is a fact. And if all we can say about the Incarnation is that it is a mystery, will it be a central part of the working faith of people?

The controversy between the Alexandrian and Antiochene positions threatened to divide the early Church and also undermined the Church's efforts to refute the heretical options noted above. Indeed, what transpired at the Council of Chalcedon was as truce between proponents of these two different Christologies. This truce is still in place today, as the differences between Alexandrian Christology and Antiochene Christology do not divide Christians. Proponents of denominations with an Antiochene Christology do not remain separate from Lutherans, Catholics, and Eastern Orthodox churches *because* they are Alexandrian, and vice-versa. But inevitably Christians must assume a position on the *comunicatio idiomatum*, and so readers are encouraged to figure out where they stand.

No matter one's position on these issues (more likely the question will arise among those with Alexandrian sensibilities), there may be a desire to find the sort of concrete images for depicting the union of Christ's Natures that we sought in understanding the Trinity. Let's look at some of the historic options.

Describing the Hypostatic Union

Of course one option in dealing with the Christology is to appeal to the concept of Mystery, that it is a concept which defies reason, cannot be explained, and that we distort the faith when we try to makes sense of it in concrete images. But if that is your preference, consider the risk just noted. And there may be others that today's theologians can develop. It is noteworthy that all but the final image provided were proposed by proponents of the Alexandrian position. All presuppose the Virgin Birth, but none offer an explanation of that mystery.

—United Like Body and Soul are One: Augustine (Epistles, CXXXV) and Martin Luther (*Confession Concerning Christ's Supper*, in *Luther's Works*, Vol. 37, p. 229) embraced this image at times.

—The Two Natures are United Like a Glowing Iron was proposed by Origen (*On First Principles*, II.VI.6) and the Lutheran heritage (Formula of Concord SD VIII.64, 66). The iron and the heat of the iron are distinct, yet no one can separate them.

—United Like Sugar in Water: Martin Luther also invoked this image (*Sermons on the Gospel of John 6–8*, in *Luther's Works*, Vol. 23, pp. 148–149).

—Activist Model: This position was advocated by Karl Barth. It operates with the supposition we have already observed that Barth used in dealing with the Trinity—the idea that a being is what it does (*Church Dogmatics*, Vol. IV/1, p. 492). Consequently on his grounds Jesus is said to have a human nature insofar as He does what humans do, and has a divine nature insofar as He does works that only God can do (*Ibid.*, Vol. IV/3, pp. 39ff.).

Readers should evaluate each of these options, determining which one/s might best communicate today in our context, and if not, seek other alternatives.

OFFICES OF CHRIST

Some, but not all theologians try to understand the Work of Christ in accord with certain emphases. In some cases a theologian may attribute more than one of these offices to Christ. In addition to the three dominant images we review below it should be noted that some Catholics and even Protestants focus on Christ's office as *Judge*. That is, He is seen primarily as a teacher of moral principles and spiritual life, laying down guidelines and laws that He expects us to obey. And He will judge us accordingly (Matthew 7:13-14; 13:41–42). We have already noticed above how Locke and Kant portray Christ this way and sometimes the Catholic Church too (*Catechism of the Catholic Church*, 1036). The problem with this image, and why it has not been one of the historic three that follow is that it may minimize the loving character of God and Christ.

Christ As Priest

Viewing Christ as Priest is to emphasize how He offered Himself for us as a Sacrifice for our sin is a construal of Christ which is especially typical of Catholic Orthodox and Protestant Orthodox theologies of the seventeenth century up to the present. A handful of examples include the Roman Catholic Church (*Catechism of the Catholic Church*, 1544ff.), Lutheran Orthodox theologian John Baier (*Compendium Theologiae Positivae*, 491), the Baptist London Confession (VIII.9, also affirming the other two offices), and almost all proponents of the Satisfaction Theory of Atonement (see Chapter 7 below). We find sound Biblical backing for this vision in Hebrews 4:14; 2:17.

As Prophet

Christ is viewed as Prophet especially when emphasis is placed on His role as Teacher, as functioning Prophetically in proclaiming a Word that challenges the status quo. In the role of perfectly revealing the Will of God John Calvin (*Institutes*, 2.15.1–2), The Shorter Catechism (Q.24) of The Westminster Assembly, and the Baptist London Confession (XVI) exemplify this outlook. But if by the Prophetic role we mean that Christ challenges the status quo like the Old Testament Prophets, has a social-ethical agenda, then Martin Luther King, Jr. (*Strive Toward Freedom*, Ch.11) and other representatives of Black Theology as well as Liberation Theology (Rubem Alves, *A Theology of Human Hope*, especially pp. 94ff.) exemplify this viewpoint. When Black Theologians refer to Jesus as Black, claiming that this is just a way of reminding us that He identified with the oppressed or that He sought to lead the nation to freedom (James Cone, "God Is Black," *Lift Every Voice*, p. 83; Albert Cleage, *Black Christian Nationalism*, p. 4), by implication they portray Him in the role of Prophet. Biblical authorization for these commitments include Mark 2:2–4; 6:6; 11:15–19 and Luke 7:16.

As King

Viewing Christ as King is to emphasize His reign over the Church and the world. Among texts supporting this model are Revelation 19:16, Ephesians 1:20–23, and Mark 15:2; 14:62.

Those embracing this model include Martin Luther (*Smalcald Articles*, II.IV.9) and others opting for the Classic View of the Atonement (see Chapter 7, below). Others embracing this model include Athanasius, in claiming the Christ as Ruler of the world needed to return it to its true allegiance (*On the Incarnation of the Word*, 10.55), Karl Barth insofar as he claims that Christ reveals all that exists concerning God and the world, including human nature (*Church_Dogmatics*, Vol. IV/2, pp. 154ff.), Friedrich Schleiermacher in claiming that Christ is the animating principle which the Church requires (*The Christian Faith*, 105), and Paul Tillich as well as Justin Martyr claiming that the New Being/Logos that Christ embodies reflects in the structures of all that is (*Systematic Theology*, Vol. 2, pp. 125ff.; *First Apology*, 23). Given how many ancient African theologians taught the Classic View of the Atonement (see Chapter Seven) and so embraced Christ's Kingship, it is interesting to note that some early African-American Christians in the South implicitly embraced this model to the extent that they regarded anyone who brought liberation as Jesus Christ (a Cosmic Christology). And likewise is not surprising that Afro-Caribbean and African Christians are believed by some analysts to understand Christ's divinity in terms of His reign and triumph over forces in the cosmos (Robert Hood, *Must God Remain Greek*, pp. 155ff.).

Is Jesus the One Who takes the punishment to save us, the One Who overcomes all the forces of evil, or the One Who courageously teaches and acts, standing up against what the establishment wants Him to do? The Biblical witness suggests He is all of these offices, but does one agenda warrant more attention than the others? If so, why?

CLOSING THOUGHTS

When thinking about Jesus Christ (Christology), we have put all the important questions on the table. First there is the issue of what to make of Who Jesus is, and if both divine and human how to make sense of that (how He can be both). Considering the Offices of Christ is just a matter of what to emphasize about His Ministry, what the theologian thinks is the heart of Jesus' Mission. How one answers that question will say a lot about (or reflect) what the theologian's sense of the heart of Christian faith is.

4

THE HOLY SPIRIT

This doctrine pertains both to the Person and Work of the Holy Spirit. Regarding the Spirit's Person, we have already indicated how the Holy Spirit is one of the three hypostases of the Triune God, of the same substance as Father and Son, and we also considered options for describing Who the Sprit is. (Think back to the many Biblical references cited in the second chapter to the Spirit of the Lord.) Also note that at least one time God Himself is said to be Spirit (John 4:24).

Regarding the Spirit's Work, we should remind ourselves that there are references to the Spirit being poured out on the faithful in the Old Testament. Yahweh's Spirit was said to be poured out on certain leaders/Prophets of Israel (Judges 6:34; 1 Samuel 11:6; 16:3). It should be noted that unlike the New Testament understanding of the Holy Spirit, the gift of the Spirit in this period was selective and temporary, not permanent and given to all. In fact in the period after The Babylonian Captivity the Spirit no longer seemed to manifest itself. (The Prophets who did arise were given a mandate by Yahweh apart from any gift of the Spirit [see Isaiah 8:11; Jeremiah 1:9].)

In the period when the Spirit was no longer manifest in Israel, the gift of the Spirit came to be deemed an eschatological hope (a sign of the realization of the Kingdom of God or of the End Times) (Isaiah 59:21). Messianic Prophecies identified the Messiah with the shoot of Jesse who would receive the Spirit (Isaiah 11:2). This correlation of the Messiah and the Spirit is certainly relevant for the Trinity doctrine and the dispute over the Filioque. Also, in this period the idea that the Spirit would be poured out on all flesh, not just Israel's leaders, is a foreshadowing of the New Testament realities (Ezekiel 36:26–28; Joel 2:28).

Early New Testament Christians of course experienced extraordinary prophetic operations of the Spirit, apparently states of ecstasy (Acts 2:4ff.; 10:46; 1 Corinthians 12:7–10; 14:1–40; 2 Corinthians 12:12; Galatians 3:5). But a combination of Pauline critiques of these practices and the development of church structures in the second century as the Church's original high expectations that Jesus would soon return began to fade led to a diminishing of ecstatic experiences thought to have been engendered by the Holy Spirit. Let's start out by reviewing the options that have developed in the Church's history regarding the Work of the Spirit.

MANIFESTATIONS OF THE HOLY SPIRIT

We immediately think of the Holy Spirit's role in inspiring ecstasy and speaking in tongues, or glossolalia. The Charts for Chapter 9 on Sanctification/Christian Life lay out the options. If we think of Christians speaking in tongues, the Pentecostal Movement and the Charismatic Movement come to mind. But these experiences have not been limited in the history of the Church to these twentieth-century Movements. Speaking in tongues and ecstasy did not first appear in the 1960s when these experiences developed in various existing denominations whose members having this experience remained in their denominations in hopes of starting internal revivals (the Charismatic Movement). Nor did the outbreak of these experiences only begin in at the Los Angeles Azusa Street Revival of 1906 when the Pentecostal Movement became an internationally-known phenomenon eventually leading to the formation of today's Pentecostal denominations.

It is well known that the famed LA Revival had precedents in the early years of the twentieth century in experiences of the Holy Spirit around Charles Parham in Topeka Kansas. But we must not forget the sixteenth-century outbreaks of tongues among the so-called Spiritualists, other Reformers, and even earlier expressions of ecstasy in Medieval Mysticism and in pre-Medieval centuries. Let's review some of these options, as well as the option of not speaking in tongues, for that is probably the majority position of theologians in the history of the Church.

Montanism

This option owes its name to a second-century leader of a movement to revitalize a Church which was no longer regularly experiencing the Holy Spirit as it had in the New Testament era, though even after the end of the New Testament era and before his crusade there seems to have been some extraordinary manifestations of the Spirit (as reported with criticism by Justin Martyr, *Dialogue With*

Trypho, LXII, LXVIII and Irenaeus, *Against Heresies*, II.XXXII.4). As we noted already in the first chapter, Montanus and his colleagues like Tertullian and Perpetua tended to speak of the Holy Spirit in the first person. In that sense they were effectively claiming to receive new revelations, which entails that the New Testament events were not authoritative for them. This is certainly attractive for those hungry for direct experiences of God. But the danger is that it violates appreciation of the authority of the Biblical witness and of Tradition. Such practices seem to undermine Paul's call for discerning the Spirit (1 Corinthians 12:10; 14:39–40). But then on the other hand it might be argued that the original Christians who did not have an authoritative New Testament operated with this kind of leading of the Spirit.

It should be reiterated that others opting for a similar understanding of the authority of the Holy Spirit include the Spiritualists of the Reformation era like Thomas Muntzer and the Peasants Revolt of the era (*Sermon before the Princes*), Caspar Schwenkfeld (*Answer to Luther's Malediction*), and Sebastian Franck (Letter to John Campanus, 17–18, 24). Later Spiritualists of the next generation included Faustus Socinus, whose views on Christ as a result of the new revelations we have he already noted. An African example is Vita Kimpa, a Kongolese Christian, who was granted a direct revelation and encounter with St. Anthony who taught her that Jesus was Black. Modern examples of Spiritualism include the Black Revolutionary of the nineteenth century Nat Turner, the famed Black preacher of the early part of the twentieth century Father Divine, and Josiah Ositelu, the founder of The Church of the Lord (Aldura) Worldwide in Nigeria.

The same points previously raised in the first chapter against an emphasis on Experience alongside Scripture are pertinent to this understanding of the Holy Spirit. A viewpoint like this one elevates attention to the Holy Spirit and is likely to result in a Spirit-centered life. But given our sinful human condition (our ability to twist the interpretation of our experience in self-serving ways), can we really trust our new revelations as much as Scripture and Tradition?

Inner Light

In the first chapter we reviewed this version of Montanism in considering George Fox and the Quaker tradition's claim that the Inner Light provides intimate fellowship with God, enabling people to develop spirituality and morality. But Quakers also make it clear that this Light is not inherent in nature, but is of divine origin. Thus this Light, it is said is the influence of the Holy Spirit (Declaration of Faith). Indeed some say members of the Society of Friends "quake" or tremble when experiencing the Inner Light possession of the Spirit.

Special emphasis is said to be placed on the Inner Light, and in that sense on the experience of the Spirit. The question is whether this "special emphasis" outweighs the authority of Scripture. The Friends' Declaration of Faith may protect them from this problem by contending that "No one can be required to believe, as an article of faith, any doctrine which is... contrary to Scriptures, though under professions of the immediate guidance of the Holy Spirit..." Perhaps the Quaker model is not Montanist, and therefore not so problematic—nothing more than ecstasy in the Lord without tongues.

Mysticism

Mysticism is a piety that posits that through spiritual discipline one is led to an intimate, even immediate relationship with Christ, something like sexual intimacy in which one feels like one with her/his lover. Though not consistently made clear, the Holy Spirit often is credited with bringing Christ or making possible the believer's loving attitude. Mysticism has been present through much of Christian history. In the Middle Ages one thinks of Francis of Assisi, Catherine of Siena, Bernard of Clairvaux, and an anonymous late Medieval tract titled *Theologia Germanica*, which deeply influenced Martin Luther. In the modern era, Howard Thurman has been among the most famous proponent.

The Mystical experience is direct and immediate. But unlike Pentecostalism there is rarely an experience of tongues, and unlike Montanism, most Mystics do not designate the experience as authoritative. Of course some Mystics have extraordinary experiences. Thus Catherine of Siena in experiencing unity with Christ reportedly had her body marked by "stigmata," Christ's very wounds.

Mysticism seems to afford the kind of immediacy with God and Christ that the other options noted provide. Indeed the concept of union with Christ as akin to sexual union may even make the believer's relationship with Christ more intimate (Catherine of Siena, *Dialogue* 134; Bernard of Clairvaux, *On the Song of Songs*, 8.1.2; *Theologia Germanica*, XXXV). And, as noted, it does not appear to make the Mystical experience authoritative. But there is still the concern with Mysticism that the faithful with direct access to God might not need the Church. Others have difficulty with the image of sexual intimacy with Christ it posits (but see the Song of Solomon). Are these concerns sufficient to render Mysticism problematic?

Modern Pentecostalism and The Charismatic Movement

What distinguishes the modern Pentecostal Movement (and Charismatics) from these various extraordinary manifestations of the Spirit's Work lies in Pentecostalism's origins in the American Holiness Movement and its concern with being born again. The Movement's founders were the first to relate the gift of tongues evidencing the outpouring of the Spirit with references to the Baptism of the Holy Spirit (Mark 1:8; Acts 1:5; especially see Acts 10:44–47) (Charles Parham, *The Everlasting Gospel*, Ch. II; Assemblies of God, Statement of Fundamental Truths, 8; Church of God in Christ, *Official Manual*, p. 46). This has led to disputes among Pentecostals regarding the relationship between the Baptism of the Holy Spirit and Sanctification. All agree on the fact that they are distinct, but the issue is whether you must receive the Baptism of the Spirit in order to be sure of your Sanctification and salvation (so called Three-Step Pentecostalism) or whether this Baptism is merely an enrichment of your Sanctification and salvation (Two-Step Pentecostalism). The differences between these approaches as well as their strengths and weaknesses will be discussed in detail in Chapter 9.

Another important difference from most of the options already considered is that at least in the official statements of Pentecostal denominations and in the case of most Charismatics, there is a break with Montanism and Inner Light thinking. Typically these denominations and Charismatics are theologically conservative and insist on the infallible authority of Scripture; they will not countenance a role for the present experience of the Spirit to critique the written Word of God (Assemblies of God, Statement of Fundamental Truths, 1; Church of God in Christ, The Articles of Religion).

Pentecostal understandings of the Holy Spirit seem to have a lot of Biblical backing and are not so readily critiqued as the previous alternatives. But the next options raise critical questions regarding the validity of Pentecostal theology.

Others With Openness To Tongues

In the history of Christian thought there have been some theologians, who though they did not speak in tongues, were not critical of it. Protestant Reformer Ulrich Zwingli is one who comes to mind. He claimed that the gift of tongues is not necessary for salvation, as it is only given to a few. But it was ordained by Christ for the benefit of providing a witness to unbelievers he claims (*Of Baptism*).

John Wesley's reflections on the gift of tongues is in the same vein. He chides a colleague for claiming that the gift has been withdrawn since Biblical times, speculating that it may have transpired at least in John's ministry to Asia Minor and Peter's mission in Italy, continuing into the sixteenth century (Letter To The Reverend. Doctor Conyers Middleton, VI). And yet Wesley himself never claimed or advocated for this gift.

This mediating position was largely forgotten in the next 300 years. However with the emergence of the Charismatic Movement in the 1960s most mainline churches in the West and for different reasons also in Africa have taken a position in line with Zwingli – not mandating tongues for all Christians but allowing it as long as its Charismatic proponents in the denomination do not violate the other theological commitments of the Church.

There seems to be a valid Biblical basis for this position. We have already noted Paul's warnings against abuses of speaking in tongues, so presumably not all Christians in this era were wholehearted proponents of this experience. Also problematic with Pentecostalism is whether it might tend to create a class of "super-Christians," those who speak in tongues and those who do not. Paul seems to embrace such a concern (1 Corinthians 13:1–2). Proponents of this position seem to ensure that we not fall prey to creating such a distinction between true believers and lackluster ones.

The Holy Spirit without Glossolalia

This is clearly the majority position in theology. Indeed, there are numerous examples of harsh critiques against speaking in tongues. Martin Luther was among the most vociferous. Regarding most expressions of tongues as Montanism, he claimed that the desire for extraordinary religious experience is an expression of sin, prioritizing the subjective experience over the Word (Smalcald Articles, III.8; *Against the Heavenly Prophets*, in *Luther's Works*, Vol. 40, pp. 146, 147). Karl Barth offered a critique in the sense of suggesting that the tongues of the Acts 2 Pentecost experience refer not to the experience of glossolalia but to the fact that the gifts of actually speaking the languages of many nations assembled at the Festival is what is intended (*Church Dogmatics*, Vol. III//4, pp. 321–

322; Vol. I/1, p. 521). He raises a fair question. If you are more liberal in your Theological Method, and believe that miracles like the Pentecost experience are mere symbols testifying to our being in a new context, this would be another reason for not embracing Pentecostal experiences (Rudolf Bultmann, *Theology of the New Testament*, Vol. 1, pp. 41, 45, 155). Luther's concern should also not be overlooked.

Does this mean that theological positions that do not embrace speaking in tongues do not take the Holy Spirit seriously? This is a challenge that all who opt for the previous two options must consider. And it is true that in many non-Pentecostal churches there is a sense that the Holy Spirit is ignored.

The answer to the questions we have raised is largely a function of how important grace is in one's theology. This will become clear at the close of the chapter. Suffice it to note for now, if a theologian believes that we are autonomous, then we don't need the Holy Spirit as much as one who posits a role for grace in doing good. And if the Holy Spirit is construed as the Agent of grace, then the Spirit has a prominent role in such theologies.

Consider Augustine's thinking on this matter. We have already noted in his treatment of the Trinity how the Spirit is the love uniting Father and Son. Elsewhere he claims that this love draws us to faith, binding us to God as it binds Father and Son (*Treatises on the Gospel of St. John*, XXVI.3; *On the Morals of the Catholic Church*, 13.22). He also says the Spirit is the Finger of God, leading us to good works (*On the Spirit and the Letter*, XIV.26). For Augustine, the Spirit works faith and good works in us. Martin Luther adds to this that no one can understand Scripture without the Spirit (*Commentary On the Magnificat*, in *Luther's Works*, Vol. 21, p. 299). This seems to fit Luther's idea of the Spirit as Listener to the conversation between Father and Son. John Calvin, another strong proponent of stressing grace also has a strong emphasis of the Holy Spirit. Like Luther, he claims that we cannot do good or understand Scripture without the Word, cannot come to faith without the Spirit (*Institutes*, 2.2.25; 3.1.4).

Even the Sacraments are dependent on the agency of the Holy Spirit, Calvin claims (IV.XIV.9). These commitments flow nicely from Calvin's idea of the Holy Spirit as the Power of God, which he posited in his Trinitarian vision. God's Power moves us to understanding, faith, and action.

It is evident, then, that when theologians emphasize God's grace, they can have a strong emphasis on the Holy Spirit. The Spirit is the One Who makes faith (Galatians 3:14; Ephesians 2:18), Biblical understanding (1 Corinthians

2:10), and good works happen (Romans 8:11–14; 1 Corinthians 6:11; Galatians 5:22). The Spirit is also involved in the Sacraments (1 Corinthians 12:13) and in prayer (1 Corinthians 14:15). Just because you do not opt for glossolalia, it need not follow that you ignore the Holy Spirit. Of course, those theologians with less of a grace orientation may want to say that faith and good works, interpreting Scriptures, and prayer are things we do. Such a theological perspective will de-emphasize the Holy Spirit. The more we go that route in theology, the more the Pentecostal and Charismatic critique of those not speaking in tongues seems validated.

If all of these actions are Works of the Holy Spirit, does that reduce Christians to mere robots? Not necessarily. Let's review the options.

THE HOLY SPIRIT AND HUMAN ACTIVITY: OPTIONS

Essentially three options on how the Spirit works in relation to human activity have developed. (See the Charts for Chapter 8 for these options.) These three represent every logical possibility on the question of divine-human cooperation.

Heteronomy

One option is to contend that when God and human abilities meet in an event, the divine will always prevails. After all, we have no free will or God overcomes what we want, even violating our will to affect His good. The Holy Spirit must then be understood to violate the human spirit in bringing about faith. Those who teach Predestination and our bondage to sin are thought to teach this position. Several Biblical texts may be cited as perhaps giving support for this position (Romans 9:16; Philippians 2:13; Exodus 9:7, 33).

I have not been able to find any prominent theologians often seen as representative of this way of thinking. Several who do deny free will (in the sense of our bondage to sin) and teach Predestination claim that God and the Sprit work through our fallen will. We see this in the case of Augustine who says that our will does what God wants (*City of God*, V.9.1). Calvin does not say that God bypasses our will but that God prompts it or bends it (*Institutes*, II.IV.7). Even the Puritan Westminster Confession claims that God does not do violence to the will (III.1). Besides these problems in finding partners for a strict determinism which posits that the Spirit violates the human will, it seems difficult to integrate this view with the many Biblical exhortations to faith (see Mark 16:16; James 1:22ff.).

Autonomy

The next option is the polar opposite of the first, and it does have some precedents. The belief that we are totally free, make our own decisions without the influence of grace and the Holy Spirit, entails that faith is our own work. We have already encountered some of its representatives like Immanuel Kant (*Religion Within the Limits of Reason Alone*, First Ed., Pref.). Ignatius of Antioch (Letter To the Ephesians, 8–16) of the early Church also embodies this model as well as Pelagians and Semi-Pelagians whom we will consider in Chapter 8 (see the relevant charts). This viewpoint makes intuitive sense in the American context stressing individual responsibility and freedom. But is the cost compromising grace and the Holy Spirit?

Theonomy

The third option is a kind of middle ground, if not a synthesis of the first two. With this model faith is understood as God's Work, yet accomplished in such a way that the Holy Spirit works through the structures of human existence. We have already provided examples of this vision in the discussion of Autonomy above. Likewise the Biblical texts cited in that discussion provide relevant backing for Theonomy.

This model is really a spectrum. It may include those who see the human will as cooperating with grace and the Holy Spirit. The Roman Catholic heritage (to some extent Eastern traditions) as well as those designated in Chapter 8 as teaching Justification By Grace and Works construe the Holy Spirit's Work in accord with this option. But as we observed above, those theologians like Augustine, John Calvin, the Westminster Confession, and others who teach the will is bound in sin and salvation by grace alone are also representatives of this point of view. Another group of theologians who belong to this genre are Radical Orthodox theologians like John Milibank who refer to the concept we are discussing as *theurgy* (*Radical Orthodoxy: A New Theology*).

A risk of this model is finding the language to keep this balance, making sure that both grace and the human vehicle through Whom the Spirit works receive due attention. Many who think that they are articulating this viewpoint, readily fall into the Autonomy or Heteronomy position. The way human love or passion for one's work operates in some people's lives might be a useful analogy to illustrate this position. We are not forced to love or forced into most vocations. The will is involved. And yet we say we "fall" in love and some of us (especially pastors who are called) cannot imagine our lives without the job we love, would do it for free. If human love can freely compel us in these ways, think what God's love can do. The Holy Spirit works through the human will. And the more a theologian wants to stress grace the more the role of the human will is to be emphasized.

One other possibility emerges in the history of Christianity in developing the concept of Theonomy, a concept that might make the prioritization of grace associated with this model more palatable. It has to do with the way Augustine (*City of God*, XI.21) and his followers Martin Luther (*Sermons on the First Epistle of St. Peter*, in *Luther's Works*, Vol. 30, p. 114) and John Calvin (*Institutes*, III.XXI.5) as well as Medieval Mystic Meister Eckhart (*Intravit Iesus*) construed time. Prefiguring Einstein's Theory of Relativity (the idea that at the speed of light there is no time), they taught that from God's perspective all events in history are simultaneous (Psalms 90:4). For our purposes this entails that though faith is the work of the electing God, from God's perspective the action of God is simultaneous with our decision to believe and the good work we do with grace. Does this make Theonomy a more or less attractive option?

CLOSING THOUGHTS

With hard work in developing one's view of the Trinity doctrine, the task of determining Who the Holy Spirit is will already be addressed by the time you get to this chapter. That means that the big job you will have if you are a theologian who sees a role for experience as a norm for Theology is to decide whether you find yourself more inclined to Montanism. You should already be clear on this matter from the work done on Theological Method in the first chapter.

The next issue is whether or not you have a Pentecostal or Charismatic perspective. Either way, you need to have your argument and witness ready. And either way you need to come to terms with what other Work you see the Holy Spirit doing in addition to tongues. And then finally you need to sort out the relationship envisaged between the Spirit's Work and what human beings do (or do not) contribute to it. The more grace-oriented you are with a loving God, the more likely you will turn over most of the things in Christian life to the Spirit.

5

CREATION AND PROVIDENCE

The doctrine of *Creation* properly addresses the issue of how God made the cosmos and what the created order is like. Part of God's creation is humanity, as we were intended to be like prior to the Fall into Sin. This topic is considered in the doctrine of *Human Nature* or *Anthropology*—what human beings were intended to be like prior to the Fall into Sin. We will therefore examine the doctrine of Human Nature in this chapter. *Providence* is a related, though distinct doctrine. It pertains to *how* God rules His creation and whether all the events that transpire in the world are God's Work or the results of human autonomy. Let's begin first with the Creation doctrine.

The Biblical witness offers at least two different visions of creation. In Genesis 1:1–2:3, we find an account that pertains to the whole cosmos, said to have transpired in 6/7 days. In Genesis 2:4b-25 the focus is more on the creation of human beings with no time-table reported. (This is the basis for historical critics contending that there are two different creation stories in Genesis.) In Psalm 104 creation is portrayed more as a process. (Also consider John 1.) These different strands contribute to the differences over the doctrine that have developed in the history of the Church.

But despite these differences, the texts just cited collectively render remarkable agreement reflected among most theological expositions of the Creation on at least six points; (1) God is the Creator of the world (Genesis 1:1; 2:4b; Psalms 105:5); (2) It is created out of nothing (Genesis 1:2); (3) The world is not eternal (John 1:1–3); (4) Christ is involved in the Work of creation (John 1:1–3); (5) Humanity is made in the image of God (Genesis 1:27); and (6) Creation is intrinsically good (Genesis 1:4, 10, 12, 18, 21, 25, 31). Inheriting most of these affirmations from Judaism (save the role of Christ in creation), the early Church needed to make these affirmations over and against some of the philosophical and religious movements of the Roman Empire. Heavily influenced by Plato, it was commonly held that God (the Good) and matter were coeternal. Also the

Good was deemed impassible, so transcendent that no direct relationship between it and the world was possible. Thus to the degree that God was identified with the Good, creation of the world by God was not readily accepted in the philosophically educated segment of the first century Roman Empire. It was more common to believe that the world came into existence through the work of some intermediate beings that gave pre-existent matter its form. Let's turn to the Christian options for describing Creation that have emerged.

Out of Nothing

Most theologians have embraced the notion that the world was created *ex nihilo*, "out of nothing," since Clement of Alexandria (*Exhortation to the Greeks*, IV). When linked to the affirmation of the Son of God's role in creation, this affirmation serves to undergird the Trinitarian commitment that the God Who creates us also saves us. We can only have confidence in the One Who purportedly saves us from annihilation if He has a track record of creating us out of nothing. Just as Christ saves us without our bringing anything to the table, so God originally created us without our bringing anything of our own (matter) to the creation.

Despite its Biblical foundations, the idea that God created everything out of nothing has some intellectual challenges. For example, Process Theology and other viewpoints teaching God's Immanence which we examined in the second chapter have difficulties with this assertion, because if God is part of creation then the cosmos cannot entirely be nothing and been created in time. For God is an eternal substance (John Cobb and David Griffin, *Process Theology*, p. 65).

On the positive side if we take physics and its Big Bang Theory into account, then perhaps creation out of nothing makes more sense.

Made From Pre-Existent Evil Substances

The alternative against which the previous option had its origins was rooted in Gnosticism and its idea that the flesh is evil. A second-century Christian Gnostic from Asia Minor named Marcion added the idea that the god who created the evil flesh was the lesser god of the Jews, not to be confused with the good God of Christianity. Though the anti-Jewish implications and the violation of the First Commandment seem problematic, in cultural contexts in which the old gods of the culture are still a force with which to reckon, one might be pressed to consider if there is some Biblical precedent for this general line of thinking (Job 1:6; Judges 11:24; Genesis 31:53).

A modern version of this model is implied by the teachings of Mary Baker Eddy and the Christian Science Church. Though some have maintained that the church rejects the Genesis account of creation not pertaining to God's creation of humanity in the divine image as "false and material," the church itself rejects links to Gnosticism (an ancient religious movement that regarded the flesh as evil). However, the silence of Christian Science regarding God's creation of the material world suggests similarities to this model.

If you join the catholic Christian heritage in rejecting this option, at least it must be conceded that this Gnostic orientation does seem to enable us to account for how a good God is not the cause of evil in the world.

The Result of Rebelliousness

A related option was proposed in the third century by Origen. He regards Creation (both the creation of the soul and of material things) as the result of rebellion. In the beginning God was All in All, he claims. The first, spiritual creation resulted when minds (apparently eternal) that had formed a unity in God Who is Reason became weary of the divine love and in response to their desire were made individual souls which later received bodies in punishment—the second, physical creation (*On First Principles*, I.VII.4; II.VIII.4).

Paul Tillich and others who employ Existentialist Philosophy posit a related, though perhaps less controversial version of this viewpoint. The argument is that creation is only actualized when what is potential in our essence comes into existence. Consequently as soon as we exist and are created we become distinct, even alienated from our potential, our essence (*Systematic Theology*, Vol. 1, p. 255). Thus Creation implies Sin. (Tillich tries to take this back by contending that in God's creative vision the individual and his essential being are present, but then notes that we have no access to the divine life.) G. W. F. Hegel seems to make a similar point contending that what is created is outside of (alienated from) God (*Lectures On the Philosophy of Religion*, III.C; III.C.I.3). The belief that we are created in sin is a position that will speak to much modern popular piety, uneasy with a good creation (Romans 5:14; 1 Corinthians 15:22). But then Genesis 1:4, 10, 12, 18, 21, 25, 31 requires allegorical interpretations.

Essentially Moral

Another, less controversial mode for understanding Creation is to construe it as having been established by God in accord with laws of nature, and that these laws or at least some of them are moral—even in harmony with the Decalogue (at least with those Commandments pertaining to our human responsibilities). From this commitment, theologians proceed to refer to the **Natural Law**—the belief that because a common morality is embedded in the structures of creation through the use of reason we can discern right from wrong. Among the historic proponents of this view have been Augustine (*City of God*, II.4/74–75), his contemporary Ambrose (*On the Duties of the Clergy*, III.IV.25), Medieval Scholastic Theology (Thomas Aquinas, *Summa Theologica*, I/II.91.3; I/II.95.2), Martin Luther (*Temporal Authority*, in *Luther's Works*, Vol. 45, p. 128), sometimes Vatican II (*Lumen Gentium*, 36; *Gaudium est Spes*, 76, 69, 48, 12), proponents of Boston Personalism (Edgar Brightman, *Religious Values*, p. 110), and Martin Luther King ("The Power of Nonviolence").

These commitments have Biblical authorization in Romans 2:14–15. There seems to be scientific support for this concept, as there is a growing body of literature which suggests that there is a natural moral sense with which we are all born, that there are certain neural circuits in the human brain (especially its prefrontal cortex) which make morality possible. But then the question must be faced, why in a moral universe is there so much evil, injustice, and chaos.

Creation in 7/6 Days

Of course in view of the Biblical witness in Genesis 1 most Christians throughout history have believed in a 7- or 6-day creation. One of the first theologians to claim that creation was in 6 days was the second-century church leader Theophilus of Antioch, who claims that others had previously made this point (*To Autolycus*, II.Iff.). A document which became later very influential on the first Fundamentalists, the Puritan Westminster Confession, IV.1), as well as the Baptist Second London Confession (IV.1) also insisted on Creation in 6 days. With the emergence of modern scientific thinking this insistence that Creation happened in this time-span continues to be asserted in many Fundamentalist (and even some Evangelical circles, such in its Institute for Creation Research) (Henry Morris, *History of Modern Creationism*, pp. 358, 339; Baptist Bible Fellowship,

Articles of Faith, V). All of these theological alternatives seem to posit a Young Earth Theory.

Another version of this theologically conservative view was even found, surprisingly in the document which gave birth Fundamentalism, *The Fundamentals* (Vol. IV, p. 101). It teaches an openness to understanding the 6–7 days as longer than 24 hours, even as ages. More recent prominent Evangelicals to take this stand include Carl Henry (*God, Revelation and Authority*, Vol. 6, pp. 146, 205) and Francis Schaeffer (*Genesis in Space and Time*, pp. 57–133). Others teaching this position have been Augustine (*On Genesis Literally Interpreted*, I.17.32–35; IV.27.44ff.; V.24.44–45) and Martin Luther (*Lectures On Genesis*, Vol. 1, p. 121).

This latter version of the days of Creation can accommodate scientific and archaeological evidence regarding the age of the cosmos and of the earth. It also has some Biblical support (Psalms 90:4). Also it is interesting to note that the order of creation outlined in Genesis 1 beginning first with light (The Big Bang Theory and so the stars), then water (which is the origin of life), then plants (reference to sun and moon is a little out of order), then fish, birds, animals, and only at the end humanity. Relating faith and science in this ad hoc manner is one option. A more systematic approach, reinterpreting the Biblical images in light of the categories and findings of modern physics with a Method of Correlation is also an option that could be pursued.

A third version, finding the preceding alternatives as too liberal, is the so-called Gap Theory of Creationism. It accounts for the age of the Earth by contending that there is a gap (of undisclosed duration) between Genesis 1:1 and the 6/7 days' creation account that follows. Championed by nineteenth-century Scottish theologian Thomas Chalmers and by *The Scofield Reference Bible*, this model posits 24-hour days of creation but is still able to account for an older Earth that geology reveals. For Genesis 1:2ff. is said to report a second creation of the Earth following the first creation reported in v.1.

Creation As Ongoing Process

The idea of Creation as an ongoing process is certainly more compatible with modern science (especially the theory of evolution). It could be related to the preceding view of the days of Creation as longer than 24 hours, depending on how long these days are interpreted. Of course the proponents of Process Theology embrace this viewpoint, since for them all reality is in process (John Cobb and David Griffin, *Process Theology*, p. 14). In addition there are earlier precedents like Tertullian (*Against Hermogenes*, XXIX), Origen (*On First Principles*, I.I.6), and Martin Luther (*The Small Catechism*, II.2). There is Biblical precedent for this view, in texts like Psalms 104. The problem with this view might be the perception that it challenges the concept of Creation as something God has completed. Indeed this and whether God's Creation is out of nothing are the major questions associated with the doctrine of Creation. Another issue might be what sort of philosophical or scientific conceptions are used to describe what God has done (and is doing).

PROVIDENCE:
GOD'S INVOVLEMENT IN EVERYDAY LIFE

We turn now to the related issue of how God rules the universe. Depending on whether you think Creation is a completed action by God you will relate this doctrine and Creation differently than you would if you think Creation is still an ongoing process. If the latter and you take the position of the option just considered, Providence is just a part of the doctrine of Creation. But if Creation is finished, then Providence is a distinct doctrine.

Essentially the other issue that divides Christians on this matter is how much happens according to God's Will. Is all that happens according to God's direction, or are we free to determine what happens in life? We examine now the alternatives.

Weak View of Providence

We begin with the viewpoint that takes human freedom more seriously. Given the impact of Western society on the theology that has been done since the Biblical era it is perhaps not surprising that this model has prevailed in the history of Christian thought. There are plenty of examples in Scripture exhorting our behavior (implying God does not determine everything we do) or implying that what we do impacts God (Genesis 6:5–6; Exodus 32:7–10; Judges 4:2; Mark 6:5). Among the numerous representatives of this orientation include the first theologians of the Church, the Apostolic Fathers (Clement of Rome, To the Corinthians, IV; Polycarp, Epistle To the Philippians, VIII–X) and the Apologists (Justin Martyr, *On the Sole Government of God*, IV–V; Tatian, *Address To the*

Greeks, XI), an architect of Lutheranism Philip Melanchthon (The Augsburg Confession, XVIII), the Anglican and Methodist traditions (The Thirty-Nine Articles, X; Articles of Religion, 8), a Reformed theologian of the same era, Faustus Socinus, General Baptists (An Orthodox Creed, XII, XX), Liberal theologians like Georgia Harkness (*Understanding the Christian Faith*, pp. 16–23, 114–120), Roman Catholics (*Catechism of the Catholic Church*, 306–308), the school of Open Theism most recently (Clark Pinnock and Richard Rice, *The Openness of God*), and proponents of Deism (John Toland, *Christianity Not Mysterious*). West African theologian Kwesi Dickson sees that a necessary tension must exist between destiny and self-determination, though insisting God has final say (*Aspects of Religion and Life in Africa*, p. 16).

Though not for most of these theologians, in some cases God is said to foreknow what we chose to do—the position of Origen (*On Prayer*, 3–4), Ambrose (*On the Faith*, 5.6.82), sometimes Augustine (*City of God*, I.28; XII.4), the Mennonite Waterland Confession (VI), and early Baptist John Smyth (A Short Confession, 6–7). One might appeal to Romans 8:29 and 1 Peter 1:2 for authorization, though it is not clear that these texts support such thinking. This view is strong on affirming human responsibility, allows us to blame ourselves and sin for evil that happens in life, but is it at the cost of God's control of and guidance in our lives?

Sovereign God

The polar opposite to the option just considered is to believe that God's sovereignty entails that God always gets His way. In short, it was determined in eternity that you would be reading this very passage when you do, and has been determined if you will pick up this book again as well as when the next severe weather event will come to your region. Even what your great grandchildren do (if they will be born) has long ago been determined.

There are two options here. Referring to a distinction made in the previous chapter on how God's Work relates to the human will, one could understand this option in terms of *Heteronomy* so that God gets the divine way in everything even in violation of His Will. A more typical way of making these points has been with the concept of *Theonomy*, the belief that when God works it is always through our will, though it is God Who is the Agent of the Work.

There have been plenty of proponents of this vision of God's sovereignty over all events in life. John Calvin and the Reformed tradition immediately come to mind (*Institutes*, 1.16.1; 1.17.1ff.; 2.4.7), and of course Jonathan Edwards ("Sinners in the Hands of an Angry God"). But at times Martin Luther (*The Bondage of the Will*, in *Luther's Works*, Vol. 33, pp. 36–39) and Anselm (*On the Harmony of the Foreknowledge, Predestination, and Grace of God with Free Will*, II.II; I.I.2.2–3) reflected this orientation. African Methodist Episcopal Bishop Daniel Payne ("Welcome to the Ransomed") expressed this position (at least he claimed that all God does is good), perhaps indicating how typical belief in a sovereign God is in the Black church, despite many advocates in its pews for freedom. Leading Black Presbyterian Gayraud Wilmore has expressly asserted the centrality of the sovereignty of God, and James Cone rejected the concept of a limited God as a way of dealing with evil in the world (*Martin & Malcolm & America*, pp. 29–30).

At times Augustine and John Wesley take a position on this range of issues that seems like a compromise, but not really. They speak of God giving permission for some events, especially evil ones, and that God fittingly orders what is lacking in creation (Augustine, Sermon 286, 6, 5; *On True Religion*, vi.11; xiv.27; Wesley, Sermon CXL, in *Works*, Vol. 7, pp. 500–501). Giving "permission" may get God off the hook for evil, but the one who backs away from action in order to let something happen is still in control. As we previously noted, some of these theologians, especially Augustine, Anselm, Luther, and Calvin understood there to be no time in God's Presence so that God's actions in the world are simultaneous with the events and human decisions themselves.

Ample Biblical authorization for this position seems to exist: Exodus 11:9–10; 14:4, 8, 17; Joshua 11:20; Job; Psalms 107:28–29; Ezekiel 13:11–13-14; Joel; Romans 9:15–23. But is a God Who sends death and catastrophes lovable? Or are we wrongly judging this God by our own feeble standards?

God As Band Leader (and Other Mediating Positions)

A mediating position has been articulated by third-century North African Dionysius of Alexandria (*Libris de Natura*, III), Athanasius (*Against the Heathen*, III.43), Process Theology (John Cobb and David Griffin, *Process Theology*, especially pp. 69ff.), and a modern scholar of faith and science, Arthur Peacocke (*Theology for a Scientific Age*, pp. 174, 176). The band leader, music composer, and movie producer are in control of the performance, involved in it even if in a hidden way, but a mistake on the part of the musician or actor can skew plans, even lead to a bad result. A related image has been offered by Martin Luther at times and also by other theologians who espouse the Classic View of the Atonement (see Chapter Seven). God is said to be in a struggle with evil, and does not always prevail (*Predigten*, in *Weimar Ausgabe*, Vol. 46, p. 495; *On the Bondage of the Will*, in *Luther's Works*, Vol. 33, pp. 70; Martin Luther King, *The Strength To Love*, Ch.III.2). In that case, all good is done by God; He only aims to do good, but like the Band Leader, evil transpires through no fault of His own.

Another image related to the Band leader image has been developed by eminent Geneticist Francis Collins. He refers to God as a Parent who has built playground equipment for children and then lets them play on it (*The Language of Science and Faith*, p. 191). In letting the children play, the parent is still observant and may intervene in what happens. The question must be posed to theologians employing this image, though, is whether they are in fact not opting for a view more akin to Deism than the models we have been considering. This image certainly seems to allow for more Autonomous Freedom that the alternatives just considered.

There are plenty of Biblical references to support all the visions associated with this model (combining the texts cited for the previous two options). But for those seeking a stronger view of Providence, not comforted if God is not fully in charge, then we need to look elsewhere.

HUMAN NATURE

The doctrine of Anthropology pertains to what human beings are like (especially how God intended us to be). The doctrine of Sin is not considered at this point, but rather what human beings would be like had they not fallen. Theologians tend to be divided on this issue pertaining to the different philosophies they use in describing human nature. There are also disagreements about how one defines the image of God (*imago dei*) (Genesis 1:27). Some claim it is our reason that reflects God's image, that we share reason with God. Others turn to our linguistic abilities that we share with God. Others think the image of God is our relational nature or the ability to love and cooperate. These are just some of the options, and readers may identify other possibilities which more helpfully shed light on who we are and Who God is. Depending on how a theologian describes God, which characteristics define the essence of God, the description of the image of God in human beings should be defined accordingly.

Employ Greek Philosophy

We have already in the first chapter outlined the core suppositions of Greek philosophy. Because reality is comprised of physical and rational elements, the human being is comprised of two substances, body and soul. This entails sharing the Greek idea that what is really essential to human beings is reason and that we are essentially individuals who participate in humanity.

In the first chapter, ample Biblical documentation for this view of human nature was provided in the section about those employing Greek philosophy in executing the Method of Correlation. Among a handful of examples of theologians endorsing this way of portraying human nature this way includes the self-proclaimed arch-enemy of philosophy from the early Church, Tertullian (*A Treatise On the Soul*, I, II, IV, teaching in VII.XXXVIII Traducianism, that the soul is formed in the womb), and a later African theologian Lactantius (*The Divine Institutes*, II.XIII; III.XII; III.XXVII; VII.V). Others endorsing this line of thinking include Anselm (*Monologion*, 67, 69, defining the image of God in terms of reason), John Wesley (Sermons CIX.5–7), the Presbyterian heritage (The Westminster Confession, XXXII; IV defining the image of God as having the Law in our hearts), Pentecostalism (Church of God in Christ, *Official Manual*, p. 62), and the Baptist tradition (Second London Confession, IV).

All of these theologians rely on Plato's ontology. The most famous theologian to employ Aristotle was Thomas Aquinas. This commitment manifested itself in his Anthropology with more emphasis on the role of habits in humans beings than those theologians indebted to Plato (*Summa Contra Gentiles*, 56, 57; *Summa Theologica*, IA.LXXXIII.1; IA.LXXVI.1).

Another example of those Christians using Greek philosophical categories to describe human nature is Mary Baker Eddy and the Christian Science tradition. This heritage not only distinguishes body and soul in human beings, but goes so far as to claim that the mind can control the body.

We have already noted the strengths and weaknesses of this way of portraying human nature. It is in line with how most Western people and so people in the pews think. But we must ask if this dualism and its inherent individualism is problematic in light of the holistic view of human nature that biology is discerning and in light of what we know about the Biblical worldview.

Regard Flesh As Evil

A heretical movement of the early church Gnosticism appropriated a body-soul dualism, but did so in a radical, controversial manner. Using Romans 8:8, 13, 2 Corinthians 7:1, and Galatians 5:16ff., Christian Gnostics could claim that humanity's heavenly element, the soul, was imprisoned in the evil body. Thus one could only achieve true spirituality, they taught, through *gnosis*, knowledge, which involves renouncing the evil of fleshly existence. In their view the larger class of humans was purely corporal with no souls (Gospel of Thomas, II.32).

This viewpoint, though condemned as heretical, was embraced by a number of white Southern US Protestants prior to the Civil War in order to justify slavery or not seeking the conversion of slaves. Were we to reject this position, can we agree that there is a certain popular piety in some Christian circles that would stress spiritual over earthly matters. Could we not consider the virtues of such an emphasis in view of the material acquisitiveness of much popular American culture? Let us not forget, though, that 1 John and perhaps Colossians 2 were written against such Gnostic thinking.

Maintain the Dualism With a More Relational Understanding

Proponents of this model largely endorse the suppositions of Greek philosophy (especially its body-soul) dualism, but with important amendments. Rather than the more individualistic basis of Greek philosophy, these theologians stress either that we have an essence which is at its core relational (we are not fully human if not in relationship to others) or in accord with African ways of thinking contend that we are shaped by the relationships we have. Among the most obvious representatives of this option include early church theological Clement of Alexandria (*Instructor*, II.XIII), Martin Luther (First Lectures On Psalms, in *Luther's Works*, Vol. 10, p. 356), Karl Barth (*Church Dogmatics*, Vol. IV/1, p. 492), Dietrich Bonhoeffer (*Communio Sanctorum*, pp. 98–100), Boston Personalism (Edgar Brightman, *Nature and Values*, p. 117), and Martin Luther King ("A Christmas Sermon On Peace"), as well as many members of the Black church tradition.

Use of Phenomenological Views of Human Nature

Several prominent modern theologians share these same sentiments but make these points by employing the philosophy of phenomenology. Recall from our first chapter that this philosophical viewpoint presupposes that there is a subjectivity that extends beyond ourselves. Edward Farley picks up this insight by contending that existence takes the form of universality. The phenomenological model even refers to our intersubjectivity, that transcendental subjectivity mirrors the structures of the world. And there can be tensions between these structures and our concrete historical situation, which can lead to bondage or chaos, or there can be world-unifying references that we interpret in the realities of the situation in which we find ourselves (*ecclesial man*, especially pp. 43–45, 128–130, 196–197, 220–222; cf. Edmund Husserl, *Ideen*, Vol. II, p. 79). A similar view of humanity is found in Paul Ricoeur (*The Conflict of Interpretations*, pp. 233–235; *Time and Narrative*, Vol. 1, p. 91), and Langdon Gilkey (*Naming the Whirlwind*, especially pp. 391–392) who posit humanity as a complex interaction of instincts, consciousness, and subconsciousness unified only through social intercourse with narratives, since language is at the core of being and narratives are the core of history.

There are clearly attractive features with this model of understanding human nature. Individualism is a more Western notion than is characteristic of the Biblical era. It is no accident that the characters of the Bible are always the son/daughter of someone of a place. There are no self-made human beings in the Biblical accounts. But insofar as the theologians subscribing to this model continue to posit the body-soul dualism of Greek philosophy, the weaknesses as well as the strengths attributed to this dualism for those using Greek philosophy pertain. We must also ask of this Anthropological model if its dualism and the inherent individualism this implies is problematic in light of the wholistic view of human nature that biology is discerning and in light of what we know about the Biblical worldview.

On the other hand, those in this group who rely on phenomenology do not typically speak of the body-soul dualism as much. But even in their case there is a sense in which human beings are construed as a substance like those with a Greek philosophical view of human nature (call it consciousness [even historical consciousness] in this case rather than a soul).

Human Beings As Priests of a Divine Temple

Late third- and early fourth-century North African theologian Lactantius offered this interesting vision of human nature. He did endorse the Greek body-soul dualism (*The Divine Institutes*, II.XIII; III.XII; III.XXVII; VII.V). But he affirmed uniquely that humans alone in the world can admire the works of God (VII.IV). In that sense they are spectators of God's works, like priests in a divine temple (XIV). This unique vision of human beings certainly suggests a purpose in life, to observe God and spend our lives leading others to worship. Humanity on grounds of this model is certainly more other-determined than the options thus far considered and compared to the ones that follow.

Employ Romantic Philosophy

We have also explained in the first chapter the core suppositions of this philosophical orientation. Applied to human nature in the hands of Friedrich Schleiermacher, Romanticism led him and others so influenced by this school and philosophy to regard human beings not primarily in terms of reason (like Greek philosophical thinking implies), but also as doing and feeling creatures. Feeling, especially immediate self-consciousness, is said to be the mediator of knowing and doing. We are really integrated, most human when this mediation happens, and piety is when all three are in operation. Faith makes us most human (*The Christian Faith*, Int. I.3.4–5). This vision of life as the alternation of passing-beyond-self and abiding-in-itself seems to be a wonderful vision for life. But does the basic "internatility" and individualism of this vision accord with the Hebraic view of the Biblical witness?

Employ Existentialist Philosophy

In the first chapter the core commitments of Existentialism were sketched. The Existentialist focus on existence appreciates that we are people who make our lives by the decisions we make. However, who we are is related to our potentialities (our essence), and we will be happiest when our potentialities are realized, when our existence coincides with our essence. A lot of Method of Correlation theologians employing psychology (especially Carl Rogers' insights) as their primary dialogue partner have similar understandings of human beings as healthiest and happiest when they become who they are. The best examples of this model have been Rudolf Bultmann and Paul Tillich.

In the case of Bultmann and Tillich, not much can be said about human beings as created. Of course Tillich can provide a lot about human essence, regarding individualization and participation in Being, freedom and destiny, dynamics and form, and the like (*Systematic Theology*, Vol. 1, pp. 168ff.). But this analysis only pertains to human potential. As soon as we come to exist, estrangement and sin set in, though we do keep the image of God (defined in terms of reason) (pp. 258–259).

Bultmann has even less to say about humanity before the Fall into sin. He defines creation as "subject to transitoriness." He does define humanity in terms of relationship to God (*Theology of the New Testament*, Vol. 1, pp. 230–231). But then in line with his reliance on the philosophy of Martin Heidegger he notes that "the chief characteristic of man's Being in history is anxiety" (*Kerygma and Myth*, pp. 24–25). For Bultmann and Tillich, actual created existence and the Fall into sin seem to be identical.

In view of how difficult the concept of Original Sin and the story of Adam's and Eve's Fall are for some people, should we praise the moves of Tillich and Bultmann? Or if we forfeit the goodness of creation, focusing more on Christ's saving work to the exclusion of attention to Creation, are we distorting Christian faith, undermining the Trinity's commitment to relating salvation and creation, and rendering Christian faith a religion only concerned about individual salvation?

Bultmann's student Gerhard Ebeling, who also relied on the insights of Martin Heidegger (in a later period) has some of the same problems, but may be less liable to the critique just issued. Recall from the first chapter the later Heidegger's teaching about the linguistic character of reality. This would imply that human beings are linguistic in nature, and that is precisely the move Ebeling makes. He proceeds to describe conscience in this way (*Word and Faith*, p. 409).

But this is essentially all he says about human nature. By implication, then, Ebeling can talk about the image of God in terms of language. This certainly accords well with Genesis 1 and John 1.

Ebeling proceeds to talk about conscience as having a futurity. Its ultimate validity lies in the future (p. 413). Does this mean that the full realization of human nature lies in the future (the realization of the Kingdom of God)? If so, Ebeling may offer a Biblically sound vision of human nature. But though he has not effectively denied the goodness of human beings as created, or is he claiming that the full goodness of human nature is eschatological?

Employ Process Philosophy

Some attention has already been given to Process thought. Its contention that the universe is always in process entails that human beings are always ontologically related to the world, much like phenomenology and pre-colonial African ways of thinking posit. There is no self apart from the world, and in that sense the world belongs to the self, like the self belongs to the world. There is no persistent plan for the self, for existence is radically contingent. Although this contingency is a lot like Existentialist ways of thinking about human beings, there is a concern with Process thinking to integrate the past in one's life. Process theologians employing this scheme for talking about human nature also in accord with scientific thinking talk about the psyche, not so much a soul distinct from the body. With evolution, this psyche now tends to use the body more than be used by the body (John Cobb and David Griffin, *Process Theology*, pp. 80ff.).

There are a lot of links with this between this Process vision and evolutionary science as well as with Old Testament general neglect of a body-soul dualism [the Hebrew term *nephesh* more properly refers to the life-force] and its tribal suppositions that did not stress individuality so much (Proverbs). But is the break with the idea of a soul so central to the New Testament problematic? And is the strength that this view of human beings links with Evolution a problem for those who want to claim that Creation is a past event?

Construe God and Human Beings With a More Holistic and Relational Understanding

This model has a lot in common with the vision of human nature we identified above, those theologians who continue to affirm the body-soul dualism but do it with a greater emphasis on the relational character of human nature. In fact two eminent theologians who were in that group, Karl Barth and Dietrich Bonhoeffer, embody this model too. The difference between these models is that the first group considered takes its bearing from Greek philosophy while in the case of Barth and Bonhoeffer and others who agree with them the starting-point for thinking about human beings is God's Revelation. That is how we know who we are. Human nature is determined by what God reveals Himself or His plans to be. Consequently, this view of human nature is more other-determined, while in the case of most of the options thus far considered (Lactantius' vision of humans as priests in the divine temple may not be privy to this critique), there is something about the human being that is essential and unchanging.

Barth's reflections on human nature begin with the Revelation in Jesus Christ (*Die Theologie und die Kirche*, Vol. II, pp. 212–239), and Bonhoeffer insists that individuals really can be changed in the Church, through Revelation (*Act and Being*, pp. 122–124). We have previously noted that for Barth God is what He does, and so this is also true for human beings, which entails that they are impacted by what happens to them (*Church Dogmatics*, Vol. I/1, p. 340; Vol. IV/1, p. 492). And Bonhoeffer's stressing the act of God in Revelation by which He binds Himself leads Bonhoeffer to note that human existence is impacted by acts done to them (*Act and Being*, pp. 82–83, 90–91, 123–124). In short, we are persons like God; who we are is shaped by what we done and has happened to us. This is a break with Greek philosophical thinking.

This break with Greek philosophy entails a distancing from its dualism. In line with Hebraic thinking and the insights of much modern Biology, the soul or mind not seen as a unchanging substance like the ancient Greeks taught. We are the souls of our bodies, Karl Barth claims in contract (*Church Dogmatics*, Vol. III/2, pp. 325ff.). The soul is part of the body, just a life-force and so is shaped by what happens to the body, just as biology teaches that the brain and the body interact.

Interestingly, in the name of facilitating Feminist concerns Rosemary R. Ruether takes a position in line with this model (in *Christianity and Crisis* [Dec. 1971]: 267–272). The two prominent Theologians of Hope also seem to endorse this sort of approach. Wolfhart Pannenberg makes clear that who we are, even the human mind, emerges only in our interaction with the world, especially the social and cultural world, shaped by spirit, the energy God has united with the evolutionary process (*Toward a Theology of Nature*, pp. 134–137, 153ff.). And Jürgen Moltmann claims that there is no given human nature at the beginning of history, but that it only exists as the goal of history (and of course that goal is the Work of God at the End of Time) (*No Man Is Alien*, p. 208). In these cases as well, human nature is becoming, but it is God's Revelation or Work that drives this becoming.

John Mbiti and much of African theology also offer a view of human nature that aligns at least to some extent with the theologians just considered. Speaking for an African worldview Mbiti claims that man is defined by the community, and this implies that there are fundamental changes at the core of one's being depending on what happens in the community, but all that transpires is in the spirit world (*African Religions and Philosophies*, pp. 141, 33–34.). To the degree that what we become under the guidance of the spirits is construed as a reference to Revelation, the connection between this African model and the theologians considered in this section is readily apparent.

This model as a whole seems to entail that the image of God is being/becoming what we have done (will do) or committed do, just as God is what He does. There are obvious strengths with this model and its break with Greek philosophical dualism. Unlike all the models considered, it does not assert a particular essence to humanity. Consequently it could be argued that this is in line with Biblical testimony and its communal orientation, as well as its claim that we make ourselves known by our acts (Proverbs 20:11). But on the other hand, it is then necessary to take into account the apparent use of Greek philosophy in the New Testament that we have noted. When we are clear about the nature of human beings our vision of Sanctification and Eschatology gets a lot clearer, since on Trinitarian grounds salvation and eternal life are related to Creation.

CLOSING THOUGHTS

When describing Creation, the first set of concerns is whether one agrees with the catholic consensus listed on the first pages of the chapter and if not, why not. Then the key questions to resolve are: (1) Length of Creation; (2) What the created order looks like; (3) The degree of God's involvement in what happens in the cosmos and the role of human action; and (4) Clarifying what set of philosophical, psychological, or sociological concepts best aid one describing human nature and what the image of God is thought to be. Be sure to address all these questions with an eye towards the implications for what you will want to say about Justification, the Christian life, and life after death (Eschatology).

6

SIN

The Church did not develop a doctrine of Sin (especially Original Sin) until relatively late. Of course the earliest theologians of the Church, the Apostolic Fathers of the late first and second centuries, had inherited the idea of sin from Judaism. But there is no concept of Original Sin in Judaism. Thus only after the Church began the practice of infant baptism, began to think about sin in terms of temptations, and as a result of Augustine's confrontation with Pelagius in the fourth century did the Church get around to formulating this teaching at the Council of Ephesus in AD 431—the idea that because of the sin of Adam and Eve we are all born in sin (Romans 5:12–15; 1 Corinthians 15:22). The history of Christian thought reveals that there have been disagreements on what Original Sin entails, how sinful we are and whether we have lost the image of God in sin or just had the image damaged.

Another disagreement, related to Original Sin and how sinful we are, also emerges from the fact that some theologians seek to identify and define what the essence of sin is. Some describe sin as the desertion of a better good for a lesser good (Augustine, *To Simplician*, II.18), as disobedience (Society of Friends, Declaration of Faith), as turning from what is right (Thomas Aquinas, *Summa Theologica*, Ia-IIae.xxi.1), as foolishness (Dionysius of Alexandria, *Exegetical Fragments*, I.II.14), as unfaith (Martin Luther, *Lectures On Genesis*, in *Luther's Works*, Vol. 1, p. 162), as loss of grace (Karl Rahner, *Theological Investigations*, Vol. XV, pp. 23ff.), sloth (Karl Barth, *Church Dogmatics*, Vol. IV/2, pp. 378ff.), as pride (Karl Barth, *Church Dogmatics*, Vol. IV/1, pp. 358ff.; John Wesley, Sermon XLIV, II.8), as selfishness (Martin Luther, *Lectures On Romans*, in *Luther's Works*, Vol. 25, p. 222), as emptiness and nothingness (Augustine, *On the Spirit and the Letter*, XII.19; Anselm, *On the Virgin Conception and Original Sin*, 5), as unjust efforts to gain security at expense of one's fellows (Reinhold Niebuhr, *Nature and Destiny of Man*, Vol. 1, pp. 220ff.), as domination of the neighbor (Liberation Theology as expressed by Enrique Dussel, *Ethics and Community*, p. 19), as loving the oppressor (James Cone, *A Black Theology of Liberation*, p. 51), as whatever denies women's full humanity (Rosemary Ruether, *Sexism and God-talk*, pp. 18–19), and as estrangement/alienation (Paul Tillich, *Systematic Theology*, Vol. 2, pp. 224ff; Vol. 1, pp. 155–157). All of these images seem to share the idea of the Greek term for sin, *hamartia*—missing the mark. Sin is missing the mark set by God. We turn now to the different options for dealing with Original Sin and its impact on human beings.

In the background of these differences is the disagreement over what sin has done to the image of God in human beings. Does Original Sin destroy the image of God or just distort it? The problem with the former position is that it might be taken as a denial of the goodness of creation on this side of the Fall into sin. But if we say that the image of God remains in us in sin, then does it follow that there is something in us for which Jesus did not need to die (a compromise of the belief that Christ alone save us)? Keep this question in mind when examining the options that follow.

TOTALLY SINFUL IN EVERYTHING WE DO OR SAY

Let's begin with the oldest approved version of Original Sin—with St. Augustine and the first Protestant Reformers. The core concept regarding Sin for Augustine and also the first Protestant Reformers who assimilated this aspect of his thinking is **concupiscence** (Augustine, *On Marriage and Concupiscence*, I.24–25; Martin Luther, *Lectures On Romans*, in *Luther's Works*, Vol. 25, pp. 292, 159; John Calvin, *Institutes*, II.II.24–25; III.III.10). Concupiscence of course is a term that refers first to sexual deviation. As employed theologically by Augustine and his heirs the term refers to selfishness, the desire for self-pleasure not just in sex but in everything one does. Just as the sex addict has no concern about the pleasure of her/his partner, but only seeks pleasure, so it is with the sinner. Even outwardly good deeds are undertaken for pleasure. As a result, we sin in everything we do.

All our deeds, even your reading this book and my writing it are sins, as liable to punishment as sloth, theft or murder. We have no free will; it cannot be avoided.

This stress on sin as concupiscence entails that Original Sin is not just a statement about everyone since Adam and Eve sinning, but a description of our condition and an explanation of why we are trapped in sin. Augustine offers the idea that Original Sin (concupiscence) has been transmitted through the birth process. The fruit of the lust of desire, what drives the sexual union, cannot but reflect this lust. If your parents enjoyed concupiscence in the sexual encounter that conceived you, no wonder that the product would be concupiscent (*On Marriage and Concupiscence*, I.XXIV.27). In these cases, of course the image of God in the sinner is said to be destroyed (*Exposition of Genesis According To the Letter*, VI.24.35; VI.27.38; Lutheran Church, Formula of Concord, SD I.10). John Calvin went so far as to speak of the human condition as "total depravity" (*Institutes*, 2.2.1ff.). We noted in the previous chapter how Paul Tillich also understands us to sin in everything we do, as he describes Sin as Existence, that as soon as we exist and are created we become distinct and alienated from our essence (*Systematic Theology*, Vol. 1, p. 255).

For Biblical backing for this family of positions, we find in Romans 7:4–23 and Ephesians 2:1–3 a clear testimony to the way in which we are caught up in sin in this way. Proponents of this vision tend to teach justification by grace alone. If you want a view of sin that continues to remind us of our need for grace, this option is the way to go. But if the feeling is that such a strong doctrine of sin will frustrate efforts at good behavior then the other options will be more attractive.

STRUCTURES OF SOCIETY MIRED IN SIN

A related version of the first option applies that option's reflections on the depths of sin to social structures. In a way, all the examples cited above belong in this group as well. Luther (*Lectures On Zechariah*, in *Luther's Works*, Vol. 20, p. 200) and Augustine (*City of God*, XVIII2; XIX.17/361–362) made the obvious move of going from understanding sin as concupiscence to understanding the structures which sinful human beings created as self-serving and mired in sin. Famed twentieth-century theologian Reinhold Niebuhr is someone we associate with this viewpoint (*Christian Realism and Political Problems*, pp. 120–127). But he made that point because he understood sin as pride, very similar to concupiscence (*Nature and Destiny of Man*, Vol. 1, pp. 190ff.). So he also embodies the first option.

Martin Luther King, Jr. certainly affirms this realism about political institutions, how in order to get things done you have to apply pressure and appeal to their leaders' self interest ("Love, Law, and Civil Disobedience"). And at times like Niebuhr he can talk about sin in an Augustinian way, as a force that traps people ("The Current Crisis in Race Relations"). Note how the emphasis, though, is still more on the self-serving sinful character of institutions more than individual sin. This trend has especially become evident in much Latin American Liberation Theology and Black Theology. The call for new language in liberation seems to exclude individual sin in the work of Rubem Alves (*A Theology of Human Hope*). Founder of Black Theology James Cone claims that Christianity must be primarily about Black liberation, and so he does not deal much with the sin for which Christ had to die (*God of the Oppressed*, pp. 126, 131–132). The sin that must concern us is white racism. We should also note Rosemary Ruether's concern to avoid all dualisms, which she claims lead to patriarchy (*Sexism and God-talk*, p. 93). But she does not have much to say about individual or personal sin.

If the theological agenda is with liberation, then the case can be made that we need to focus on social sin, interpreting Christ's Work primarily as the remedy for such injustice. But then the question comes, what are we to make of the Biblical references previously cited. Perhaps the answer is to be found in interpreting these texts as references to social sin, to how we use the structures of society to oppress and to advance our own economic agendas.

INCLINED TO SIN

There are several alternatives to this option. Proponents belonging to the first sub-group believe in original sin. But either they dodge the concept of concupiscence or like the Roman Catholic tradition they interpret the concept as referring to the "tinder" of sin, what can make sin possible if we act on it (*Catechism of the Catholic Church*, 1264). In short, just because you have concupiscence in you or are tempted by it that does not mean you are sinning. This in turn entails that the image of God is not totally destroyed for these theologians, just damaged.

Sin Can Only Be Avoided With the Help of Grace

By far this is the most advocated option in the history of Christian thought. As we will see in Chapter Eight it is the characteristic position of the Roman Catholic Church. (See below for further elaboration of its view of sin.) Most Protestant bodies other than Lutheran and Reformed heritages embrace this line of thinking. Thus, for example, Episcopalians (The Thirty-Nine Articles, IX–XI), Methodists (The Articles of Religion, VII–IX), and Southern Baptists (The Baptist Faith and Message, III, IV) teach Original Sin, without dealing with concupiscence, and rather than stating that we sin in all we do only speak of our being "inclined" to sin. But all affirm that only by grace through faith can we overcome sin enough to do good works.

In view of the many exhortations to avoid sin in the Biblical witness (Leviticus 16:30; Jeremiah 7:23; Romans 6:1–2) and even references to being "inclined" to evil and death (Psalms 141:4; Proverbs 2:18), this viewpoint seems most valid. It takes sin and grace seriously. But if we are not sinning in every deed, a reality that is neither affirmed nor denied with this vision, then we seem not to be in need of God's grace and forgiveness in all aspects of our lives.

We Can Choose To Avoid Sin

A number of theologians prior to Augustine embraced this way of thinking—Clement of Rome (Letter To the Church in Corinth, 7.5, 26, 58.2), The *Didache* (I–IV), The Epistle of Barnabas (18-21), John Chrysostom (*Homilies on the Epistle To the Hebrews*, XII.5), and Athanasius (*Four Discourses Against the Arians*, III.XXVI.33). The Society of Friends still takes this position in the sense of speaking, like many Baptists, of an age of accountability before sin is imputed (Declaration of Faith). There are certainly many Christians in the pews who think this way. The idea has ancient roots, appearing as early as the fourth century in the writings of Timothy, Bishop of Alexandria (Canonical Answers, XVIII)

The strengths and weaknesses of the previous option pertain to this viewpoint. In addition, there is even less a concern about grace and the need for constant forgiveness. In effect, this approach seems little different from the heresy of Pelagianism, which we will consider below.

Temptations Are Not Sin

Both early Christians Polycarp (Epistle To the Philippians, VI) and Origen (*On First Principles*, III.IV.2), writing before Original Sin was received as a doctrine, took this position. If we do not submit to our temptations we have not sinned. Thus of themselves, temptations are not sin. James 1:12 and the fact that Jesus endured temptation (Mark 1:12–13; Matthew 4:1–11) but remained sinless might be cited in support. It could also be argued that this viewpoint relieves sincere Christians of guilt, for who of us is not tempted? But on the other side it could be argued that such a position rejects the concept of sin as concupiscence and as a result does not make us dependent on God in all we do.

SPIRITUAL SICKNESS

This model, typical of the Eastern traditions of Christianity, portrays sin as a terminal spiritual sickness, rather than a state of guilt like the preceding models imply (rooted in Augustine, Sermons, XXVIII.13–14; cf. John Wesley, Sermons, LXXIV.21). As self-perpetuating, sin distorts the whole human being, corrupting (not eradicating) the image of God that we bear in our humanity. This sickness distracts a person from fulfilling her or his natural potential to become deified. (More on deification in Chapter Eight.) Another description employed is sin as chasm, separating God from humanity (Christoforus Stavropoulos, *Partakers of Divine Nature*, pp. 20ff.).

These Eastern images seem to take Original Sin quite seriously, but avoid the concept of concupiscence. We can recover from sicknesses and bridge chasms. And so there is a little more optimism about the chances to overcome sin. The door is open for us to do something about Sin. As we shall see in the Chapter on Justification this is precisely what the characteristic Eastern position on Justification and salvation affords, a chance with grace for us to do something. Those with a theology that includes this sense of our role in overcoming sin will find this as useful model. See the Biblical references cited above. But is the cost that one has forfeited an emphasis on the role of grace?

SIN IS CHOICE

Most Christians find the first two options in particular as overdoing pessimism, preferring to describe sin as misdeeds that we can avoid. And this also entails the rejection of Original Sin. The early church heretic Pelagius is the best example of this option (Epistle to Demetrias, 16). We have already noted that this teaching is a heresy, but a most popular one in American pews, polls tell us. Once again we note that this is a viewpoint that stresses human responsibility. It has a high regard for what human beings can accomplish, a good message in our culture of self-esteem. But what are we to make of an emphasis on God's forgiving love and Paul's message in Galatians 3:1–14 as well as Romans 7:4–23?

DIFFERENCES IN THE CHARACTER OF SIN

Not all sins are equal. This is a viewpoint of the Roman Catholic Church (*Catechism of the Catholic Church*, 1456, 1458, 1852–1863) originally inspired by the great scholar of the early Church, Jerome (*Against Jovinianus*, II.30). Some Eastern Orthodox churches seem to endorse this position (*The Holy Catechism of Nicolas Bulgaris*, p. 282). A distinction is made between **Mortal Sins** (grave violations of God's Commandments which offend love) and **Venial Sins** (everyday faults which offend love and God's grace, but do not quench it).

This model just makes common sense. Not all sins are equal. But not if you understand sin not just in terms of misdeeds, but as denials of God. In that case whether you sass someone or hurt that person, in either case you have denied the mastery of God over your life. The issue at stake here seems to be whether we quantify grace, whether some sins do not require as much grace as others. Both sides need to consider the relevance of Matthew 12:31–32.

CONCLUSION: MAKING SIN KNOWN, ITS IMPACT, AND OUR ACCOUNTABILITY FOR IT

Three other issues need to be addressed. There is general agreement that the Law of God in its Theological Use condemns sin and makes it known. But a handful of theologians with a Christocentric perspective, namely Karl Barth and to some extent Martin Luther, contend that because of the depth of sin and its corruption, we are likely to think when we hear the Law alone that we can measure up to its demands. Only when the Law is accompanied by the Gospel are we likely to understand the depth of our sin (Karl Barth, *Church Dogmatics*, Vol. IV/1, pp. 358ff.; Martin Luther, *Christmas Sermons*, in *Luther's Works*, Vol. 52, p. 22). Only when we see Christ on the cross and His love for us can be sure of the depth of our sin. Is this the way we should always preach and teach? Or is preaching the Law alone sufficient to make sin known?

Related to how we know our sin is the question of when we are accountable for our sins. Most theologians teaching Original Sin opt for the sinfulness of infants and their accountability for sin (Psalms 51:5). But, as we've already noted, those traditions teaching believers' baptism are not inclined to want to contend that unbaptized infants are damned, and so teach an "age of accountability" for sin, that only at a certain age when we are able to be born again is our sin charged to us (Southern Baptist Convention Baptist Faith and Message, II). Mark 9:34–36 and 2 Samuel 12:21–23 are cited in support. Which viewpoint has strongest Biblical support and best expresses the logic of Christian faith?

The previous discussion of the different accounts of how to portray or depict sin has already led us to consider sin's impact, especially whether the image of God has been destroyed or only been distorted. On that matter theologians need to decide whether it is more important to maintain a certain optimism about an appreciation of the goodness of human nature (then refer to the image just being distorted) or to protect a total dependence on God's grace (then it is preferable to speak of the image of God as destroyed in sin).

CLOSING THOUGHTS: WHAT TO MAKE OF THE DIVERSITY OF OPTIONS

In addition to addressing the question just raised, the primary issues that need to be resolved about Sin is how deeply mired in it we are, what Sin does to the image of God in human beings, and whether God is complicit in this. (This matter should already have been addressed, at least implicitly, in the theologian's doctrine of Providence.) The positions taken on the first two issues determine the role of grace required in saving us, whether we can contribute to our salvation by what we do. If thoroughly mired in sin, then salvation by grace alone becomes the only option. Once this issue has been clarified it is important to make sure that the images employed to describe Sin and Original Sin actually convey the theologian's agenda regarding how deeply mired in sin we are. Finally, it needs to be considered whether what is said on these issues still allows for an affirmation of the goodness of Creation, that humans were created as essentially good. With these maters addressed, the theologian is ready to address the questions of how we are saved.

7

ATONEMENT

The doctrine of the Atonement pertains to the Work of Christ, what Jesus did to overcome sin and ensure that we can or will be saved. Of course Jesus' death and its rationale are essential to the way in which this doctrine is addressed.

Jesus' death posed a problem for the early church. There is growing agreement among scholars that the need to explain how and why Jesus died may have stimulated the earliest theological endeavors, even those which shaped the canonical texts. Clearly the idea that the Messiah of God had met death on a tree was as source of embarrassment for the early church (1 Corinthians 1:23).

The embarrassment is reflected in the failure of some of the Church's earliest theological literature to speak much of the Cross and in the tendency to focus instead on Christ's exemplary life. Consider how the Fish (*Ichthus*, an acronym for the first letters of the Greek words in the phrase "Jesus Christ, God's Son, Savior"), not the Cross, was the original Christian symbol. Yet the Cross and its importance for Christian faith were indelibly etched in the early church's life. One finds the language of Christ's sacrificial death and suffering in some early Christian and pre-Christian liturgies.

ATONEMENT THEORIES

This way of nurturing an awareness of the significance of the Cross necessitated further theological reflection about the Atonement. Although no formal consensus defining the nature of the Atonement has been achieved in the Church, it is possible to identify five distinct ways in which Christians have explained the doctrine.

Moral Influence Theory

This Atonement model is the product of the earliest theological reflections. These early theologians like Clement of Rome (Letter To the Church in Corinth, 17–19, 36), Ignatius of Antioch (Epistle To the Magnesians, VI.IX,XI), Lactantius (*A Poem On the Passion of the Lord*), and the Constitutions of the Holy Apostles (I.13; II.xxiv) at least sometimes, if not on all occasions understood Christ and His Work primarily as an example, as the ideal man. His life makes it possible for believers to repent, amend their lives, and so be reconciled to God. Biblical justification is evidenced in 1 Corinthians 11:1 and Luke 6:36.

This way of dealing with the Atonement was not just limited to these early Church Fathers. It is a theological mode that has been influential in a Protestant movement stressing Christian spirituality called Pietism and also in the thought of modern Liberal Theologians like Friedrich Schleiermacher (*Christian Faith*, 100), Albrecht Ritschl (*The Christian Doctrine of Justification and Reconciliation*, pp. 450–452), and Paul Tillich (*Systematic Theology*, Vol. 2, pp. 172–176, though not expressly embracing the model). Not only did it reflect in the theology of Peter Abelard in the Middle Ages (*Exposition of the Epistle to the Romans*, II), but today it is perhaps the dominant model of academic theologians. Liberals find the next three models we will describe too rooted in mythological worldviews. And many modern Feminist theologians and Womanist theologians like Delores Williams find the other models guilty of reflecting patriarchy—either war-like models (the Classic View) or those which portray God as a crotchety old man (the Satisfaction Theory) (*Sisters in the Wilderness*, pp. 161–167, calling her version the Ministerial Vision).

The strengths of this understanding are that in addition to the modern issues noted above that it addresses, it also allows a strong emphasis on Christian life and responsibility, on the appropriation of Christ. Its problem is that ultimately the Atonement is made to depend upon what humans do (albeit with the aid of the Holy Spirit). And since salvation is up to you and me, we will not be confident about it. The next alternatives seek to make us more certain of the Atonement, portraying Christ's saving Work as a done-deal.

Satisfaction Theory

Proponents of this alternative, also termed the *Penal Substitution Theology* by some Orthodox Protestants understand Christ's death in terms of a sacrifice. The sacrifice must be offered in order to placate God's wrath against humanity or to set right the moral order. Sin is understood to have offended God's justice. Because God is just and righteous (cf. Isaiah 45:21), sinful humanity cannot be accepted until the debt of sin has been paid. By dying on our behalf Christ wipes away this debt and so restores a right relationship between humanity and God.

Some proponents of this orientation, often Reformed advocates of what they term the Penal Substitution View, contend that the Satisfaction Theory employed by Medieval Catholic theologians does not concern redeeming God's righteousness, but only pertains to restoring His honor (Anselm, *Why God Became Man*, I.15). On this basis these Orthodox Reformed theologians contend that their Penal Substitution Theory is distinct from the Satisfaction Theory. It is true that in the Catholic model one does not find the stress on legal transaction between God and humanity like proponents of the Penal Substitution Theory. Rather than regarding Christ's Atoning Work as paying a legal penalty like these Reformed theologians do, Catholic proponents of the Satisfaction Theory tend to regard Christ's work more medicinally, as healing (*Catechism of the Catholic Church*, 613). But in each of these versions of this Atonement model, a Sacrifice is paid to God in order to procure salvation.

This view of the Atonement is also Biblical (Ephesians 5:2; Isaiah 53:4–6, 10, 11; Hebrews 10:12). It unambiguously asserts the importance of Christ's death, inasmuch as apart from His sacrificial death humanity is not right with God. As such the objective character of the Atonement is affirmed, since it is in no way dependent on what believers do as in the case of the Moral Influence Theory. Christ alone atones for sin on our behalf. The power of God, His justice and honor, His control of the universe are also endorsed.

The only problem with the Satisfaction Theory is that it can connote a kind of legalism that does not take the radical newness of the Gospel seriously. According to this theory God's legal order is not overturned by Christ's Work. The Law is still the basis for God's relationship with humankind. It is simply that Christ fulfills the Law's demand on our behalf.

This legal framework may lead to a tendency to interpret the Gospel in light of the Law, as manifested in the medieval church's association of this Atonement theory with its system of Penance (see Chapter Twelve). Yet the Satisfaction Theory has had a venerable history of use in the Church. Besides Medieval Scholastic theologians, it predominated in John Calvin's thought (*Institutes*, 2.16.5), Protestant Orthodox Theology (some of whose theologians, as noted, prefer to speak in terms of Penal Substitution thinking [John Quenstedt, *Theologia Didactico-Polemica*, III.228, 579; Formula of Concord SD, III.56]), and it has roots in the early Church in Tertullian (*An Answer To the Jews*, 13) and even is deployed by Augustine at times (*On the Trinity*, IV.13.17). The impact of this model on Catholicism remains to this day, and it is the dominant Atonement model in most every Protestant body. But Scripture has more to say about the Atonement, especially with reference to the devil (forces of evil) and Christ's conquest of that which impedes the fellowship between God and human beings (see Colossians 2:13–15 and Christ's continual confrontation with demons in the Gospels).

Classic View

The Classic View of the Atonement picks up these Biblical themes, understanding Christ's atoning Work as God's victory over the devil and the forces of evil. This conquest sets us free from the dominance of evil and sin over our lives, and so saves us. Even Biblical references to the wrath of God (Romans 1:18; 1 Thessalonians 2:16) and the Law (Galatians 3:13) are interpreted in this scheme. This victory is understood to manifest itself most clearly in Jesus' Resurrection. Among the most famous proponents of this viewpoint have been Martin Luther (*Church Postils on the Gospels*, in *Complete Sermons*, Vol. 1/1, pp. 38–39), famed ancient theologians like Irenaeus of Lyons (*Against Heresies*, VI.1), Gregory of Nyssa (*Address On Religious Instruction*, 21–24), and Athanasius (*On the Incarnation*, 6ff.), the twentieth-century Swedish Lutheran, Gustaf Aulén (*Christus Victor*), and various modern Liberation Theologians.

Although this dualistic framework of God and evil may at first glance appear mythological and archaic, the Classic View has much to commend itself for conceptualizing our understanding of God's redemptive work in our present cultural context. The breakdown of our old social institutions has given people a sense that things are out of control. No matter how hard we try we do not seem capable of ordering the impending chaos. We are trapped by it, by all the injustices that oppress people, and by our sin. Only God can re-create order. Thus it seems like Christ's struggle with evil and chaos in order to create new good is a meaningful image in our day, notably for all who feel oppressed by social (racism and poverty) and by their psychic enslavement.

The relevance of the Classic View for today and its ability to affirm the core Biblical themes noted above seems indisputable. But questions may be raised about its ability to account adequately for the full scope of the Biblical witness, particularly with reference to those texts noted above which describe the atonement in terms of sacrifice or substitution. A fourth theology of the Atonement, which we might understand as something like a combination of the Classic and Satisfaction models warrants attention in closing.

Governmental Theory

This Theory is not well known, probably because it seems to have its origins in the nineteenth-century American Holiness Movement (A. M. Hills, *Fundamental Christian Theology*, Vol. 2, pp. 44ff., 88ff.). In the modern period we find Wolfhart Pannenberg (*Jesus—God and Man*, pp. 274–280) and Regin Prenter (*Creation and Redemption*, especially pp. 197–198, 218–219, 403, 417) speaking of the Atonement in a similar way. Sometimes Martin Luther (Large Catechism, II.2) seems to employ something like this model, but he never fully describes the theory in the way that follows.

A fundamental commitment of this fourth model is that the Law must be understood first, not as God's enemy, but as an expression of God's mercy. The Law is good and perfect; it orders creation (see Psalms 19:7–8; 1 Timothy 1:8–9). Essentially these theologians regard the Law in terms of the natural law (the idea that the Law is built into the structures of creation).

The Law is structured, however, in such a way that there exist necessary connections between punishment and an evil deed. Thus our sin naturally brings punishment upon us. It is important at this point to recognize that the punishment that the Law inflicted on sin is not something externally added by the wrath of God. The very structure of creation demands such punishment. As such the Law has become a kind of enemy to God's loving purpose. In His role as cosmic King, God could not simply overlook our sin. The only way to restore humanity to covenant fellowship is to conquer this Law that is out of control. (The language here suggests the Classic View's understanding of the Law as God's enemy, which Christ overcomes in the Atonement.) Yet the Law in its original intention cannot be destroyed by Christ's conquest, for to destroy the Law in that way would be to destroy creation, which is founded on the Law. Thus Christ's conquest of the Law's punishing function, which is out of control, must take the form of a substitutionary sacrifice, bearing the Law's punishment on behalf of humanity.

Despite similarities, significant differences between the Satisfaction Theory and the Governmental Theory were evident in the thinking of the original Holiness proponents of the theory. Unlike proponents of the Satisfaction Theory, they did not believe that Jesus bore the actual punishment due human beings for their sin. But Christ's suffering publically demonstrated God's displeasure with sin, they argued. It was a substitute for the punishment humans might have received from the Law. On this basis God is able to offer forgiveness while maintaining His governance of the created order. For only thanks to Christ's taking on its punishment can the Law be restored to its original intention. This sacrifice of Jesus regains for God the full control of the Law. It no longer functions in a way He does not desire. His governance over it and the cosmos has been restored.

This language of sacrifice suggests the Satisfaction Theory, and God's restored governance of the created order converges with the Classic View. Thus in this fourth way of talking about the Atonement we can clearly see a synthesis of the preceding two views.

The strengths and weaknesses of the preceding two options apply to this Theory. And as a synthesis it would seem to deserve some consideration. In view of this fact, though, it is all the more intriguing that this model has received so relatively little attention from theologians in the Church's first two millennia.

Black Easter Theory

One of the African Independent Churches, The Harrist Church, maintains that the salvation of African people is sealed in the encounter of Jesus with Simon of Cyrene (Mark 15:21; Matthew 27:22; Luke 23:26). Also called "The Ultimate Alliance," Harrist Christians teach that in this encounter the Body and Blood of Christ are assimilated with Simon's body and blood. This is said to manifest God's alliance with Africa. What is not clear in this intriguing example of indigenization is whether Christ's saving work creates alliances with others.

The very fact that all five ways of describing the Atonement seem to have authorization in Scripture certifies the validity of each model. Presumably Christians are justified in using the first four, if not all five models in describing the Atonement. As each view has particular strengths and weaknesses, each has been or could be used in certain specific circumstances in the life of the Church. All share one very basic commitment (noted already in Chapter Three). It is a necessary presupposition of the models that Jesus Christ can only be the Agent of the Atonement if He is both God and Man.

In the Moral Influence Theory, Christ cannot function to exemplify the life of faith unless He is human. In the Classic View He cannot be truly engaged in overcoming the forces of evil unless He is fully immersed in the human condition. Likewise in the Satisfaction Theory and Government Theory, it cannot be said that Jesus has acted as humanity's substitute in bearing punishment for our sin unless He is truly human. In the Black Easter Theory, Jesus must be human or Simon could not have his body and blood assimilated with Jesus' Body and Blood. Jesus cannot but be human if He is assimilating with the man Simon and his fellow Africans. All five views correspondingly necessitate the affirmation that Jesus is God. If He were not, then it would follow that humanity, not God, is the agent of reconciliation. Only if Jesus is both God and human can the doctrine of Justification understood as God's Work and the Biblical witness that it is God Who saves (Jeremiah 30:10; 1 Samuel 14:39) be affirmed.

WHAT DOES CHRIST'S SAVING WORK ACCOMPLISH?

One more consideration remains on this doctrine. We have considered what the Atonement is. Now we must grapple with the question of what it accomplishes. This first issue we must sort out is whether Christ's Atoning Work is only relevant for saving the faithful or whether it might transform all aspects of Creation (*Recapitulation*). Many Christians tend to opt for the focus on saving souls, but among proponents of Recapitulation include the early Church Father Irenaeus (*Against Heresies*, V.1), the twentieth-century Reformed theologian Karl Barth (*Church Dogmatics*, Vol. II/2, pp. 7–8), and Process Theologians like John Cobb (*Process Theology*, especially pp. 142–158).

Once this issue is addressed, the question remains regarding whether human beings must still appropriate the benefits of Christ's Atoning Work. Only two answers can logically be given to this question.

Possibility of Salvation

This option contends that Christ's Atoning Work creates a situation whereby salvation can be *offered* to humanity, such that it will be theirs if they believe and/or live a certain way. It is like a parent holding a gift in one hand, and all the child has to do is grasp it in order to make that gift her own. In short, salvation is contingent on faith (or faith and works). There are certainly Biblical passages that suggest this point of view (Mark 16:16; 1 Corinthians 15:2).

Among the numerous proponents of this vision include the Apostolic Fathers of the Church's first centuries (Ignatius of Antioch, Epistle To the Magnesians, IX; Clement of Rome, Letter To the Corinthians, 8), Catholic theologians from Ambrose (*On the Christian Faith*, II.27) to Augustine (at least sometimes [see *Enchiridion*, 33]) to Thomas Aquinas (*Summa Theologica*, III.Q.49, Art.1) to Benedict XVI (*Introduction To Christianity*, Excursus, 5), and Eastern theologians from Irenaeus (*Against Heresies*, XXI.2) to John Chrysostom (Homilies On First Corinthians, II.9) to Christoforos Stavropoulos (in *Eastern Orthodox Theology*, pp. 189ff.). Such commitments help the Church emphasize the importance or response to the great things God in Christ has done for us. But this is not a good vision for those in doubt about their salvation, as it might lead to concentrating more on what we must do than on what God has done.

Anonymous Christianity

One possible mode of this way of thinking is a concept developed in modern Catholicism: The belief that because by grace some who have not accepted Jesus (especially through no fault of their own) yet strive to live a good life may be considered to have prepared for the Gospel and may achieve salvation (Vatican II, *Lumen Gentium*, 16; Karl Rahner, *Pastoral Approach To Atheism*, pp. 75ff.). This position is reminiscent of early Church Apologist Justin Martyr, whom we previously considered. Recall he claimed that all rational human beings in principle have access to Christian truth as must believers do (*First Apology*, 5, 36). This Word of universal hop embodied in these views seems to feature grace in the case of Vatican II more than others teaching the Possibility of Salvation (though you still have to do good works to be saved as an Anonymous Christian.)

Actuality of Salvation

The alternative way of thinking about this range of issues takes its bearings from New Testament texts that refer to the universal thrust of God's grace (Romans 11:26; 2 Corinthians 5:19; 1 Timothy 2:4; 1 John 2:2). This model contends that the Atonement has placed all people in a situation of salvation, regardless of their response of faith. To return to the analogy used above, with this viewpoint the loving parent is no longer holding the present for the child, waiting for the child to reach out and accept the gift. Now the loving parent puts the present in the child's lap, without the child ever having to reach out to grab it.

This model can be interpreted in several ways. Some theologians like John Calvin, the Puritans, Particular Baptists, and even Augustine and Martin Luther at times will claim that only some people are given this gift, placed in this situation (see Chapter 8 on Double Predestination for references). Others like Origen (*On First Principles*, III.VI.5), Gregory of Nyssa (*Address On Religious Instruction*, 26), and the Unitarian Universalist tradition have asserted that all are saved (placed in this new situation). And several theological strands like the Lutheran Confessional heritage (Formula of Concord, SD XI) and perhaps The Anglican Thirty-Nine Articles (XVII) posit something like this idea that all are placed in this new situation of salvation but link it with the possibility that the gift can be thrown away (the unforgivable sin against the Holy Spirit—Matthew 12:32; Mark 3:28–29). If the interest is in assuring the faithful of their salvation, this model is definitely the right one. Others might find this model problematic in inviting passivity in the faith.

CLOSING THOUGHTS:
WHAT TO MAKE OF THE DIVERSITY OF OPTIONS

In constructing your own theology, the crucial questions about the Atonement are: (1) How much of the responsibility is God's, and how much of as role (if any) do we play? (2) If the answer is that it is all the Work of God in Christ, then we need to determine how best to construe Sin, as a force against which God and we contend or as a problem that will go away once someone takes the punishment? (3) Related to the preceding question is how we view God, as One Who is in control of things, Whose justice demands punishment, or as One Who is in the trenches with us fighting evil (only Eschatologically [ultimately]) in control?

Once these issues are addressed, the next matter to address is to determine what has happened to us in the Atonement. If confidence and/or inclusivity in salvation is essential to you, the Actuality Model described above is the way to go. But if a priority is on individual Christian responsibility and the importance of faith, then portraying the Atonement as creating only the Possibility For Salvation is a better commitment. Another related issue is whether Christ's Atoning Work just impacts us and our salvation or whether it also changes/transforms the whole created order. If the latter, then Recapitulation is a position worthy of attention. Once again, as in the case of all the other chapters, make sure to think about what you make of those Biblical texts used to authorize the positions you reject (see the first Chapter on Theological Method).

8

JUSTIFICATION/SALVATION/PREDESTINATION

The doctrine of Justification has been among the most disputed doctrines in the Western church, but it also has as history of being largely ignored for many centuries and has never been so much of a concern for Eastern Christianity. Even its definition is disputed. Perhaps the safest, most neutral way to proceed is to describe it as the doctrine that teaches how we are freed from sin, reconciled with God, or made righteous. In short this is the doctrine that teaches how we are saved and what the life of a saved and reconciled Christian looks like here on earth. In that sense it is a doctrine that can be of great personal significance for those concerned about their own salvation, how it is obtained and whether they have received it. It is also a doctrine that can be deployed to address one's value and worth, for if we understand ourselves to be good in God's eyes it is easier for such believers to live with themselves. If you have ever asked such questions, you will want to attend carefully to this doctrine.

In a sense all Christians agree that Christ's atoning work is crucial to their salvation (see the doctrine of the Atonement in Chapter Seven). But the question of how the benefits of the Atonement are appropriated and what happens to the faithful when they are justified still needs to be addressed in this doctrine.

Of course the doctrine of Justification is rooted in the Letters of St. Paul (see Romans 2:13; 3: 20, 26, 30; 4:25; Galatians 2:16, 17; 3:11, 24; Ephesians 2:8). It appears elsewhere in Titus (3:7), James (2:21, 24), and even in the Old Testament (Isaiah 53:11; Psalm 143:2; Job 25:4). The concept justification (*dikaiosis* in Greek and *tsadaq* in Hebrew) is closely linked with the term "righteousness" (*dikaiosune* in Greek and *tsedeq* in Hebrew). Biblically, when one is justified, she/he is righteous, and the action seems to be related to God's righteousness which in some way or other makes it possible.

In the first centuries of the Church's life after Paul's martyrdom the Church does not seem to have given much express attention to the doctrine. This may relate to the fact that the first post-New Testament theologians (especially The

Apostolic Fathers) did not pay much attention to Paul. It is true, though, that we can find some express references to justification in the writings of Apostolic Fathers like Clement of Rome (*First Epistle*, XXXII) and The Shepherd of Hermas (II.C.I) , and one of the earliest Apologists, Clement of Alexandria (S*tromata*, I.IV,XX). And of course whenever the theologians of the first centuries dealt with salvation (like today) all the theologians of this era were in effect dealing with the doctrine of justification.

Augustine was the first to deal in detail with the doctrine of Justification, an issue that his controversy with Pelagius (see below) forced him to consider expressly. Augustine's influence was so great on the Catholic Church that the doctrine continued to receive at least some attention throughout the Middle Ages and the Scholastic Theology that dominated in the period. With the waning of the Middle Ages, the doctrine continued to receive attention from the Nominalist Theologians developing in this era, though in ways different from the Scholastics. But the doctrine became the lynchpin of the Reformation, *the* issue for the first of the Protestant Reformers, Martin Luther (*Lectures On Galatians*, in *Luther's Works*, Vol. 26, p. 106). And he influenced the other Protestant denominations that later emerged, so that the entire Protestant family officially rejects a role for good works in justification, an affirmation largely neglected by Christians until the sixteenth century (except for Augustine sometimes).

Until well into the nineteenth and twentieth centuries Justification continued to receive much attention from the Protestant family, as it was a point of division from Catholicism. And on the Roman Catholic side, it also received attention as a way of distinguishing the teaching of *the Church* from Protestant heresy. However, the Enlightenment and its optimistic view of human nature (see Chapter Six, above) was effectively a critique of the Protestant vision of the doctrine. Faith was equated with morality by many of these scholars (like John Locke [*The Reasonableness of Christianity*, 213–214] and Immanuel Kant [*Religion Within the Limits of Reason Alone*, 1C]). Again the Pelagian option described below is relevant. In the 20th century, even when liberal scholars had broken with such modern Pelagianism, a theologian like Paul Tillich could argue that modern people were no longer concerned about the sorts of questions which preoccupied the Protestant Reformers, like the doctrine of Justification, but with apologetic issues of how to find meaning or whether God exists at all (*Systematic Theology*, Vol. 3, p. 227).

The Neo-Orthodox reaction to this Theological Liberalism, led by Karl Barth but also by various Lutherans like Gustaf Aulén and Regin Prenter, did restore attention to the doctrine. But even Barth's main concern was more with divine transcendence ("An Introductory Essay [On Feuerbach]"). Since World War II, though, except in Lutheran circles for several decades and more recently as a result of controversial readings of Martin Luther led by some Finnish scholars, the real action in theology has not been with this doctrine, but rather over Hermeneutics, Eschatology, or liberation and Social Ethics. This de-emphasis on interest in Justification has been assisted by developments in contemporary New Testament scholarship. A movement, the so-called "New Perspectives On Paul," with roots in nineteenth-century scholarship, has mounted assaults on Protestant understandings of the doctrine, arguing that Paul's use of the term had little to do with matters of individual salvation or as a critique of Jewish legalism (E. P. Sanders, *Paul and Palestinian Judaism*; James Dunn, *The Theology of Paul the Apostle*). For the Judaism of Paul's era was not "legalistic," it is alleged; it combined the demand for obedience to the Torah with a covenantal emphasis that expresses a priority on God's electing grace. It is also argued that references to Justification apart from works are efforts by Paul to justify his mission to the Gentiles, to make a distinction between the distinctive character of Jewish faith and that of the Gentiles, that it is an attempt to undermine ethnic presumption and disdain of the Gentiles.

In the analysis of the various options that follow we will assess the validity or invalidity of these theses. The bottom line in reaction to these "New Perspectives On Paul" is that these critics have failed to note that the Protestant stress on salvation by grace alone in the name of St. Paul seems to have been a reaction against a soteriology very much like the one against which Paul reacted. Contrary to the critics' contention that the Reformers reacted against a pure legalism, the popular piety of Catholic soteriology of the sixteenth century was a lot like first century Judaism, one in which God's work was mixed with human works. Consequently, it could be argued that Protestant Reformers and their heirs have been using Paul's insights responsibly.

In any case, another factor in the relative inattention of late to the doctrine of Justification relates to the ecumenical movement. Since the Roman Catholic Second Vatican Council of the 1960s, and even prior to that, scholars and their churches from both the Protestant and the Catholic sides have tried to emphasize that historic differences on this doctrine are not church dividing. It is argued that the differences are compatible (Lutheran-Catholic Joint Commission, Joint Declaration On Justification). Once again, readers will need carefully to assess the options that have appeared and make their own judgments. It is to that task we now turn.

HOW JUSTIFICATION HAPPENS

Christians have disagreement about how Justification happens, how it is received, since all agree that Christ's Atoning Work is essential. We begin with the characteristic Protestant positions.

By Grace Alone

Of course most all Christians agree on the essential role of God's grace in salvation. (Grace may be defined as the supernatural assistance of God, God's redemptive Work, or as His forgiving love, but as we shall note below, different models of how we are justified regard Justification differently.) A characteristic Protestant viewpoint, notably taught by John Calvin, the Puritans, and Karl Barth, is to assert that in justifying us God does it all (*sola gratia*) (*Institutes*, 3.21.7; Westminster Confession, XIII; *Church Dogmatics*, Vol. IV/1, pp. 514ff.). Any good works we might do play no role in contributing to our salvation.

Among the clearest Biblical references include Romans 3:24, Galatians 3:21–31, Ephesians 2:8, 5 and Titus 2:11. Sometimes the phrase is "salvation by grace through faith." Faith then plays the role of the receptor; it is the glove that catches or holds salvation. It is grace, then, that is said to be the agent of salvation. Though there have been quarrels about precisely how faith and grace are understood, with this model of interpreting Justification, faith is construed as a work of grace, a Work of the Holy Spirit (John 14:26; 1 Corinthians 12:9).

This is a theological position that can be a great comfort to the faithful. Salvation is not something we must accomplish. No matter how weak or mired in sin we are, there is hope.

Some theologians holding this position like Martin Luther celebrate the freedom and joy that are entailed by this sort of confidence in the grace of God (*The Freedom of a Christian*, in *Luther's Works*, Vol. 31, pp. 360–361). Salvation is a done-deal on these grounds. It is ours. It is not something still on the way

(Romans 6:2ff.), though some Theologians of Hope may contend that Justification is a future reality (Jürgen Moltmann, *Theology of Hope*, pp. 207–208).

Such an orientation also affords a better chance to extol the power and sovereignty of God, to give the Lord the credit for all happens in life. John Calvin (*Institutes*, 1.16f.1ff.), modern Reformed theologian Karl Barth (*Church Dogmatics*, Vol. III/3, pp. 52–53, 93ff.), Puritans (Westminster Confession, V), as well as certain Baptist thinkers like the early Baptist Confessions of seventeenth-century England (Second London Confession, II.1) and the official position of the Southern Baptist Convention (Baptist Faith and Message, II.1) endorse this way of thinking.

This position of course has its critics. Some critique its proponents for effectively denying free will. Of course not all advocates of this position teach *Predestination* (especially Methodist, Holiness, as well as many Pentecostal and Baptist denominations do not teach that God has elected us in eternity and determined our eternal fate). But as we shall note later in the chapter, such an affirmation (Predestination) is logically implied when we give God credit for everything in salvation, even our faith, which only saves us by grace.

Another critique of this viewpoint is that it is said to undermine the importance of good works, since it is believed that they play no role in saving us. The grace-alone perspective leads to sloth in the Christian life, it is argued. Scripture (see Biblical texts associated with views below, which assert a role for works in saving us) has been distorted, the critics contend. The response to this critique is discussed in the section below titled "What Happens."

We have already noted the critique of this viewpoint by the New Perspectives on Paul by New Testament scholars. The argument is that proponents of this grace-alone position and the *faith-alone* viewpoint (see below) have distorted Paul. As already suggested, this allegation could be refuted by claiming that these critics misunderstand the circumstances in which the Reformation controversies began. It may be that St. Augustine's use of Paul to rebut the heretic Pelagius in the fourth and fifth centuries did trade on incorrect assumptions about Judaism being Pelagian-like. But the Protestant Reformers were in tension with a Roman Catholic theology that never abandoned a role for God's grace in saving us any more than the Judaism of Paul's era neglected God's action in electing the faithful. Catholics were teaching some role for both grace and works in saving us, not unlike the Jewish faith. On these grounds it could be argued that Protestants opting for grace alone do interpret Paul correctly, that the Apostle's target (the Judaism of his day) was very similar to the Protestant critique of the Catholic teaching of Justification.

The grace-alone perspective is officially the dominant position of Protestantism (Philip Melanchthon, The Augsburg Confession, 4; Westminster Confession, XIII). It could be argued that the next option is really more characteristic of most Protestant denominations. And polls verify that the theology of the American Protestant pew is more inclined to embrace the Justification models, which insist on a role for good works in saving us.

By Faith Alone

A similar version of the preceding option stresses faith as the means of salvation. Certainly the New Testament speaks of the necessity of faith for salvation (see John 3:16; 6:47; Luke 18:42; Mark 16:16; Galatians 2:16). Most Pietists (a Protestant movement of the seventeenth-century whose proponents stress spirituality and spiritual discipline more than doctrine) embrace this way of thinking. Mystics (those theologians emphasizing an intimate union of the faithful with Christ as the ultimate expression of faith) typically embrace this model. Many of the Anabaptists of the Reformation era, like Menno Simons, taught this (*Meditation on the Twenty-Fifth Psalm*, 14; Dordrecht Confession, 6). Certainly the model seems in line with the Protestant stress on salvation by faith (*sola fide*).

The model differentiates itself from the previously considered grace-alone model by highlighting the need for an active faith in living the Christian life. God does not force salvation on us, it is asserted. We must accept what is offered.

The strength of this viewpoint can also be a weakness. Without intending it, these commitments can lead to introducing works into Justification, even lapse into Pelagianism (see below). This happens when faith is described as what we do, not as a Work of the Holy Spirit. Proponents of this view need to be on guard for this distortion. But when the Spirit plays a central role in all aspects of Christian living for a theologian, then all the strengths of the grace- alone model previously noted accrue to this model as well—the fidelity to the Pauline testimony, the peace and confidence that one need not earn salvation or must establish one's worth by what one does.

A related potential abuse of this model is that since faith becomes the means of salvation, the faithful may begin to fret about the strength of their faith, fret about whether they believe enough to merit salvation (Romans 12:6; 2 Thessalonians 1:3). This can best be remedied by stressing again that faith is a Work of the Holy Spirit and that the Spirit's Presence makes up for our lack of faith, restoring the believer's confidence and joy in salvation that the grace-alone model provides (Mark 9:24; Romans 8:26).

By Grace and Works, But Grace Must Precede All Works

Typically Roman Catholics dating back to Scholastic Theology and to the Middle Ages and even back to Augustine's views sometimes assert a role for works in combination with grace as the means of Justification (*Catechism of the Catholic Church*, 1996ff; Augustine, *On the Spirit and the Letter*, 5). Just as Augustine could be read both in this way and also as the proponents of salvation by grace alone, so we can find things written by Paul about repentance as supporting this viewpoint and the more characteristic Protestant model (Romans 6:19–22; 2:4; cf. Psalms 85:7). Even Martin Luther early in his career affirmed this viewpoint (*Lectures On Romans*, in *Luther's Works*, Vol. 25, p. 186), just as the Catholic Second Vatican Council in one document has affirmed the Justification By Faith or the By Grace model (*Decree On Ecumenism*, 3).

This approach to salvation seems to combine the best features of the Protestant models just described while taking seriously the importance of good works. Yes, it is asserted, good works must be done by those who are saved. But on the other hand, God's grace is given full credit. Without the divine initiative, none of us can be saved.

We are not alone in our journey to salvation. God initiates and accompanies us in the justification process, proponents of this position contend. This last point represents a significant difference from the first two, characteristically Protestant options considered. Justification is not construed with this model as a completed event, but as a process. We are on the way to salvation, but not there yet.

There seems to be Biblical authorization for this point of view. Certainly the Biblical texts that authorize the grace-alone position can be combined with those testifying to the importance of works like James 2:14–16 and the call to an obedient faith in Romans 1:5. For salvation as a process, see Philippians 3:12–14.

The strengths of this position as a mediating point of view have already been noted. It seems to give God credit for saving us (though perhaps not as much as when one teaches Justification by grace alone). Personal responsibility is demanded, since we are called on to make a contribution to our own salvation. In fact in the case of the Medieval Scholastic Thomas Aquinas and many Catholic theologians, our works done through *prevenient grace* (grace given *before* any works are done) *merit* (are rewarded with) more grace. The grace received is something inserted into the believer. For Aquinas it is a substance, one which establishes habits that lead to the good works which merit more grace (*Summa Theologica*, I/2 QQ110, 111–114).

The potential shortcomings of this approach to Justification relate both to its demand to do works in order to be saved and also this model's insistence that we are in a process towards salvation. If a process then we are not saved yet. This can create anxiety about whether we can be sure of salvation. And the fact that works are still required is likely to cause more doubt, to raise the question for faithful people if they have done enough good works to qualify for salvation. It is precisely questions like this that led the first Protestant Martin Luther away from conceding a role to works in saving us and insisting that justification is not a process but a completed event. That way you do not have to worry about your salvation. It is a done deal (*Disputation Against Scholastic Theology*, in *Luther's Works*, Vol. 31, p. 12).

Luther's critique of this and the next model raises another problem related to this and the others that follow. If you closely relate the Good News Gospel of God's love to the Law (the demand that we do good works), then if Luther is right, the Law always prevails (*Lectures On Galatians* [1535], in *Luther's Works*, Vol. 26, p. 115). In short, it can be argued, this model is ultimately about salvation by your works, that the witness of grace gets lost. Of course the response might be that this model is truly balanced, taking seriously both the roles of grace and works in saving us.

By Grace and Works In No Particular Order

In the first centuries of the Church's history (reflected in the theologies of most of the Apostolic Fathers [The Epistle of Barnabas, 6.11; 14.3–4; Clement of Rome, Epistle To the Corinthians, 7.5; 32.4; 49] and the Apologists [Tertullian, *Prescription Against Heresies*, XIV; Clement of Alexandria, *Stromata*, I.VIII; VII.11]) as well as today in the Eastern Orthodox churches [Christoforos Stavropoulos, in *Eastern Orthodox Theology*, pp. 189ff.] a related viewpoint was and is espoused. Like the dominant Roman Catholic mode just discussed, this formula for Justification posits a role for both grace and our cooperating works. But unlike the prior model, a prioritization of grace over works is not posited. Instead, in the spirit of much Eastern Christian thinking, mystery is celebrated (Mark 4:11; 1 Corinthians 2:7; Ephesians 6:19). How grace and works relate cannot and should not be explained, proponents contend. Some times one prevails over the other or one of them works alone. The mystery of the divine-human relationship can never fully be sorted out. Luke 9:23f and Matthew 7:18–20 seem to testify to the complexity of the grace-works relationship. But most of the texts cited in the preceding section could be used to authorize this position (also see texts cited below to authorize the teaching of deification, which also trades on this complex relationship between grace and works).

The same strengths and weakness of the preceding model seem pertinent to this characteristic Eastern Church point of view. More than the characteristic Roman Catholic position, which prioritizes grace, proponents of this vision can argue that we have a true integration of grace and works with this view. However, in turn it seems easier to make the charge that grace has been minimized with this point of view. And this commitment then also seems to put more pressure on the faithful to do enough works in order to ensure salvation. But on the other hand, when we consider the dominance of this model in the theology of the early Church and that that was a golden age of faithfulness and even Martyrdom, we may be pushed to ask if these theological commitments nurtured the kind of passion lacking in many churches of the West today.

Another version of this model seems to emerge in the implicit theology of famed Prosperity Gospel preacher Joel Osteen—a view that no doubt embodies much American popular theology and also seems to posit Justification by Works and Faith, contending that we are saved by faith but that our works have a great impact on the degree of our blessings and the favor of God (*Your Best Life Now*, pp. 221, 231; cf. T. D. Jakes, Fund-Raising Letter" [2012]). In view of the popularity of this way of thinking and its alleged Biblical basis (Malachi 3:10; James 4:2), we must give this option attention, but is it much different in terms of weaknesses than the historic Eastern position?

Pelagianism

The next option is a logical progression from the previous two alternatives considered. It bears the name of an early English Christian Pelagius, who locked horns with Augustine and was eventually declared a heretic (*For Free Will*). Many Enlightenment scholars like Immanuel Kant (*Religion Within the Limits of Reason Alone*, 1C) and John Locke (*The Reasonableness of Christianity*, 213–214) think this way.

We have already encountered Pelagius. He was concerned about the sloth he was facing in the English church, was determined to try to initiate a revival. Like many today in such circumstances he became convinced that too much emphasis on grace (like St. Augustine was teaching) would undermine a revival. His alternative was to stress the role for works in saving us, that it is our responsibility to avoid sin in order to be saved—more so than the previous options.

It is not that that Pelagius and those who agree with him completely discard a role for Christ and grace. They argue that our ability to do good is a gift of free will by God to do good. And they then point to Jesus' giving His followers commands as another indication of grace. Jesus' teaching is salvific, for He offers us extra encouragement and clarity on what God expects of us in order to be saved.

Some Biblical backing can be found for this viewpoint. James 2:14–26 is invoked to support it. And many of Jesus' directives could be cited for further authorization (Luke 6:27–28; Matthew 22:37–39). The Ten Commandments could also be cited (Exodus 20). If you are inclined to talk about Jesus primarily as a Law-giver or example, you may be operating with these Pelagian tendencies. It may be in that case that your faith will be more lively and visible. But in several ancient Church Councils the Church has found this way of thinking to be guilty of minimizing grace and of compromising the confidence the faithful can have in salvation.

Semi-Pelagianism

This final option is in its origins a self-conscious attempt to reconcile the concerns of Pelagianism with the Church's commitment to preserving a central role for grace in Justification. In fact, proponents of this model insist that without God's grace none can be saved. But unlike the other models, they insist that grace must first be earned. Whoever turns to God of their own free will, whoever repents, will be saved (see Luke 13:3, 5 and Zechariah 1:3 for Biblical authorization). If you do these things, do good, God will reward you with His forgiving love (with grace), and you will be saved. Much like the characteristic Roman Catholic model already noted, we are Justified by grace and works, but on grounds of this approach, works precede grace. There is a fine line distinguishing this model from the Prosperity Gospel teaching of Salvation by Works and Faith that we have noted above, especially when such preachers exhort: Tithe and [then] you will be blessed (Johnnie Colemon, *It Works If You Work It*, Vol. 2, p. 8).

The Nominalists of the Late Middle Ages offered a more sophisticated (perhaps more grace-oriented) version of this model than the way it is usually deployed in the pews or the pulpit. For while the mere assertion that you must do good works to merit grace clearly falls prey to the criticisms we noted against Pelagianism, Nominalist theologians spoke first of a covenant that God had established with people. It was an agreement He initiated whereby meritorious works without the assistance of grace would be given grace to make them acceptable. In short, God in His love makes the first move by setting up this covenant, which makes our good deeds, though flawed and sinful, count as good. But is the stress on God's graceful action a significant amendment?

Even with this effort to give God and His grace a more essential and active role in our salvation, this version of Semi-Pelagianism continues to be plagued by some of the same problems as Pelagianism. The same uncertainty about whether I have done enough to be saved (in this case to merit the grace which saves) remains. But given American and Western capitalist preoccupation with individual responsibility, is this approach not likely to resonate with the suppositions of many?

The historic options for describing how Justification/Salvation happens boil down to where we want to place our emphases—more on the Work of God and His grace (entailing placing more emphasis on God's love), on our individual responsibility (entailing a construal of God as a Just God), or some effort to bring the two poles more in collaboration. There seems to be some Biblical backing for all of these options. If so, theologians must determine in formulating this doctrinal theme how God is best glorified, whether it is better to risk uncertainty about one's salvation in order to stress individual responsibility or to stress confidence in salvation and affirm the faithful as they are.

WHAT HAPPENS: WHAT IT MEANS TO BE BORN AGAIN

Christians have disagreed not just on the question of how Justification happens, but also over what happens when you are Justified. In examining the options on this topic, we begin with the viewpoint that tends to dominate in Protestantism.

Forensic Justification

Romans 4:4,5 (along with Old Testament precedents in Psalm 32:2 and Genesis 15:6) seeks to assert that sin remains after we have been justified. Justification does not heal us. For virtually all the Protestant denominations and most Protestant theologians until the nineteenth century, Justification is more like a proclamation or decree that changes our situation. On these grounds we come before God full of sin and guilt. But He looks at us differently, in light of what Jesus has done. God in His righteousness declares us righteous. In fact, it is argued by Augustine (*On the Spirit and the Letter*, 9.15) and Martin Luther (*Preface To the Latin Writings*, in *Luther's Works*, Vol. 34, p. 337), that God is righteous because He declares us righteous (and in their thinking He does this by grace through faith). We remain sinners with this model and our righteousness is external (really God's).

Usually this model for describing what happens in Justification is paired with the grace alone or faith alone views of how Justification happens ([Anglican] Thirty-Nine Articles, XI; [Methodist] Articles of Religion, 9; National Baptist Convention, Articles of Faith, V). But some proponents of the Semi-Pelagian position (especially the Nominalists [Gabriel Biel, *Canonis missae exposition*, 31B]) have employed this vision. Likewise, the Forensic model could fit those teaching Justification by Grace and Works in No Particular Order. For with that approach there are times when grace predominates over works or when like the Nominalists God declares our flawed works sufficient to merit grace.

Protestant readers were likely nurtured with this way of construing Justification. Besides the Biblical backing noted above, this way of thinking about what Justification accomplishes entails a very clear distinction between grace/faith and works, between Justification and Sanctification. (Some appropriations of this way of thinking, but not most, even separate Justification and Sanctification as two different realities. Some branches of Protestant Orthodox Theology [John Quenstedt, *Theologia Didactico-Polemica*, 632] and Holiness Theology with respect to Entire Sanctification [Church of the Nazarene, Articles of Religion, 12, 15] teach this. See the implied difference between those justified and exhortations they receive to move on to perfection in Matthew 5:48, Colossians 4:12, and also Romans 8:23.) The forgiven sinner need not be so tortured about his/her shortcomings. When you are Justified you remain a sinner; it is just that God considers you righteous and holy (simultaneously saint and sinner). This way of describing what happens to you when you are justified fits logically with the grace alone and faith alone understandings of the doctrine.

The Forensic view's distinction between Justification and Sanctification entails for some theologians, like seventeenth-century Protestant Orthodox Theology and its modern heirs, as well as Holiness Theology that the two are distinguished in time—first we are justified and then sanctified. We will turn to that issue and its implications in the next chapter. But here we need to examine the implications of the Forensic View of Justification. It protects the integrity of grace, offers the security that our works (our deficiencies on that score) do not count against us. But critics contend that this leads to cheap grace, a minimizing of good works and of the transforming powering of grace. The options that follow in different ways seek to remedy these alleged shortcomings.

One way the Forensic model seeks to address these concerns is with the insistence that works must follow the declaration of our righteousness. Some theologians go so far as to claim that good works are *necessary* for the faithful. But the issue at stake is what "necessary" means. For some like in the Lutheran Confessional heritage it means that the works stemming from Justification are logically necessary ([Lutheran] Formula of Concord Ep. IV). Good, righteous trees cannot but bear fruit. For other Christians (especially those of the Reformed, Methodist, and Baptist traditions), works are necessary in order to verify that you are justified.

Made Righteous
(given new qualities of holiness or grace)

A polar opposite of the Forensic Model of Justification is evident in much Roman Catholic theology and Pietism. This model contends that something has happened to us in Justification, that we are not the same. We have been changed internally, not just externally, by Justification.

Among the Biblical references which seem to authorize these conclusions include Ephesians 4:22–24; 2 Corinthians 7:1; 1 John 4:12–13. A number of denominational heritages affirm this construal. We begin with the Catholic vision, especially as embodied by the great Medieval Scholastic theologian Thomas Aquinas.

This Catholic model proposes that justified sinners are substantially different. Grace is construed as a substance now infused in them and that is what makes them essentially different from what they were like prior to Justification. Likewise, because they are substantially different, they behave differently too.

This view is related to Justification by Grace and Works with Grace First. Consequently, the change that comes in Justification is gradual, a process. The grace given us changes us, we do more good works, and then these works are rewarded with more grace which makes us more God-like and so pushes us to do more works (*Summa Theologica*, I/2 Q.113).

Belief that we are substantially changed in Justification is also a Protestant view, at least it is evidenced in Quaker and some Baptist circles. Baptists often refer to the faithful being born again in Justification. They have new hearts (National Baptist Convention, Articles of Faith, VII; Southern Baptist Convention, Confession of Faith, IV). They are in that sense substantially different. And Quakers speak of experiencing the divine light (Declaration of Faith). Both of these traditions combine these commitments with a model of Justification by grace alone or by faith alone.

Deification/ Theosis

A related, though perhaps more ancient and even more radical model is notably evidenced in the Eastern Orthodox traditions (Christoforas Stavrapoulos, in *Eastern Orthodox Theology*, pp. 183ff.), as well as in the very first centuries of the Church's life from Irenaeus (*Against Heresies*, 5.36.3) and Athanasius (*On the Incarnation*, 54) through to the twenty-first century in these churches. Some late Medieval Mystics of the West like Meister Eckhart (*Sermons*, 1) , Johannes Tauler (*Predigten*, 55; 5), to some extent Bonaventure (*Collectiones de septem donis Spiritus Sancti* III.5), and even at times John Wesley (*Sermons*, 141.2) and Martin Luther (*Christmas Sermon*, in *Luther's Works*, Vol. 52, p. 157) occasionally endorse this image. Essentially this teaching often termed deification teaches that "God became Man [in Jesus Christ] so that man may become like God."

By taking on the flesh of Jesus (human flesh like your and my flesh), we are all born with a spark of Jesus' divinity (the divine energies in us). Christian life is then nothing more than the exercising of these divine energies in us, putting them to work through faith and good works, so that more and more those divine energies become reflected in our lives and assume control of us. Over the years, then, as we live this way we will become more and more like God.

This manner of describing Justification makes our salvation a process, not complete. But when living faithfully it teaches that we are on the way to a closer fellowship with God, on the way to perfection (see the next chapter for a discussion of how this viewpoint links with the Methodist/Holiness heritage). Its proponents almost always teach Justification By Grace and Works in no particular order, which follows logically from this construal. On its grounds Christians are already of God, have God in them. Thus their activities (works) are always with grace. But the more works they do and faithfulness they demonstrate, the more God-like they are becoming—the more grace takes over in their lives.

The attractiveness of this way of portraying our relationship to God, as well as the way in which this model affirms the faithful (they are already God-like) are clearly strengths. This viewpoint nicely converges with models for describing the relationship between God and world, which are compatible with modern scientific speculations (see the discussion of *Panentheism* in Chapter 5). But on the other hand, the idea that we might become like God is likely to be problematic for some Western eyes. It seems to border on polytheism, at least to entail the abolition of the distinction between God and humanity. It is for these reasons, and because St. Augustine (the main influence on theology in the Western church) rejected it that Protestants and Catholics have not historically embraced this vision. But on the other hand, the blurring of distinctions between God and humanity is precisely the kind of celebration of mystery that is so attractive to the Eastern mindset. Ecumenical conversations between denominations espousing this view with those maintaining the model to follow or the one previously considered are raising questions about whether the difference between these models and deification might not be so great (not church-dividing). Like these other models, deification helps explain what grace has to do with good works, because in becoming like God we cannot but be good. Of course like the previous model of Being Made Righteous Internally, the problem might be that we are not sure if we are saved, since in the case of deification we are only on the way to becoming like God, not there yet.

Intimate Union
  (Conformity to Christ)

A related, though less radical version of thinking about what happens to us in Justification has been developed among Christian Mystics like Bernard of Clairvaux (*On the Song of Songs*, 3.3.5) and Catherine of Siena (*Dialogue*, 148). Drawing upon Pauline texts like Galatians 2:20 and Ephesians 3:17 as well as the Song of Solomon, these theologians contend that in Justification the believer is united to Christ, in a kind of marital or sexual relationship.

Christian Mystics have been the primary proponents of this way of thinking. But we also find it affirmed at times by St. Augustine (*Enchiridion*, 31) and Martin Luther (*The Freedom of a Christian*, in *Luther's Works*, Vol. 31, pp. 351ff.) as well as perhaps in Pietists like P. J. Spener (*Pia Desideria*, pp. 64–66) and Nikolaus von Zinzendorf (*Twenty-One Discourses on The Augsburg Confession*, 9) (though some would claim that what they teach is closer to deification). Occasionally, though not characteristically, this model appears in John Calvin and the Reformed heritage that springs from him (*Institutes*, 3.1.3; 4.15.6). Essentially this model compares Justification to the wedding day of a good marriage or the first encounter of a fulfilling sexual union. In both cases, there is an unequivocal sharing and union. The partners truly become one.

We may speak of a "blessed exchange." All that the partners bring to the relationship become properties or characteristics of the other. This is evidenced in that the lovers share parts of their bodies with each other in the sexual union, even leave something from their bodies with the lover. In marriage (in the days prior to pre-nuptial agreements) there is community property.

All that each owns belongs to the spouse as well. And so it is that in our marriage to Jesus, He gets all we bring to the marriage—nothing, but our sin. This is why He went to The Cross. But we get all He has—His righteousness, faith, holiness, and loving nature. With this endowment, becoming part of the family heritage into which we have married, we cannot but become more loving.

Think of the long-term relationships in which you find yourself. Is it not the case that living together with loved ones changes you? The good qualities and ways of living of your loved one become yours gradually. But that sharing had a starting point, which in your relationship with Jesus is like Justification. So likewise is in your relationship with Jesus, on grounds of the Conformity to Christ model, there is this kind of sharing of all possessions and qualities from the very beginning. But of course this does not mean that you stop being who you are or that what you bring into the relationship is no longer yours. We bring our sin into the relationship, and the common heritage of love and goodness that has become ours through marriage to Jesus is still properly speaking His. And so this model does not deny the fact that we are simultaneously saint and sinner (*simul iustus et peccator*) or that properly speaking the gifts of righteousness, goodness, and love we have from Christ are not our own. Such gifts are external, properly belonging to Christ. But they are ours now, but only because of Jesus.

The strengths of this model for describing intimate relationships with Jesus and the Holy Spirit are evident. (The Spirit is usually interpreted as bringing Christ to us.) And obviously this construal makes evident what Justification has to do with good works (with Sanctification). The believer, saturated with all of Christ's holiness, goodness, and faith that He brings into the marriage will spontaneously do good, like lovers do all sorts of loving things to and for each other.

Potential weaknesses: The intimacy with Jesus could be taken by some as too much familiarity with God, as violating the distinction between God and humanity, despite Biblical precedents. In fact a related version of this model is to speak of God in one's body, identifying oneself with God, claiming "I am God," like Father Divine ("As a Man Thinketh In His Hear So Is He And You Act From That Angle...") and the Early Christians Gnostics did (The Gospel of Truth, 42, in The Nag Hammadi Library). But this is not what is intended with the Intimate Union Model. On its grounds we remain too sinful and finite to take the Gnostic position.

The other risk is that the analogy this model makes between Justification and marriage or sex leads to the conclusion that Justification is a process. In fact this model is only properly understood when the analogy is to marriage as a ceremony (the living together refers to Sanctification) and the analogy is to a single sexual encounter, not an extended sexual relationship.

Regardless of which model for describing what happens to you when you are Justified, we still need to come to terms with the question of how the acceptance or rejection of this gift of faith (and works) happen. The doctrine of Predestination was designed to address that issue.

PREDESTINATION

Predestination is certainly one of the most controversial of Christian doctrines. It is frequently confused with Providence. But as noted in chapter five that Providence refers to what happens in the world, to whether it was ordained that you would use this book and I would write it, to what you will eat tomorrow and who your parents were, etc. Predestination only refers to salvation, whether you will be saved or not, and whether that has been determined by God in eternity. Obviously the doctrine is related to Justification, an elaboration on how it is we come to faith or fail to do so.

Predestination Denied

Several denominational traditions, especially those influenced by Pietism (see [Methodist] Articles of Religion, 8; Assemblies of God, Statement of Fundamental Truths), Catholicism (Catechism of the Catholic Church, especially 323–324, 1037) and most of the first theologians of the Church prior to Augustine fail to endorse Predestination, focusing instead on our role in coming to faith. Certainly the numerous exhortations to faith found in the Biblical witness (see Mark 16:16; John 12:46; Romans 4:24; 1 Corinthians 1:21) seem to authorize this position. And this orientation is certainly appealing to our sense of individual responsibility and a desire to think that God gives everyone an equal chance to be saved. But on the hand, unless it is made clear that faith is a gift of the Holy Spirit, this model can turn faith into a work and lapse into Pelagianism.

It is not easy to make clear how faith can be something we do and also God's Work. (See the concept of *Theonomy* described in Chapter 4.) But if one opts for this idea that God works through our wills, then faith functions rather like love does in having its way with us when we do nice things for our lovers, parents, or children. We do the good deeds towards them, but are we not compelled by love to do what we do? And if we think this way, then it seems that we may be presupposing that whether we have faith or not has in fact been determined (predestinated) by God. See below.

Arminianism

In order to avoid the problems noted above associated with an outright rejection of Predestination, the seventeenth-century Dutch Reformed theologian

Jacob Arminius spoke of everybody having a chance to be elect because God *fore-knows* in eternity who will want to believe (they are the ones to whom God then bestows faith) and those who are not open to faith (and those are the ones whom God rejects) (Five Articles of the Remonstrants). Romans 8:29; 11:2 in speaking of God foreknowing whom He will predestine seems to authorize this position, and then all other Biblical references to Predestination (see below) are interpreted in this light.

Besides Arminius this viewpoint has also been held by the General Baptist tradition (A Declaration of Faith of English People [in Amsterdam], 5; A Short Confession of Faith By Thomas Helwys, 7), a certain strand of Norwegian-American Lutherans (Friedrich Schmidt, in *Lutheriske Viidnesbyrd* [1883]: 5–15), late Medieval Nominalist theologian William of Ockham (*Ordinatio*, D.XXXVIII, Q.unica), and early church theologians Ambrose (*On the Faith*, 5.6.23) and Ignatius of Antioch (Letter To the Ephesians, Address). The strengths and weaknesses of this position are akin to the previously considered option. This viewpoint is strong on individual responsibility. But unless our decision of faith, which is the basis for God's election, is deemed a Work of the Holy Spirit, then we effectively save ourselves by our faith like the Pelagians teach. And if we give credit to the Spirit for our faith, then are we not effectively teaching Unconditional Double Predestination like the next option?

Double Predestination

The approach to Predestination which most of us associate with the doctrine is to believe that in eternity God made *two* decisions (thus *Double* Predestination): (1) Decides who will receive faith and gain salvation; and (2) Decides to whom He will not give faith and therefore be damned. (Note that unlike the previous option, this option does not refer to God's foreknowledge as the ground for God's decision.) From the perspective of this model, God only foreknows because He has already decided. Biblical texts authorizing this position seem to be Romans 9:15–21 and Exodus 33:19; 7:14; 8:19; 9:7. They speak of both an election to salvation and an election to damnation.

Of course one associates this teaching with John Calvin (*Institutes*, 3.21.1, 7; 3.23.1) and the Puritan heritage (The Westminster Confession, 3). Augustine also at times taught this (*On the Gift of Perseverance*, 35) and even Martin Luther a few times (*Bondage of the Will*, in *Luther's Works*, Vol. 33). Thomas Aquinas

(*Summa Theologica*, I Q.23, Art.5), Anselm (*On the Harmony of the Fore-knowledge, Predestination, and Grace of God with Fee Will*, II.II), and the Particular Baptist theological strand (Second London Confession, III) have affirmed this.

The strengths and weaknesses of this model are similar to those of the Strong Doctrine of Providence model described in Chapter 4. On the one hand, it provides a clear witness to the First Commandment, powerfully affirms the sovereignty of God, giving God all the glory and credit for our salvation. But it also seems to make God responsible for unfaith and damnation. The response to such a charge is that the damned are merely getting what they already deserve (their sin warrants damnation) and, besides, we should not be judging God (Calvin, *Institutes*, 2.21.1–2; 3.24.17). If He does something it is good, even if it does not seem good by our finite standards.

Another way of making this model a bit more palatable to modern eyes is to opt for insights by Augustine (*Confessions*, 11.11.13), Luther (*Sermons On the First Epistle of St. Peter*, in *Luther's Works*, Vol. 30, p. 114), and Calvin (*Institutes*, 3.21.5) which are most suggestive of Einstein's Theory of Relativity. All of them, like Einstein, claim that time is relative depending on your perspective. So from God's point of view, they add, all time (like the speed of light) is simultaneous. This entails that the moment one is deciding for or against faith is simultaneously the moment that God in eternity determines the person's faith. (See the discussion of *Theonomy* in Chapter 4, which also provides examples in the history of Christian thought.) Such insights seem at least to make us seem less like robots, and can be applied to the other Predestination models. And yet if Christian faith is understood in terms of the faithful's responsibilities and if God is to be portrayed as unambiguously loving, the problems with this doctrine and this particular way of construing it may still remain.

Single Predestination

A less well known approach to Predestination has been developed in the Lutheran tradition, though something like it has also been affirmed by the Anglican tradition (in The Thirty-Nine Articles, XVII) and by Menno Simons (*Meditation On the Twenty-Fifth Psalm*, 14). Modern theologian Karl Barth does not himself expressly endorse this option, though his idea of an election in Jesus Christ seems to approximate it (*Church Dogmatics*, Vol. II/2, pp. 59–60, 94ff.; Vol. IV/3, pp. 477–478). This view is called *Single* Predestination, because it teaches that God just makes *one* decision in eternity, to bestow faith and save. Biblical texts used in support of this commitment include 1 Timothy 2:4 and Ephesians 1:11 which speak election to salvation with no reference to damnation.

Because this view may seem to create logical conundrums (how if only some are elected to salvation this position can still avoid Double Predestination), two ways of making sense of this position which are not Arminian and do not appeal to divine foreknowledge have emerged. One is typical of the heritage of The Lutheran Church—Missouri Synod and its sister Lutheran denominations worldwide. These theologians typically speak of Single Predestination as God selecting only some to salvation (C. F. W. Walther, in Synodal-Bericht, Western District; Missouri Synod [1877], p. 24; this is implied by Robert Jenson, in *Christian Dogmatics*, Vol. 2, p. 134ff.) As noted, this seems to imply that some have been rejected. But although Double Predestination seems implied by such a construal these theologians will never concede that. Double Predestination is not Lutheran, they will insist. This is just one of the reason-defying paradoxes of Lutheran thinking, they argue.

The other way of construing Single Predestination avoids this range of issues by contending that *all* are elect. All human beings are elect in Jesus Christ. All have the gift of faith. Salvation is in our laps. It is not necessary to reach out for it or embrace it (much like the Actuality Model of Salvation described in the previous chapter on what the Atonement accomplishes). But this is not necessarily to say that all are saved. Some may throw the gift of faith away. This is the one unforgivable sin, the Sin Against the Holy Spirit (Matthew 12:31–32; Luke 12:10). On these grounds, presumably, since all have the gift of election which is not thrown away, a Buddhist, Muslim, practitioner of an indigenous religion of Africa or the Pacific Isles who has never heard the Gospel in a meaningful way and so not had opportunity to reject it might be saved. (This view is at least implicit in George Lindbeck, *The Nature of Doctrine*, p. 59; see his article in *Dialog* [Summer, 1973]: 182–189. He may be opting for the possibility of a second chance to embrace Christ is offered such persons in hell as a result of Christ's descent into hell, Whose preaching reverberates there for eternity. (See Chapter Thirteen, and below.)

Some might accuse proponents of this vision of teaching universal salvation (see below). The model then seems guilty of overriding numerous Biblical references to hell (also noted in the option below) or encouraging cheap grace. But as Karl Barth pointed out, this model does not teach universal salvation "Even though theological consistency might seem to lead our thoughts and utterances most clearly in this direction." But then he adds, "there is no good reason why we should forbid ourselves, or be forbidden, openness to the possibility that in the reality of God and Man in Jesus Christ there is contained much more than we might expect and therefore the supremely unexpected withdrawal of that final threat..." At least we may hope and pray for it (*Church Dogmatics*, Vol. IV/3, pp. 477–478).

Universal Salvation (Apokatastasis)

Some theologians (notably early church theologians Origen [*On First Principles*, III.VI.5], Macrina (in Gregory of Nyssa, *On the Soul and the Resurrection*), and Gregory of Nyssa (*Address On Religious Instruction*, 26), famed modern theologian Paul Tillich [at least in a veiled way in *Systematic Theology*, Vol. 3, pp. 415–416, 418, 422], and Black Pentecostal mega-church preacher Carlton Pearson) and the Unitarian-Universalist Church endorse this final alternative, characterized by the Greek word *apokatastasis*. Relying on the texts noted in authorizing Single Predestination (especially 1 Timothy 2:4) as well as 1 Peter 3:19, 1 John 2:2, 2 Corinthians 5:19, and Romans 11:26 (which teaches that all Israel will be saved), these theologians affirm that *everyone* is saved. Not that everyone has a chance to be saved (the Possibility For Salvation Model discussed in the previous Chapter). Rather this approach asserts that all of us (the devil included) will be saved.

The strengths and weaknesses of this model are almost intuitively obvious. Of course the idea that all might be brought home to God is a majestic vision. But despite the Biblical texts cited above in support of this position, there are numerous texts that seem to refer to hell (Deuteronomy 32:22; Psalms 9:27; Acts 2:27; 2 Peter 2:4; Revelation 1:18; 20:13). And then there seems to be the danger of cheap grace should this view be espoused (why does it matter if I follow Jesus since I am saved anyway). Of course the models described in the What It Means To Be Born Again Section, which relate Justification to Sanctification, might address this concern. Another way it has been addressed was by Clement of Alexandria (*Stromata*, VI.VI), Martin Luther (*Lectures On Genesis*, in *Luther's Works*, Vol. 2, p.86), and others who explore the possibility of interpreting the reference to Christ preaching to the spirits in prison in 1 Peter 3:18–19 as teaching that when Christ descended into hell He preached to the dead souls living there in condemnation. This entails that all those in hell who are to be saved by this "second chance" are saved by faith. Grace does not seem cheap after all on these grounds, as it includes a response.

CONCLUSION
WHAT TO MAKE OF THE DIVERSITY OF OPTIONS

In constructing a theology, each of us must determine how important for Christian life we deem the doctrine of Justification to be, learning how we gain freedom from sin. Is Christian faith primarily about our salvation, or are other issues like behavior, justice, and freedom, or are God and His relation to the world more crucial for Christian faith? The starting point for theology, what we think is most important about Christian faith, is a crucial agenda for you to decide in developing your own theology.

Another set of questions is crucial in helping you determine what it is you believe in this doctrine. That is, we need to sort out whether God should get all the credit in saving us or whether we need to pay a role as well. (The options described in the section on the Holy Spirit and Human Activity in Chapter Four should be considered.) Once one is clear about how to answer that question, the position one takes on the options considered in this chapter will be a little easier to sort out. In reflecting on this matter, another issue is the confidence one has or needs to have in her/his salvation. If you want to be confident, find positions that make us fully depend on God. If you feel pretty good about your faith or the need to exhort response in others, then one of the models positing a divine-human cooperation is the way to go. Review the relevant Biblical texts. Which ones seem most convincing? And like in the case of all the other chapters, make sure to know what to make of those texts used to authorize the positions you reject. (See Chapter One on Theological Method.)

9

SANCTIFICATION/CHRISTIAN LIFE

Sanctification (*hagiasmos*) literally means to be "made holy," "set apart." Believers are made holy and set apart. To belong to the Church is to be set apart from the world.

The term also refers to the Christian life. In Greek, the root for this term entails "consecrated for service." And so when we are dealing with this doctrine we address the issue of what the Christian life is like, what it looks like. Already we have guidance from the Greek terms. The Christian life is a life of being holy, set apart, and service. But a lot of different options in understanding how to live this way, its relationship to God's grace and justification, as well as how successful you can be in living holy have developed.

A concern with holiness and being set apart was part of the Christian inheritance from Judaism. Though the concept of holiness and being set apart primarily pertains to ritual and holy sacrifices in the Old Testament (Exodus 13:2; 29:33, 37; 40:10–13; Leviticus 8, 11; 2 Chronicles 5:11; Ezekiel 44:19), read in light of Pharasaic suppositions as were in the air in the Church's first century, one can find references to individuals living holy before God (2 Chronicles 29:34; Ezekiel 18; Micah 6:8). And since there was a strong inclination among the Church's first theologians (the Apostolic Fathers and the Apologists) to stress the practice of the Christian life, this early concern with holy living is not surprising. The early theologians stressed the Christian life by linking Justification and Sanctification, sometimes teaching salvation by faith alone, but on balance insisting on both grace and good works (Clement of Rome, Letter to the Church in Corinth, 32.4; 26; 7.5; the *Didache*, 1–5, 11; Justin Martyr, *First Apology*, 10, 43). As we have noted, the characteristic Roman Catholic position as well as proponents of deification insist on a role for good works in saving us. Consequently, Sanctification is not a distinct doctrine for these options, but is included along with Justification under the Christian life (*Catechism of the Catholic Church*, 2012f.). Thus, the options considered in this Chapter are largely Protestant, asso-

ciated with theological options that teach Justification By Grace Though Faith
and distinguish Justification from Sanctification. However, the analysis of these
options is still relevant for Catholic and Eastern proponents, since characteristics
of the prevailing Protestant options do pertain to Catholic and Eastern visions of
the Christian life.

Even in the case of Protestants and others who distinguish Justification and
Sanctification, the two doctrines remain related. For the vast majority of those
considered in this Chapter, Sanctification is said to begin in Justification. The
Wesleyan Pietist traditions go so far as to relate conversion and Sanctification,
regarding both as processes (Wesley, *Sermons*, XLV.3). Only in Holiness and
some Protestant Orthodox traditions are the two separated in time—with a belief
that Sanctification comes *after* Justification. Readers need to examine these options. However, at the outset one should consider if by insisting that Sanctification begins in Justification one eliminates the concern of those teaching a role for
good works in Justification, that those distinguishing Sanctification from Justification (teaching grace alone saves) still take a concern with the Christian life seriously, and are not teaching "cheap grace."

GOOD WORKS SPONTANEOUS

Many of the theological heirs of Martin Luther (*Lectures On Deuteronomy*, in *Luther's Works*, Vol. 9, pp. 179, 184) (including the later Dietrich Bohoeffer [*Communio Sanctorum*, pp. 22–23, 44]) and sometimes Augustine (*Ten Homilies On the
Epistle of John To the Parthians*, X.4, 3, 2) as well as Martin Luther King ("Letter
From a Birmingham Jail") embody this option. They argue that since Sanctification begins in Justification, when you are justified, considered righteous and holy,
you will *want* to start acting that way. Grace and the Holy Spirit compel you to
do so. Indeed, it is like you are intoxicated with the things of God, Luther says
(*The Freedom of a Christian*, in *Luther's Works*, Vol. 31, p. 349). Romans 6:1–14
and Ephesians 2:8–10 offer this testimony to the spontaneity of good works. And
if you teach Justification As Intimate Union With Christ then it follows that you
have become like Christ (part of His family), a "little Christ" (*The Freedom of a
Christian*, in *Luther's Works*, Vol. 31, pp. 367–368; Romans 6:2, 8; 8:5, 10–11; 2
Corinthians 5:20; Galatians 2:20; Colossians 3:16; Hebrews 3:14)

The spontaneity of good works and stress on freedom of the Christian entails that there is no role for the Law in guiding Christian life (no Third Use of the Law, as described in Chapter One). Consequently, the corresponding Ethic of this option is a **Situational Ethic**, the idea that one determines the good in a situation and not on the basis of fixed laws. Consequently this may involve disobeying God's Commandments if the disobedience serves God's will. Luther advocated this on some occasions, like deceiving enemies with lies (*Lectures On Genesis*, in *Luther's Works*, Vol. 5, pp. 150–151; Vol. 3, pp. 257–262; *Kirchenpostille*, in *Complete Sermons*, Vol. 3/1, p. 166). And Bonhoeffer's efforts to assassinate Hitler also illustrate his perceived freedom from the Command against killing in order to do more good. Jesus might be cited as precedent for this position (Mark 2:23–3:6; Matthew 12:1–14). Obviously there is a joyful, daring way to live associated with this way of thinking about Sanctification. Being a Christian is no burden, because no one, not even God, tells you what you must do.

This vision does not entail "cheap grace" or "a do your own thing" Christianity. Luther spoke of the Christian life as a life of sacrifice, of denying oneself (dying to self) and rising with Christ (*The Freedom of a Christian*, in *Luther's Works*, Vol. 31, p. 371; cf. Bonhoeffer, *The Cost of Discipleship*, p. 45–58). Closely related to this idea of "Living Your Baptism" (taught in Romans 6:1-14) is the concept of **Vocation**, taught especially in the Lutheran and Reformed heritages. This is the idea that we all (even laity) have a calling from God in which to serve Him by living the Christian life in that position (Luther, *Kirchenpostille*, in *Complete Sermons*, Vol. 1/1, p. 242; *Sermon On Baptism*, in *Luther's Works*, Vol. 35, pp. 40–41; Calvin, *Institutes*, III.XI.6).

If you understand your job as a call from God, then you have all sorts of opportunities to live the Christian life of dying to sin and rising for Christ in love. The difficult boss or customer (student or professor) with whom you interact provides great opportunities to deny oneself for Christ and the neighbor. (Other Protestant bodies and even Catholics and Eastern churches affirm the **Priesthood of All Believers**, but not with such an appeal to the doctrine of Vocation. More on that in Chapter 10 on Ministry.)

Simultaneously Saint and Sinner

Luther and his heritage differ from other alternatives in his characteristic unwillingness to allow for the possibility of growth in grace. This is a function of his endorsement of the Augustinian concept of Sin as concupiscence. If we sin in everything we do, then even Christians remain sinners—as much as they ever were or they will not feel themselves as dependent on grace as they were when they first came to Christ. Consequently Luther and his heirs teach *simuliustus et peccator*, that we are simultaneously saint and sinner, not just partially saint and partially sinner but 100% saint and 100% sinner (*Lectures On Romans*, in *Luther's Works*, Vol. 25, pp. 258, 332, 340f., 434).

How can this paradox be affirmed? God considers the Christian a saint even though he/she is as selfish as ever. Romans 7:14ff. seems to provide Biblical authorization for this viewpoint. As a result, on Luther's grounds, the best a Christian can do is to **Sin Bravely** (Letter To Philip Melanchthon, in *Luther's Works*, Vol. 48, pp. 281–282; *Heidelberg Disputation*, in *Luther's Works*, Vol. 31, p. 63). Being a brave sinner is not an invitation to do whatever you wish. But it is a call to confess your sin boldly, to concede that your sin is great, impinging on the good deed you seek to do. Living that way will make you clearer about your dependence on grace (*Lectures On 1 Timothy*, in *Luther's Works*, Vol. 28, p. 245).

Theologians attracted to this utter dependence on grace and the freedom that comes with a Situational Ethic will be attracted to this model. But for those who believe that Christ's Atoning Work makes a difference in how we live, the second alternative is more in line with that point of view.

GOOD WORKS MUST BE EXHORTED

The typical position of almost every other theologian outside of Lutheranism (and Augustine as well as even Luther sometimes) who embraces this approach is that even when we are Justified, even if Sanctification is complete, good works must be taught to the faithful, or they must be exhorted (Augustine, *On the Correction of the Donatists*, 1.3.5; Luther, The Large Catechism, I.Con.). Dietrich Bonhoeffer took this point of view as well, especially in his critique of cheap grace (*The Cost of Discipleship*). This position involves the employment of the Third Use of the Law (the Law used as a guide for living the Christian life). The New Testament (notably James) and Old Testament texts relating to instruction support this point of view. (Also see Romans 15:1–13, Galatians 6:1–10, 1 Peter 1:13–2:10, and 2 Peter 2:7–11; 3:1–18.) There are several different versions of this option, and so we examine them individually.

Growth in Grace

By far, the majority of theologians in the history of the Church have taken the position that though sinners we can advance in the Christian faith with enhanced obedience to the Commandments. Biblical backing for this position seems provided in Matthew 6:28, 2 Corinthians 9:10; 10:15, and 2 Thessalonians 1:3. Among a handful of the numerous examples of this viewpoint include the Eastern understanding of deification, which presupposes progress in becoming like God (Athanasius, *On the Incarnation of the Word*, 8; Anthony, 33, in *Fathers of the Church*). Progress in the Christian life is also presupposed in the Catholic conception of Justification as indebted to Thomas Aquinas (*Summa Theologica*, I2ae, Q.114, Art.8; Council of Trent, "Decree Concerning Justification," Ch.X).

Early pre-Augustinian theologians making this point include Polycarp (Epistle To the Philippians, XII) and Clement of Rome (Epistle To the Corinthians, LVI). Almost all of the Reformers like John Calvin (*Institutes*, III.VII.5) and the heirs of Menno Simons (The Dordrecht Confession, VI) believe in the possibility of progress in the Christian life.

Baptists (Southern Baptist Convention, Baptist Faith and Message, V.2), Anglicans/Episcopalians (The Thirty-Nine Articles, XVI) and even some Pentecostals not impacted by the Holiness Movement (Assemblies of God, Statement of Fundamental Truths, 7) or some denominations influenced by Pietism (Brethren in Christ, *Doctrine & Government*, p. 12; Evangelical Covenant Church, *Covenant Affirmations*, p. 10) teach this growth in grace and progress in the Christian life. Most Pietists and those influenced by the Holiness Movement also teach growth in grace, as we will note below. But unlike these traditions, the theologians affirming the option we have been considering continue to teach that the faithful always remain in sin, though they can overcome sin (remain only partially sinful and increasingly saint).

One African Independent Church, The Celestial Church of Christ based in Nigeria, even has a purification rite to help female members. Rooted in Leviticus 12:16–30 and Mark 5:25–34, female members are purified after their monthly periods and after giving birth (Doctrines and Services).

Proponents of this Growth in Grace option are likely to seek signs that they are making progress in the Christian life, even signs that they can be assured of Justification or their Election. This is especially evidenced in the case of theologies that embrace Double Predestination. In the case of John Calvin, his theological heirs and Baptists joining him in teaching Predestination, the **Perseverance** of the believer is a sign of election (Calvin, *Institutes*, III.XXII.7; III.XXIII.10; The Westminster Confession, XVII; [Baptist] Second London Confession, XVII; Southern Baptist Convention, Baptist Faith & Message, V). Such a teaching offers comfort for those with anxiety and might be said to have Biblical roots (Philippians 1:6; Ephesians 6:18). The longer you walk the walk of faith, the more confident you can be of your salvation.

Another sign of salvation or obedience to God (faith) that proponents of Prosperity Gospel tend to highlight is **Prosperity** or at least staying out of poverty (T./D Jakes, "Twitter Account, 9/24/17; Joel Osteen, *Your Best Life Now*, pp. 265–266). Job 36:11, Psalms 35:27, and Jeremiah 29:11 might be cited in support. This sign of election/faith too may be a way of gaining confidence for one's faith. But in all cases, when you seek assurance of spiritual matters from yourself (what you are doing) you unwittingly put more focus on yourself than on God. And more than likely that can lead to insecurity rather than assurance.

This Prosperity Gospel sign of assurance seems problematic for other reasons. In the previous chapter we have already pointed out the Pelagian propensities of this theological approach. It gets the focus off God and puts more on us. In addition, from the viewpoints of Liberation Theology, Black Theology, Womanist Theology, and the Theology of the Cross, the Prosperity emphasis seems to get the focus off God's concern for the poor and oppressed, that He has a thing for the poor.

Perfection

We have already alluded to the fact that some Christians, who think that we must exhort living the Christian life and believe that the faithful may grow in grace, believe that the process of spiritual growth should have the goal of perfection (Entire Sanctification) as per Matthew 5:48, 19:21, and Philippians 3:12. Those not subscribing to Perfection (the majority of Christian theologians) see no need for it, believing that we have already been entirely sanctified in Christ, that what remains is merely the appropriate process and that sin will prevent its full completion until the End. Besides references to perfection in the texts cited by proponents are literally translated "completeness," "maturity," or "wholeness," these critics contend.

Proponents of Perfection in ancient times include teachers of deification like Anthony (see Athanasius, *Life of St. Anthony*, 74), Macarius the Egyptian (*The Spiritual Homilies*, 15.37; 27.11, 5), and Gregory of Nyssa, (*On Perfection*). In the Middle Ages such striving for perfection was advocated by famed Mystic Catherine of Siena (*Dialogue*, 47) and during the Reformation era so did the Anabaptist Hans Denck (*Whether God Is the Cause of Evil*). Pietism also nurtured the idea of striving for perfection, as did the Holiness Movement in a different way. Philip J. Spener, the first of the Pietists, though a Lutheran, taught perfection as a goal for which to strive (*Pia Desideria*, 2). He was joined by the founder of the Moravian Church Ludwig von Zinzendorf (*Remarkable Conversations between a Traveler and Various Other Persons*, 1) and of course by John Wesley (*Plain Account of Christian Perfection*). His teaching of the concept explains why Methodist churches teach this doctrine, as well as the Quakers. The Holiness Movement beginning in the nineteenth century in the United States also teaches perfection, but in a different sense than Methodists, Quakers, and pre-Modern theologians mentioned.

We need to elaborate on what is meant by Perfection by these theologians. Perfection in their sense does not entail what those influenced by the Holiness Movement mean, and so we will return to that option in a moment. In any case for none of these theologians does perfection entail never making a mistake. It is not an exemption from ignorance or temptations. As John Wesley contends, it is simply another term for holiness; it is nothing more than entire sanctification (Wesley, *Sermons*, 40.I.7-9; *Late Conversations*, V.1-2). It is the ability not to sin, a desire not to sin (*Sermons*, 40II.20; *Plain Account of Christian Perfection*, 10). Perfection means to love God with all that we have, manifest when all thoughts and deeds are governed by love (*Plain Account of Christian Perfection*, 2.5 Q.6; 19). For Wesley, perfection in this life is a goal, but most of the times he claimed that it only happens in death (*Sermons*, CXXVII.Int,; II.3–6; CXXXV).

For Wesley and most of the theologians considered, Christian perfection is a process, not a state. It is an instant but also "a gradual work" *(Brief Thoughts On Christian Perfection*, 2). The process begins in justification (simultaneous with it in the case of those teaching deification) (*Sermons*, XLIII.1.4; XIV.V.2; I.I.16). However, as we shall see, there is another side of Wesley on these matters that has dominated in the Holiness Movement. For the present, suffice it to note the strengths of this viewpoint. It has some Biblical backing (Matthew 5:48; 19:21; Philippians 3:12; Hebrews 6:1) and it certainly calls the faithful to high standards. No cheap grace is associated with this vision. In fact, most proponents of perfection advocate for life-style codes, from abstaining from alcohol to dress codes and even strictures on dancing. Are such standards violations of Christian freedom or admirable ways of saying "no" to rampant secularism?

Protestant versions of this model also emphasize the role of grace in drawing the faithful towards perfection. But it must be asked whether this view effectively minimizes the power of sin and in so doing both compromises the importance of grace and sets such a high standard for Christians that it effectively lays a guilt-trip on them.

As An Event

As previously noted, the Holiness Movement and its theologians have a different understanding of perfection and when it happens. In their view Methodists have distorted Wesley on these matters and as a result the Methodist interpretation of these concepts has diminished the importance of perfection. (In its origins, another concern of the original leaders of the Holiness Movement was that American Methodists had compromised John Wesley's opposition to slavery, a movement that the Holiness leaders linked to the strong emphasis on Christian perfection that they believed they and Wesley affirmed.

In response the Holiness Movement understood perfection not as a process like the Methodists had, but as an event. They made this point clearer, they thought, by insisting the perfection is a "second work of grace," something that comes *after* justification. Entire Sanctification or perfection is identified with the baptism of the Holy Spirit (H. Orton Wiley, *Christian Theology*, Vol., pp. 471ff.; Hannah Whitehall Smith, *The Christian's Secret to the Happy Life*, especially p. 28); Charles G. Finney, *Lectures On Revivals*, II; The Wesleyan Church, Articles of Religion, IX, X; Christian and Missionary Alliance, Statement of Faith, 7). Even John Wesley at times described Sanctification in a manner like the Holiness tradition, referring to it as a "second work of grace" (*Sermons*, V.II.1).

The texts cited above in support of the doctrine of perfection are relevant to authorizing Holiness thinking. Also suggestive of the need for Sanctification in order to be saved are 2 Thessalonians 2:13; I Thessalonians 5:23. A baptism of the Holy Spirit that comes after Justification seems authorized by Acts 1:5; 8:14–17; 10:44–48; 19:1–6. Regarding Perfection As an Event, this model exhibits the same strengths regarding the high standards and individual responsibility we observed among those teaching Perfection As Process. In addition, this approach clearly gets the Church away from an undue reliance on rituals like Baptism. But the same weaknesses as anyone teaching Perfection emerge with this model. More so, than those teaching Perfection As Process, this model challenges our confidence in salvation. Because Sanctification is said to happen *after* Justification, we cannot be sure of our salvation when we come to faith (and are justified). Only when we enjoy the experience of Sanctification (termed the baptism of the Holy Spirit) can we be assured. Thus, the Holiness model can cause strong doubts about one's salvation.

This last weakness of the Perfection As Event Model gave rise to the Pentecostal alternative. For the first Pentecostals were all members of the Holiness Movement, seeking assurance that they indeed had been saved had received the Baptism of the Holy Spirit. These Christians and their theologians devised a different vision of Sanctification in response.

Pentecostal and Charismatic Theology

We have already described the origins of the modern Pentecostal Movement and its theological core—relating the Baptism of the Holy Spirit to the gift of tongues understood as the visible manifestation of this Baptism. Likewise we reviewed how while Pentecostals start denominations that are Pentecostal in character, Charismatics remain in their original denominations in hopes of inspiring a religious revival.

This insight about the nature of Pentecostalism helps explain how and why this theological perspective was so relevant to those who believe in striving for Perfection but were despairing over whether they had received this gift. Equating the Baptism of the Holy Spirit with Entire Sanctification (Perfection) entailed that if one was assured he/she had been baptized in the Spirit then the believer could be certain of having been sanctified and so saved. Finally a Bible School preacher in the Midwest whom we've already noted, Charles Parham, made the connection between tongues and the Baptism of the Holy Spirit. This entailed that if one spoke in tongues he/she could be assured of salvation. The problem of finding assurance of one's salvation posed by the Holiness Movement had been addressed. The resulting theology has come to be known as Three-Step Pentecostalism.

Three-Step Pentecostalism. This oldest version of Pentecostalism (also known as Holiness Pentecostalism) is properly named. There are three steps on the way to salvation. We are already aware of the first two steps from our study of the Holiness option: (1) Justification (or Conversion). This is a Forensic understanding of the doctrine, the view of Justification employed by all the options studied in this Chapter which posit that Good Works Must Be Exhorted; and (2) Entire Sanctification (Perfection) which transpires *after* (in time) Justification. The Third Step, transpiring after Sanctification, is then Baptism of the Holy Spirit, whose outward sign is speaking in tongues. Because this third Step only transpires after Sanctification, being born again in the Holy Spirit and speaking in tongues is evidence that Sanctification has happened. Speaking in tongues, then, is the assurance that one has been made perfect, that the believer is saved.

W. J. Seymour the leader of the famed Azusa Street Revival was an early proponent of this viewpoint ("Receive Ye the Holy Ghost," in *The Apostolic Faith*). A number of denominations continue to teach this viewpoint, notably the Church of God in Christ (*Official Manual*, pp. 56–58) and the Church of God (Cleveland, Tennessee) (Declaration of Faith, 6–7). This viewpoint can cite the texts noted above for the Holiness position as well as Hebrews 10:14,15 and Ephesians 3:16 in support. In addition to the same strengths that characterized the Holiness Movement and anyone teaching Perfection, the Three-Step model's strength is also a potential weakness. It places more emphasis on speaking in tongues than its Pentecostal alternative. But this emphasis might in turn encourage the faithful to claim the experience of tongues for themselves without quite being sure of it (to fake the experience). But is this risk worth taking given the obvious strengths of this vision?

Two-Step Pentecostalism. After some time the Pentecostal Movement began to attract followers not raised in a Holiness ethos. More like Baptists, Reformed Christians, and all other Protestants they rejected perfection and believed that Sanctification began in Justification (W. H. Durham, articles in *Pentecostal Testimony* [Summer, 1911]). Consequently the Baptism of the Holy Spirit (manifest in tongues) is a Second Step (Justification and Sanctification constituting just one event). This position continues to be maintained by the Assemblies of God (Statement of Fundamental Truths, 7–9). It is also the position of most Charismatics, since their churches teach the idea that Sanctification begins after Justification (is part of Justification in the case of Catholic Charismatics). It is called the Completed Work view because it posits that since Sanctification begins in

Justification, then Christ's Work in saving us got the job done. It is not like the confirmation of salvation had to await a later Baptism of the Holy Spirit.

What then becomes of speaking in tongues? It is the Second Work on grounds of this option, following Justification and Sanctification that constitute the First Work. To be sure, the Baptism of the Holy Spirit is still equated with speaking in tongues, which is the evidence of this Baptism. But we do not need this experience in order to be assured of our salvation, since those with faith already know that they are Sanctified. In short, the faithful do not need to speak in tongues as badly. It and the Baptism of the Holy Spirit are enrichments of the gift with which one can find comfort.

In addition to the texts on Pentecost in Acts 2, which can be taken as indicating that the Disciples had already been saved prior to the outburst of tongues and Paul's warnings about too much emphasis on tongues (1 Corinthians 14), several Biblical texts which indicate that Sanctification is not a later work following Justification (Hebrews 2:11; 1 Peter 2:24) may be cited in support of this position. This option clearly alleviates anxiety the faithful might have about their salvation which is associated with the Holiness commitment to teaching that salvation is not assured until we have experienced perfection (the Baptism of the Holy Spirit). But the yearning for standards in the Christian life, high goals for which to strive along with the importance of speaking in tongues, is not so strongly asserted in Two Step Pentecostalism.

There is a rich variety in how to regard the Christian life, how to nurture it. The importance one places on gaining confidence in one's salvation, how important Christian freedom is, very much sets the agenda for one's view of Sanctification. Whatever one says on the subject, how the Holy Spirit is involved in the works we do needs to be clarified. Most positions dealt with in this chapter claim that the Spirit works theonomously (see Chapter on the Holy Spirit).

CLOSING THOUGHTS

In dealing with the Christian life, theologians must first determine the precise relationship between Sanctification and Justification—whether the two are distinct, and if so precisely when Sanctification begins—and also sort out to what extent the works done in the Christian life are works of the Holy Spirit (see the earlier discussion of the difference between Heteronomy, Autonomy, and Theonomy). After that matter is dispatched, the following issues demand attention: (1) Do we live as Christians spontaneously, moved by grace alone, or do we need to be exhorted to live in a joyful Christian manner? How you answer that determines whether Christian living is portrayed and experienced as a game to play or a duty; (2) Can one make progress in the Christian life? (3) If so, how much progress can you make, and how do you know when you have done enough to feel assured? What are the signs of Christian life? You might want to think about how **Prayer** fits the images employed. If you are more inclined to stress Christian faith as exhortation, then Prayer is a duty for Christians, something we need to do with the Holy Spirit's help. If you came down on the side of good works as spontaneous, then Prayer is something God does to us and for us, that the words don't matter so much because the Holy Spirit will give them to us. (As for invoking Mary and other saints, we have already noticed how in prayer they may be petitioned to intercede on our behalf, from a Catholic and Eastern standpoint. We address this again further in the Chapter on Eschatology.) Answer all the preceding questions, elaborate images for describing how you see Christian life, and that language can be most useful to you in your preaching and teaching, in the tone you aim to set for faith in Church and society.

IO

CHURCH

The two terms used in the New Testament to designate the Church (*ecclesia* and *soma Christou* [Body of Christ]) summarize the Biblical witness to this doctrine. The term *ecclesia* literally means "called out." It has its roots in ancient Greece where it referred to an assembly of citizens "called out" to elect magistrates. Paul may have borrowed the term from Athens and applied it to Christian gatherings as a way of communicating the fact that Christians have been "called out" from the world and the world's people (see 1 Thessalonians 2:14). The Church is "called out" in the sense that membership in the Church entails a radically new mode of existence (just as Sanctification entails being "set apart"). As such, the term *ecclesia* connotes the Church's eschatological character as a community that has been "called out" of the old realities to give witness to the new reality of God's Kingdom.

The term Body of Christ conveys another dimension of the Church's character. It provides a powerful witness to the fact that Christians are bound together in a kind of organic community in which everything is shared in common (Romans 12:4–8; 1 Corinthians 12:12ff.). To say that the Church is the Body of Christ (see Ephesians 1:23; Colossians 1:18) is to say more than that the Church is institutionally organized. Rather the Body of Christ is a living reality. The image conveys the fact that Christians are united to each other and to Christ as a vine to a branch (John 15:3–5). All that Christ has is given to the Church, to Christians, and all that they have is to be shared with each other (see 2 Corinthians 1:5ff.; Romans 6:1ff.). It is quite clear then how to refer to the Church as Body of Christ is to emphasize the Church's character as a community, as the **Communion of Saints**. A similar image stressing that the faithful share all Christ has is the idea of the Church as the Bride of Christ (Ephesians 5:25–27).

This word study demonstrates that Christians can agree that the Church is an eschatological community—one which bears witness to God's ultimate purpose for the world and which transcends the limitations of space and time. (The term *ecclesia* is used in the New Testament at some points to refer to the universal Church [Acts 15:3; 2 Corinthians 1:1; Galatians 1:13]).

Because the Church has an eschatological character it is also identified in terms of being an eschatological fulfillment of the Old Testament. This is evident in the Church's identification as *People of God* (Romans 9:25–26; Titus 2:14) or *Israel of God* (Galatians 6:16). In this sense it could be argued that the concept of Church is presupposed in Jesus' Ministry, in His gathering His Disciples around the theme Kingdom of God (Matthew 4:23; Mark 1:14–15). As His Body, later-day followers have the sort of fellowship with Him, sharing all He has, just as this was enjoyed by the Disciples (Luke 22:28–30; Mark 2:19). Obviously, then, if Jesus' Ministry is a paradigm for the fellowship of the Church, then one cannot be a Christian apart from fellowship with Christ and other Christians. In that sense, there really is no salvation outside the Church (*extra ecclesimm nulla salus* [Cyprian of Carthage, Epistles, LXXII]).

Of course this does not connote that the reality of the Church is to be absolutely identified with the Kingdom of God, as an eschatological fulfillment of all that Jesus proclaimed. But in the midst of these general ecumenical agreements, differences emerge among theologians over the degree to which the visible institutional Church can approximate the Kingdom of God and also over how to identify what the true Church is. We will consider the various options for addressing this matter and for portraying the points of agreement just noted.

One other set of common convictions about the Church: The Nicene Creed refers to the Church as "one, holy catholic, and Apostolic." We will note that the options that follow have different construals of those marks.

THE CHURCH AS GOD'S WORK, CREATED THROUGH WORD AND SACRAMENT

We begin with what is likely the oldest way in which the Church seems to have been construed, as God's Work (though Word and Sacrament), gathered around those Apostles who knew Jesus, could proclaim His Word and preside over the Meal He had instituted (Acts 1:12ff). Of course, proponents of the final (the fourth) family of modes for the Church that I will introduce would argue that theirs is the oldest model, that the Church is the gathering of people like at the first Pentecost (Acts 2).

All of the options that fall into this category of understanding the Church share a common understanding of the Church's holiness. For them the Church is holy in virtue of God's holy actions. His Word, which founds the Church, makes the Church holy. Indeed among its members include sinners and hypocrites (in contrast to the last family of models we will consider whose advocates understand the Church in terms of its members).

Built On the Foundation of an Apostolically-Ordained Ministry

The development of an ordained ministry in the Church was largely a function of the failure of Jesus to Return as quickly as His first followers expected, and the consequent need of the Church to begin to get organized as long-lasting communities. In the same period as Gentile membership was growing in the Church and in some local churches the Jewish roots of the Christian movement were being overlooked, a self-conscious appropriation of Jewish roots began to develop. The Church began to turn away from worshipping in a free, spontaneous manner, awaiting insights of the Holy Spirit, as it had at its outset, in favor of structured, liturgical worship. The model for this was quite naturally the worship styles of the Jewish Temple. This inevitably entailed the appreciation of the need for Christians to have priests, as the Jewish Temple liturgy was presided over by a priest. We will elaborate further on the polity (church structure) that developed in the earliest era (the Three-fold View of Ministry) in the next Chapter.

One of the developers of this polity, Ignatius of Antioch, first insisted that without Bishops, Presbyters, and Deacons there is no Church (Letter To the Trallians, 3.1). In the third century Cyprian of Carthage made a similar point asserting that the Church is in the Bishops (Epistles, LXVI/LXVIII.8). To this day the Catholic Church continues to teach that the Church is founded on the Apostles (*Catechism of the Catholic Church*, 857, 861–863). Eastern churches define the Church as gathered by the Mysteries (Sacraments) founded on Apostolic doctrine and polity, which includes the priesthood with Metropolitans/Bishops as successors of Apostles (Liturgy of Basil; Irenaeus, *Against All Heresy*, 4.26.5; *Catechism of Nicholas Bulgaris*, pp. 44, 46–47). The Church of England is an interesting mix on this matter, as it defines the Church in a manner like a number of other Protestant traditions (in terms of Word and Sacraments, see below), but adds that an Episcopal polity is characteristic of the Church.

All of these theologians and churches define the Church's unity and catholicity in relation to the Bishops: apart from the Episcopacy (and the Pope for Catholics, the Ecumenical Patriarch of Constantinople for the Eastern churches) there is no Church. Fellowship with these Bishops guarantees Apostolicity, because all teach Apostolic Succession (the idea that there has been a line of the consecration of Bishops through the laying on of hands dating back to one of the Apostles) (Ignatius of Antioch, Letter To the Philadelphians, 1–3, 8; *Catechism of the Catholic Church*, 816; *Catechism of Nicholas Bulgraris*, p. 44). Biblical precedents cited are Acts 8:18; 13:3 and 1 Timothy 4:14.

Several distinct ways of construing this model of the Church as Built on the Foundation of an Apostolically-Ordained Ministry have developed. We next revisit two of these alternatives, which are options for all theologians who in some sense appeal to Tradition as one of the norms of theology

On This Foundation the Church Is Infallible

The Roman Catholic Church has been led to conclude that an ecclesiastical hierarchy that has been duly established by Christ (Apostolic Succession) cannot err on matters of faith and morals. This takes two forms: (1) **Ordinary Magisterium**, which is exercised when the Bishops make binding decisions in Council (Vatican II, *Lumen Genium*, 25; *Catechism of the Catholic Church*, 884); and (2) **Extraordinary Magisterium**, which is exercised by the Pope, but only when he speaks *ex cathedra* ("from the Chair," as an authoritative interpreter of the Tradition) (Vatican I, Enchiridion *Symbolorum, definitionum et declarationum de rebus fidei et morum*, 3074). Non-Catholics need to be clear that the Catholics do not claim that the Pope never makes a mistake. Only when speaking authoritatively as Teacher of the Church are his decrees infallible, and that has only happened twice in history (in establishing the doctrines of the [Mary's] Immaculate Conception and her Assumption Into Heaven).

It may be that humans err, but do we want to say that God makes mistakes? And since God has established the hierarchy through Apostolic Succession and conferred such authority on Peter and his successor the Pope, it seems logical to conclude that they do not err on faith and morals.

After all, as the Body of Christ the Church cannot err since Christ never errs. Another way of arguing this point is by appealing to Matthew 18:18. Of course the response may be that the faithful need assurance in their beliefs, that none of us except Unitarians and Arians want to think that the Church erred in the Conciliar decisions made by the Councils of Nicaea, Constantinople, or Chalcedon.

On This Foundation the Church Is Indefectible

A softer version perhaps (for Protestants) emerges from the segments of the Eastern Orthodox tradition. They refer to the Church's "indefectibility," rather than its infallibility. This view claims that the Church has no defect and will forever be a trustworthy instrument of salvation. Some of these segments of the Orthodox tradition, notably in Russia and Slavic nations, differ from the Catholic Ordinary Magisterium by asserting that the Councils in themselves may not be infallible, but that they gain authority by being received in the Church everywhere and at all times (George Florovsky, in *Eastern Orthodox Theology*, p. 118; John Meyendorff, "What is an ecumenical council?," *St. Vladimir's Theological Quarterly* 17 No. 4, 1973, p. 270).

This idea is sometimes termed the **consensus fidelium** (consensus of the faithful). Several Protestants open to a role for Tradition affirm something like this notion. Lutherans seem to take this position insofar as arguments for infant baptism are based on the fact that God would not have deceived the Church so long given the allegedly ancient character of the practice (Martin Luther, The Small Catechism, IV.49). The invocation of the ancient Creedal formulations by the Anglican heritage (The Thirty-Nine Articles, VIII) along with Lutheranism (Philip Melanchthon, The Augsburg Confession, I) also seem to indicate these traditions' endorsements of something like the authority of Church teaching when there is consensus about it among the faithful. Methodism is another Protestant tradition relying on Tradition as a source. Not much is said about its content, but the church's willingness to endorse the traditional teachings of the Church which concur with Scripture seems to entail that the heirs of Wesley find value in what the Church has had consensus about everywhere and at all times (*The Book of Discipline of The United Methodist Church*, 104). The same may be the case in John Calvin's veneration of Councils of the Church, mixed with his claim that not every interpretation of Scripture by a Council is true and certain (*Institutes*, IV.IX.3).

Inclusion of a role for laity as a whole along with clergy in determining authoritative teaching may have some appeal. We have previously noted that a role for consent of the faithful seems to receive Biblical testimony in Acts 15:22. But the appeal of a more hierarchical approach, one allegedly commissioned by Christ Himself, seems undeniable in our relativistic context in which many yearn for certainties.

There are some indications in the Biblical witness that the Church may be founded on the Apostles (see reference above in Acts 1:12ff. and also Matthew 16:18; Acts 15:6, 22; I Corinthians 12:28). And as long as this model is understood as God establishing the Church through His Spirit's Work by means of the Episcopal structure of Apostolic Succession (this is implied by Vatican II's assertion [in *Dei Verbum*, 10] that the Magisterium is to serve the Word of God), then this model clearly testifies to God's Work in establishing the Church. But for those inclined to want to stress the responsibility of all people for keeping and maintaining the Church, that its holiness depends on the holiness of the faithful, there are problems with too much emphasis on God's Work. Proponents of this alternative contend that the Eastern and Catholic grounding of the Church on an ecclesiastical hierarchy as well as all the other ecclesiological models which we consider under this rubric of The Church as God's Work, as Mother, as House of God with a Lamp-Light, as Culture, as a Hospital, or as an Exodus Church are susceptible to the critique of not stressing the faithful's responsibility enough. In fact, the common emphases of these latter models on God's Work entails that they have been and may be combined so that theologians may and have espoused several of them together, along with the model we have been considering this far. We proceed to examine these other options.

Openness To Protestants As Separated Brethren

For those who find the first group of models too exclusivist, the Catholic Church and its leading theologians in the twentieth century found a way to inclusivism. The logic of the positions thus far considered is that other believers in Jesus who do not have a valid Ministry in their communities are not Christian, but heretics (Council of Trent, "Canons On the Sacrament of Order"). But in Vatican II the claim is made that one can find among Protestants "truly Christian endowments" in their "ecclesiastical communities," and so they may be considered "separated brethren" (no longer heretics) (*Unitatis Redintegratio*, 3–4).

In a sense this move was related to another decree, which seemed to make a distinction between the visible church (the institutional expression of the church) and the invisible Church (the spiritual essence of the Church) a distinction that is typical of most Protestant traditions (see below). It is claimed by the Council that the Church merely "subsists" in the Catholic Church (Lumen Gentium, 1–3.6). Consequently it follows that a given community like Protestant bodies can have many of the core elements (especially God's Word and many of the Sacraments) in its life (have the Church "subsisting" in it) and yet because of not having a valid Ministry (the Catholic version of it), the Protestant community in which the elements of the Church subsist is not fully a Church (the Roman Catholic Church). Protestants may not like this new status of not being fully members of the Church, but it sure beats being a heretic (their status for more than 400 years).

This model is obviously not one that either Catholics or Protestants would want to embrace long-term. In order for Church unity to be implemented with this mode it will demand that Protestants and even the Eastern churches eventually "regularize" their Ministries/Polity by accepting an Episcopal polity (the Threefold View of Ministry, see the next chapter) with Apostolic Succession and subordination of all Bishops to the Bishop of Rome. (Note the precedent for Lutheran openness to accepting a "reformed Papacy" in The Smalcald Articles.) Is this a model for theology today? Note Jesus' appeal for unity in John 17:20–21 and also Ephesians 4:3ff. This model for the Church is heavily dependent on the one that follows.

A Sacrament

Some progressive Roman Catholic theologians influencing Vatican II offered another model that the Church cannot be unequivocally identified with the Roman Catholic institutional Church. Progressive modern Catholic Henri de Lubac had contended that the essence of the Church is a Sacrament in the sense that She [note the Church is female for him] represents Christ and that He is Present in Her—like a Sacrament (*Catholicism*, p. 29). De Lubac was joined in this commitment by Karl Rahner *(The Church and the Sacraments.* p. 317) and the concept reflects in Vatican II (*Lumen Gentium*, 48; *Sacrosanctam concilium*, 26). This model was also taught in the early Church by Cyprian of Carthage, speaking of the Church as a "Sacrament of unity" (*On the Unity of the Church*, 7).

The preceding reference to unity fits du Lubac's claim that Christ (and then the Church in turn) represents the single goal of humanity. Much like we have already noted, a distinction is made in this model between what the Church is in its essence (Christ's Real Presence in the "stuff" of the Church) and its visible character as an institution. This concept seems entailed by Biblical references to the Church as Body of Christ. Catholics claim that this model can be held together with their episcopal polity. If so, is this a model for Christian unity?

Built Only On Word and Sacrament

This is the most characteristically Protestant way of describing the Church. As much as the Catholic and Orthodox versions, the intention of this model is to proclaim that the Church is more than what we do for it, but without insisting on an episcopal polity. It is through God's Word and the Sacraments that the Church is One (the same Word is preached everywhere), catholic (the Word establishing the Church is the Gospel taught everywhere), Apostolic (in the sense that this Word goes back to the Apostles), and holy (in the sense that God's holy Word makes the Church holy). By not identifying the Church with a Polity or with other institutional expressions and insofar as the Word is not visible, a distinction between the true "Invisible Church" and its institutional expression, "the Visible Church," is implied by this model. Among those denominational heritages embracing the model to some extent include Lutherans (Philip Melanchthon, The Augsburg Confession, VII; Martin Luther, First Psalm Lectures, in *Luther's Works*, Vol. II, pp. 373–374), The Episcopal (The Thirty-Nine Articles, XIX), and Methodist heritages (Articles of Religion, XIII).

This model has all the strengths of the Catholic and Orthodox stress on God's Work in creating the Church that we have noted, but without the clericalism and hierarchicalism implied in founding the Church on Ministry. In fact there is an openness on polity with this model, which is why many different traditions can embrace it. Because different polities can embrace this vision of the Church, implicit in it is a distinction between the invisible Church (God's Work in gathering the Church) and the visible church (the church's organization, institutional structures) (Philip Melanchthon, Apology of The Augsburg Confession, VII–VIII12ff). There also seems to be some Biblical support for this vision in Ephesians 5:25–27 and 1 Corinthians 12:12–13.

This is not to deny that an Episcopal polity cannot fit this view of the Church. In fact Anglican/Episcopalians, Methodists, and some Lutherans combine such a polity with understanding the Church as marked by Word and Sacrament. Of course Catholics and Eastern Christians will object that not mandating an episcopal polity can easily lead to chaos and a lack of unity, as Protestantism's history seems to illustrate (for once the historic episcopate rooted in Apostolic Succession was lost, Protestant denominationalism and schism have prevailed). In addition, others might challenge this vision for not taking seriously the need for personal holiness among its members.

Also Marked By Discipline

This model is related to the preceding model, in complete agreement with it but adding one mark—discipline—which is a response to the critique raised to the previous model. This position was advocated by John Calvin. He completely agreed with the foregoing model (*Institutes*, IV.1.10–12), simply adding discipline as a third mark of the Church (*Reply To Sadolet*; also see The Scots Confession, XVIII). This addition fits his commitment to construing Christian life with a Third Use of the Law. Certainly this model addresses the concern that in positing God as the source of the Church's life we not forget Christian responsibility. The consistent advice given to the churches addressed by the Epistles seem to be in line with this way of construing the Church (Romans 14; 1 Corinthians 5:3–5; 1 Timothy 3; 1 Peter 1:13–2:10; Titus 1:7–16). But it might be argued from the viewpoint of one who teaches Sanctification in terms of the Spontaneity of Good Works that this vision of the Church leads us to legalism, not implicit in previous models considered.

None of the options that follow expressly refer to the role of Word and Sacrament in forming the Church. And yet insofar as each one, except the last one, does presuppose that it is God working in creating the Church they could be considered as families of our first category.

THE CHURCH AS THE BODY
OF THE PREDESTINED

While not directly referring to the role of God's Word in gathering the Church, the emphasis here is still on God's role in creating the Church. True enough, the Church is the people on these grounds, but they only got into the Church because of God's action of predestining them. In that sense they are united and certainly catholic because God elects all sorts of people. His election ensures holiness. But it is less clear how on these grounds the Church is Apostolic.

This position has been held by Pre-Reformer John Wycliffe (*On the Pastoral Office*, II.2.a) and famed Protestant Reformer Ulrich Zwingli (*Exposition of the Faith; Reply To Emser*). Ephesians 1:22 might be cited in support of this vision. On the other hand, one might critique this vision for not providing much guidance on the way in which the Church should conduct its mission. Zwingli seems to respond to this concern by insisting on discipline of members. But in that case this model falls prey to the same weaknesses pointed out with the previous model.

THE CHURCH IS THE FAITHFUL UNITED BY THE SPIRIT

This model also aims to emphasize God's role in gathering the Church, this time with an emphasis on the role of the Holy Spirit. Certainly the Acts 2 account of Pentecost supports this image. Not surprisingly a Pentecostal denomination, The Church of God in Christ (*Official Manual*, pp. 60–61), and a Holiness denomination, The Church of the Nazarene (Articles of Faith. 10), embrace this model. Like the preceding model it is not clear how this position provides guidance on the way the Church should do its mission. But in the case of The Church of God in Christ references are added to the spiritual power of the Church and to the responsibility to preach the Word and administer Ordinances (Sacraments) as well as to enforce discipline. In that sense the charge of legalism might be leveled against this option too, and yet its stress on the Holy Spirit is in line with biblical testimony. The Spirit's Presence makes the Church holy and in calling on all members, unity and catholicity seems implied. Perhaps we can say the Church is Apostolic on these grounds in the sense that the Spirit fulfills the apostolic message.

THE CHURCH AS THE HOUSE OF GOD
WITH A LAMP-LIGHT

Early church African theologian Didymus the Blind offers this interesting image (*Commentary On Zechariah*, 4:1–3). There are Biblical texts identifying the Temple as the house of God (John 2:16) or the Church meeting in houses (Romans 16:15; 1 Corinthians 16:19; Colossians 4:15). And insofar as Johannine literature relates Christ to Light (8:12; 12:46) and He is Present in the Church, regarding the Church as a lit house make a lot of sense. The image is especially powerful in view of Didymus' blindness. This is a model that combines concern to affirm God's initiative in founding the Church but also implies what the Church might be doing, shining the light that it has. There is no elaboration of how one would regard the Church as One, holy, catholic, and Apostolic on these grounds. But Didymus as a Catholic prior to Papal Supremacy would use most of the explanations of these terms we noted in the Church Founded On An Apostolically-Ordained Ministry model above.

THE CHURCH AS MOTHER OF ALL CHRISTIANS

A number of prominent theologians have preferred to focus on the Church's role in nurturing Christians, and so the Church in its nurturing role seems well described as the Christian's Mother. This largely overlooked model has been employed by Clement of Alexandria (*The Tutor*, I.VI), Cyprian of Carthage (Epistle, LXXIII/LXII.24), Augustine (*On Holy Virginity*, 2), Martin Luther (*Sermons On the Catechism*, in *Luther's Works*, Vol. 51, p. 166), and John Calvin (*Institutes*, IV.I.1, 4). The virtues of this model are obvious, both for its ability to express what the Church does and also for its gender inclusivity. The Church is One because it is the Mother of all Christians. We inherit Her holiness. As for Apostolicity we might speak of the Church as Mother as the fulfillment of Prophecy (Isaiah 40:11). The priority on God's Work is also here preserved, since with this model the Christian as passive like the child is ultimately passive in growing up. One might argue that this model does not give guidance on how Mother speaks, but it is no accident that Luther and Calvin relate this model to the concept of the Church as Word and Sacrament while the ancient Africans noted above embraced the model of the Church As Founded On An Apostolically-Ordained Ministry.

THE CHURCH AS A HOSPITAL FOR SINNERS

Martin Luther most famously advocated this model (*Lectures On Romans*, in *Luther's Works*, Vol. 25, p. 263). It nicely portrays our sinfulness and also that the Church's holiness, like all else that is good about it, is God's Work. God gets all the glory for the Church on these grounds. The same strengths, weaknesses, and ways of addressing the shortcoming that we noted in the model of Church as Mother is relevant to this image.

THE CHURCH AS A CULTURE

There are two different approaches to implementing this model. In both cases, theologians recognize that there is no such thing as an individual Christianity, no "spirituality" apart from an ecclesiastical community. We consider first those who only focus on the Church's role in nurturing Christian faith.

The major proponents of this position, Dietrich Bonhoeffer (*Act and Being*, B.3; *The Communion of Saints*) and George Lindbeck (*The Nature of Doctrine*), claim that the Church nurtures us much like a culture does. Just as American culture and the family civilize us (not always successfully) to obey laws, wait our turn in line, expect freedom, see things from an American point of view and stand for the National Anthem, so the Church civilizes us to expect good things from God, venerate Jesus, and behave in certain ways appropriate to the Decalogue and the Bible. Theology on these grounds is like the grammar for the cultural norms of the Church. Again we see with this model a strong emphasis on God's Work in making the Church happen. Bonhoeffer in particular understands the Church functioning as a culture to be Christ in the community (see 1 Corinthians 1:30; 3:16; Colossians 3:10). Other Biblical texts supporting this way of thinking include Ephesians 6:4 on bringing people up in the Lord (also see 1:22–23 and 4:22–24). This is not a viewpoint for those who think that we can be Christians on our own, be spiritual without being religious. That may be a vice or virtue of this model.

The other, compatible approach using this model is evident in what happens in ethnic churches which exist in cultures where they are the minority. In America, the historic African-American church dating back to the Pre-Civil War "Invisible Institution" is a fine example.

These churches function as cultures not just to socialize Christian values as we have been describing. They also preserve the native culture of the membership, pass it to the next generation. The music, the manners, the language, and sense of ethnic pride get passed along. At their best churches providing this second aspect of socialization do not interfere, but merely enrich the Christian nurturing of the primary task of the Church. In rare cases where they do not, the Church becomes just a social club. (In some churches populated primarily with the majority culture, this sociological dimension may be activated by weaving together faith and patriotism, often in unseemly ways.)

This is a risk with regarding the Church as a Culture. But is it worth that risk? Note that this model can lend itself to either an episcopal polity or to any of the Protestant options we have already noted and will consider in more detail in the next chapter.

EXODUS CHURCH: COMMUNITY FOR THE FUTURE

This model wants to take the Church's mission in the world more seriously, especially what it can do as an agent or vehicle of God for the future. Theologians of Hope like Jürgen Moltmann have employed this model. With an Eschatological, future orientation for their theology as a whole, it follows that Christians and the Church cannot allow the world to remain as it is. And so as a community of the Church it cannot allow the world to stay as it is, but must seek to transform it (*Theology of Hope*, pp. 327–328). This entails that the future-looking Church is not at home in a world not looking forward. It is an "Exodus Church" (p. 304). This entails that the Church will function as crusader for justice, sometimes a Servant (a counter-cultural orientation to the ways of the world). Others with a similar orientation in include Wolfhart Pannenberg (*Theology and the Kingdom of God*, pp. 74–75), Eduard Schillebeeckx (*God and the Future of Man*, Chapters 5–6), and Johannes Metz (*Theology of the World*, p. 116).

The reference to an "Exodus Church" is most suggestive of the role of the Exodus account in the Black church. Consequently this model may also typify its piety. Martin Luther King, Jr. (*Stride Toward Freedom*, Ch. 11) seems to have endorsed a model of the Church like this, and it is clearly present in the writings of Latin American Liberation Theologian Rubem Alves (*A Theology of Human Hope*, pp. 65–66).

The Eschatological emphasis of Jesus' proclamation (Mark 1:14–15) and some links between the Church and Kingdom of God in 2 Thessalonians 1:4–5 along with the many references of the New Testament church's concern for the poor (Romans 15:26; Galatians 2:10; cf. Isaiah 41:17; 58:7) provide some Biblical background for this model. This is an ecclesiological vision that prods social engagement. But is a Church always becoming stable enough to endure? What of the question for holiness? Or is the Church always to be dying institutionally like Christ overcomes evil with death?

THE CHURCH AS COMMUNITY
OF THE FAITHFUL

This model is the primary counter to all the models we have been describing. This one focuses less on the Word of God's role in gathering the Church and more on its members. The Church is defined in terms of the quality of the spirituality of its members (and in that sense the Church is holy). Their harmony makes it one. It is catholic in that all who are born again may belong to the Church, and its Apostolicity is evidenced in the self–conscious efforts of its proponents to restore New Testament Christianity in the present, a Christianity that is modeled on the way in which the Apostles lived and taught. Membership requirements also aim to ensure that its members live in holiness. Baptist churches and traditions rooted in the Anabaptist Movement like the Mennonites are best exemplars of this model. For example, the Church is said to be a community of the converted by Menno Simons (*Why I Do Not Cease Teaching and Writing*). The Church is defined in terms of believers by the National Baptist Convention (Articles of Faith, XIII) and by the Southern Baptist Convention (The Baptist Faith & Message, VI).

Some Liberal Theologians employing a Method of Correlation embrace something like this model. Friedrich Schleiermacher spoke of the Church in terms of fellowship, a fellowship of believers in which all the regenerate are found (*The Christian Faith*, 6, 113). In a similar manner Immanuel Kant referred to the Church as an "ethical commonwealth" under divine law (*Religion Within the Limits of Reason Alone*, CCC.IV).

Biblical support for this vision of the Church as defined by its members is provided in Acts 2:41–42, 1 Corinthians 1:2, Philippians 1:1, Hebrews 11:39–40. We have with this model precisely what its adherents wish to emphasize – Christian responsibility with an emphasis on being born again and maintaining the holiness of the Church. As a result, in the strictest applications of this vision excommunication is practiced, even shunning in the case of the Amish. The challenge is what adherents of this view make of the Scripture cited on behalf of other models considered and also if there is not a concern that there is too much legalism in their view. The response is that of course these Baptists and Mennonites still believe and affirm that it is only because of the grace and the Work of the Holy Spirit that born-again belief is created and that they then gather to form the Church.

CLOSING THOUGHTS

In articulating what one means by the Church, the first question must be whether to focus more on what God does to make the Church or whether the focus should be on what the faithful should do to contribute to the Church's formation. Does the Church nurture Christians, or do we comprise the Church with the Work of the Spirit? Once that decision is made, be consistent to that commitment in the way you explain the Church's unity, holiness, catholicity, and Apostolicity.

A number of the models for describing the Church that we have considered are compatible and have been held together by some theologians. Those stressing God's role in constituting the Church can also readily endorse the concept of the Church As Mother of All Christians or the Church As Culture. As a Catholic, Augustine endorsed both the Church As Built on the Foundation of an Apostolically Ordained Ministry and Church As Mother. Martin Luther affirmed both the Church as Created Through Word and Sacrament and As Mother. Likewise Ethnic Protestant churches have operated with both the Church As Created through Word and Sacrament model and the model of Church As a Culture. In

African-American Christian circles, both the Church As a Culture and either the Church As Created Through Word and Sacrament or the Church As the Faithful models have been linked to the Exodus Church option. Many other examples of synthesizing models could be provided. These ways of dealing with the doctrine of the Church are all available to budding theologians. But if synthesizing models, care must be given to explaining how they fit together.

The question of Polity next emerges, first whether it is essential to the nature of the Church. But then the question is how central a role should the way the clergy are structured play in Polity. When you have those matters sorted out, your ecclesiology will be well on the way to being formed, and that will be a great first step towards clarifying your congregation's and denomination's mission.

II

MINISTRY AND POLITY

The Hebrew and Greek equivalent terms for "Ministry" [*shareth* and *diakonia*] refer to service, an interesting equation for an office that is supposed to be about leadership in the Church. It is significant to keep this in mind as we remind ourselves of the Biblical roots of the Office of Ordained Ministry.

Of course in its origins, the Church was largely led by the eyewitnesses of Jesus—the Apostles (presumably those who had seen the Risen Christ [see 1 Corinthians 15:4ff.]). We see the leadership role of Peter and also of James the brother of Jesus testified to on a number of occasions (Acts 12:17; 15:7–17; 1 Corinthians 15:7; Galatians 1:19; 2:9). But the typical way in which church life was conducted was locally in homes with a free, spontaneous style, apparently accompanied by expressions of ecstasy (perhaps in line with the experience of receiving the Spirit at Pentecost) (Acts 2:44–47). It is reported that in these homes, anyone could assume a leadership position and instruct others (presumably if seized by the Holy Spirit) (see the analysis of Celsus, in Origen, *Against Celsus*, III.55). Indeed it seems that the early first-century Christians frequently met in the homes of women who then exercised leadership in the assembly they hosted (see Acts 12:12; 16:14–15; Romans 16:3-5, 15; Philippians 4:2–3; Colossians 4:15).

As the Church became gradually more institutionalized as Jesus' Second Coming was delayed, awareness developed that the leadership responsibilities needed to be assumed by certain persons. Thus we find Biblical references to Bishops (Philippians 1:1; 1 Timothy 3:2; Titus 1:7), Deacons (Philippians 1:1; 1 Timothy 3:3:8, 12–13), Presbyters (1 Timothy 4:14; 1 Peter 5:1–4), Pastors (Ephesians 4:11), Prophets (Acts 13:1; 1 Corinthians 12:28; Ephesians 4:11), Evangelists (Acts 21:8; Ephesians 4:11), Teachers (Acts 13:1; 1 Corinthians 12:28; 1 Timothy 2:7), and Widows (Acts 9:39, 41; 1 Timothy 5). Of course all Christians were deemed priests (1 Peter 2:9; Revelation 20:6). The various **poli-**

ties (ways of structuring the Church) that we now examine try to come to terms with these various offices and images.

POLITY

We have already noted that when controversy began to develop with the need to organize and as the growing Gentile majority in the Church in the late first century threatened a diminution of the Church's Jewish heritage, the Church's move towards liturgical forms of worship inspired by Jewish Temple worship mandated a worship leader, a priest like the Jewish priest. Accepting the Jewish priesthood as a model for Christian leadership entailed an end to women's leadership in the Church, since there was no precedent for Jews ordaining women as priests. In time, polities that developed later allowed for Women's Ordination. We shall deal with that issue in more detail in the final chapter on Social Ethics.

The early Church from the outset of the development of a priestly ministry recognized that the priest would not do all the supervision and other ministry tasks. We move to consider the first polity that was developed and then proceed to later options.

Threefold View of Ministry

Although there had been offices of Bishops, Deacons, and Presbyters in the New Testament era (see Biblical references above), this model specifies the tasks of each office in a way the Biblical witness does not. In the preceding chapter we noted the role of theologians of the late first and early second century, the Apostolic Fathers, in the development of the clergy-lay distinction and in constructing an understanding of the Church as founded on an Apostolically Ordained View of Ministry. One of the primary developers of this polity, Ignatius of Antioch opted for a hierarchy conferring much authority on the Church's leadership. Ignatius claimed that Christians are to follow the Bishop as Christ followed the Father, to fallow the Presbytery [literally "elders," equated with Priests] as they would the Apostles, and to respect the Deacons as they would a Commandment of God (Letter To the Smyrneans, 8). The authority conferred on these offices is obvious. But it is also clear that the Bishop is credited with the highest authority of the three, that the Bishop is the leader.

Subsequently this formula has been maintained in the churches that continue to structure the Ministry with these three offices. Thus in the Roman Catholic Church, Bishops are given a governing role and Priests in turn are assigned a subordinate role to the Bishop (*Catechism of the Catholic Church*, 894, 1562; see 901ff., 1546–1547 for references to the priesthood of the laity). The lowest level is Deacons, appointed to serve (1569–1571) and dedicated to works of mercy (*Gaudium et Spes*, 29). The same hierarchy of arrangement of offices with similar assigned tasks is endorsed by Eastern Orthodox churches (*Holy Catechism of Nicolas Bulgaris*, pp.19–20). In this tradition as well as in the Catholic Church, men practicing lives dedicated wholly to God (Monasticism) may be ordained as Deacons, if not as Priests.

These churches endorse clerical celibacy for Bishops (though it is not required in the East). And the Catholic Church has insisted on celibacy for all ordained clergy, at least since Pope Gregory I urged its adoption in the sixth century with the practice fully established 500 years later by Pope Gregory VII. Biblical support includes Matthew 19:12 and 2 Corinthians 7:32. Only in the Eastern Catholic churches (Catholic congregation historically permitted to maintain Eastern Orthodox practices) is a married priesthood permitted by Catholics (*Catechism of the Catholic Church*, 1579–1580; cf. Domiskinos Papandreau, "The Orthodox churches and priestly celibacy;" Nikolaos Bougastos, *The Married and the Celibate Bishop*). By contrast, based on texts suggesting that some of the Apostles were married (1 Timothy 3:2; Matthew 8:14–15) and also the ancient practice of the Church, Protestant churches have remained open to the marriage of all who are ordained.

To some extent, with the exception of clerical celibacy just noted, every Protestant church with an episcopacy (Anglicans, most Lutherans, Methodists, Church of God in Christ) has a polity similar to the Catholic and Eastern versions of the Threefold View of Ministry. But they differ in that most do not ordain Deacons, and so do not have a Threefold Ministry in the strictest sense. Except for the Episcopal/Anglican churches they also do not exhibit Apostolic Succession, which will be described in the next section.

The ancient character of this polity certainly seems to commend it, and the offices themselves seem to have Biblical roots. But the Protestant response may be that the specific tasks of these offices are the result of Tradition, not Biblical. Besides, it may be contended, the stress on clerical authority (especially Bishops) undermines the Priesthood of All Believers (the belief that all Christians are priests [see Biblical references above]. Perhaps, but it must be noted that the Catholic Church maintains a Threefold View of Ministry with something like the Priesthood of All Believers (see reference above in the preceding paragraph). This is also the Polity of Tertullian (*Exhortation To Chastity*, VII), Ambrose (*Commentaries On Twelve of David's Psalms*, 4.1), and even Augustine (*City of God*, XVII.5).

Apostolic Succession

In the previous chapter we have already explained this concept and provided relevant Biblical sources. Again all the same churches noted including The Anglican/Episcopal heritage (*Responsio* [1897]) endorsed this practice (as well as the Lutheran State Church in Sweden). In view of the visible way of demonstrating continuity in Ministry and its Apostolicity, this seems to be a most valuable tradition. But on the other side we might challenge whether just because Apostles laid hands on some of their Successors there is no Biblical promise that the line of laying on of hands would guarantee an unbroken succession to this day.

Collegiality of the Bishops

The hierarchical character of Roman Catholic polity can lead to some Bishops showing deference to others, notably the papacy. Jerome, the translator of the Bible into Latin, *The Vulgate*, sought to mitigate this, arguing that the strength of the Church depends equally on all the Bishops (*Against Jovinianus*, 1.26). In a manner suggestive of Protestantism, He went so far as to maintain that the office of Presbyter and of Bishop are identical (Letter To Evangelus, CXLVI.1). Vatican II made this position regarding the collegiality of the Bishops official, still making it clear that the Pope is head of the Bishops (*Lumen Gentium*, 22-23, Exp.). Matthew 18:18 and 28:16–20 are cited as Biblical support. Pope Francis seems to be an advocate of this point of view. But if one embraces this model, the question is why not embrace the one that follows?

One Bishop Designated the First Among Equals

In principle this model could be employed naming any Bishop, including the Bishop of Rome as the first. But in fact Catholics do not opt for this model. It is essentially the model of the Eastern Orthodox churches. Largely as a result of competition between the Bishop of Rome and the Metropolitan/Bishop of

Constantinople, which began in the fourth century, the churches of the East have long been inclined to look to Constantinople for leadership in adjudicating disputes among Orthodox churches. After the fall of Rome it came to be regarded as the "New Rome." The office came to be known as the **Ecumenical Patriarch**. But the kind of primacy ceded to the Metropolitan is as a first among equals, the Chair of the Board if you will, who judges in disputes among Bishops.

The Coptic Church of Egypt has a similar polity with the Bishop of Alexandria (titled Pope) as the primary Bishop of the Church, the Chair of Synod meetings. This primacy was a function of its reputation as the church founded in Africa by her first missionary, St. Mark (Eusebius of Caesarea, *Church History*, XVI). Since the eleventh century this Bishop has resided in Cairo.

Neither of these churches has much Biblical basis for their practice. But there are rich traditions justifying the primacy conferred on these episcopacies, and all of these churches rely on Tradition along with Scripture as a source of authority. Is this model a way of keeping order without chaos, not unlike Protestant bodies with episcopal polities which elect a Presiding Bishop?

Papal Primacy

Of course only the Roman Catholic Church embraces this polity. The Bishop of Rome came to play an increasingly significant role in adjudicating conflicts among Bishops as early as in the Roman Empire period. Eventually Pope Leo I developed the idea of **Petrine Supremacy** based on Jesus' response to Peter's confession of faith, that the Church would be built on Peter (Matthew 16:18). Since tradition indicates that Peter was the first Bishop of Rome, his spiritual heirs in that office should then be the head of the Church.

In previous chapters we have noted that in the nineteenth century the doctrine of Papal Infallibility developed. But we have also observed how qualified and rarely employed this infallibility of his proclamations have been. Protestant prejudices against this polity are of course deep-seated in popular perceptions of the Reformation. But what then are we to make of Jesus' words to Peter, and the strength of this polity is difficult to refute given its long-term success over centuries. (Note: As a result of certification by the Third Lateran Council of 1179 the formula for electing Popes is by ballot of the College of **Cardinals** [Bishops selected by Popes who are authorized to function as his representatives].)

Reformed Papacy

Contrary to the suppositions of many, Martin Luther and his heritage were not anti-Catholic, but sought to retain many aspects of the Roman Catholic heritage, including the papacy. In fact in one official Lutheran document, a willingness is stated to concede the Pope superiority over other Bishops which he possesses by human right if he would allow the Gospel [of Justification by Grace Alone] to be preached (Philip Melanchthon, "Signatures," *Smalcald Articles*). Of course this reformed papacy (reigning by human right) would not have infallible authority. Consequently, if all the teachings of your church were affirmed by the papacy, why not designate the Pope as the head of a united Church that includes the Catholic Church, given the long history of that polity?

Primacy of the High Priest

The African Church of the Holy Spirit founded in Kenya is led by a clergyman designated High Priest, even though it has pastors leading congregations. This high office is elected by members of the Church. This Polity may be more akin to the Connectional Polity discussed below. But clearly the High Priest is an office of much Biblical precedent (Hebrews 7:28; Acts 26:10, 12; numerous Gospel references). And so it should be asked if perhaps this African model integrates the best democratic elements of the Connectional Polity (voting for leaders) with an ancient office. Of course one could argue in a Protestant vein that since Christ there is no need for a Priest, but then when the role of priests in African indigenous religions is considered, should we not praise this polity for its indigenizing of Christian faith in Kenya?

Primacy of the Head of the Church

In The Kimbanguist Church based in Zaire there is an office called Head of the Church (*Diagngienda*), which has profound authority because that person is regarded as the body of Holy Spirit. Recall that this Church (officially titled Church of Jesus Christ on Earth by His Special Envoy Simon Kimbangu) believes that Christ has been incarnate again in the person of Salomon Diangani Dialungana second son of Simon Kimbungu). Obviously the Head of the Church, then, has great authority in the Kimbanguist Church, for he speaks in the Name of God with direct revelations. The Montanism associated with the model may be problematic for many, but perhaps not if we wish to take seriously the authority of the Holy Spirit and respect the traditions of direct revelation from God which are part of African spirituality.

Five-Fold Ministry

Study of the New Testament has lead several denominations, mostly of African origins, to discern other offices in the Biblical witness in addition to Bishops, Priests, and Deacons. There are three different versions of this Polity. We examine each individually.

Pastors/Bishops/Elders; Deacons; Apostles; Prophets; Evangelists

We have already noted Biblical references to Bishops, Pastors/Elders. Of course there are also New Testament references to Apostles (Mark 6:30; Acts 8:14, 18; 1 Corinthians 9; 2 Peter 1:1; 3:2), Prophets (Acts 15:32; 21:10; 1 Corinthians 14:29), and Evangelists (Acts 21:8; Ephesians 4:11; 2 Timothy 4:5). Pentecostal-oriented churches are among the primary practitioners of this polity—the Church of God in Christ and on some occasions the Assemblies of God. Praise should be given to proponents of this model for the careful identification of these offices in the New Testament. But as in the case of the Threefold View of Ministry, the Bible itself does not clearly specify the expectations/duties of each office. And could it not be argued that since the Threefold View has a longer history its venerability should take precedence. Is not the work of Evangelists and Prophets covered by Pastors and Priests?

Pastor; Prophets; Evangelists; Shepherds; Teachers

In the previous section we noted Biblical references for the first three offices. There are also Biblical references for Shepherds (John 10:2) and Teachers (1 Corinthians 12:28, 29; Ephesians 4:11; 2 Timothy 1:11). This unique model is embraced by the Celestial Church of Christ of Nigeria and The Cherubim and Seraphim church also originating in Nigeria. In the case of the Celestial Church, its Five-Fold Structure is hierarchical. There is only one Pastor, the Supreme Head of the church. Shepherds represent the Pastor to congregations. Evangelists and Teachers support the Shepherd in congregations, and Prophets, filled with the Spirit from time to time emerge by communicating dreams and visions of God to the faithful.

With regard to The Cherubim and Seraphim Church there is a similar but distinct hierarchy. For this body, the *Baba Aladura* is the head of the Church, also called the General Superintendent. But Ordination takes place for various Ministries—Pastors, Prophets, Evangelists, Shepherds, and Teachers.

Two very different understandings of these offices have been presented. The Cherubim and Seraphim Church's version seems more in line with what the New Testament intended for these offices. Whereas the Celestial Church of Christ certainly understands the role of the Pastor differently, reinterpreting its function in very exclusive terms. In both cases, we need to ask whether in formulating church structure it is better to follow Biblical precedent and traditional practice or to structure the Church in accord with the needs of the context.

3. Bishops; Pastors; Disciples, Apostles; Primate

The preceding analyses have already provided Biblical warrants for the first four offices. But there are no clear Biblical references to Primates. This version of the Five-Fold Ministry involving these offices is embodied by The Church of the Lord (*Aladura*) Worldwide of Nigeria.

This model finds a place for a Primate with another hierarchical arrangement of offices, with the Primate at the top. (The Primate is an elected office, selected by a Council of Prelates, to which the Primate continues to report.) The holder of this office may be designated an Apostle. Next in the order of authority are Bishops/Archbishops, who are leaders of the local Provinces of the Church. Archbishops may also gain the title of Apostles. They supervise Sr. Pastors in the congregation, who may be assisted by Disciples (those in training for Ministry). Another interesting feature of the church's polity is that women are ordained for these posts like men. Though it must be noted that no woman has served as Primate and that ordained women must abide by Old Testament prescriptions about purity and so are not allowed to approach an altar during their menstrual periods.

Obviously it seems that the tasks assigned by the Bible to Disciples are not being observed in this polity and the running together of Bishop and Apostle is much in line with those traditions opting for Apostolic Succession. Another aspect that seems very Catholic and Eastern Orthodox is the special priestly function of the Head of the Church (the Primate). An annual Tabierorar Festival is celebrated when, after 13 days of praying and fasting in seclusion, thousands come to an open space to receive divine blessings from the Primate. And yet at the same time the function of the Primate seems suggestive of the Connectional Polity, as he is responsible to interact with various Councils comprised of church leaders. This Polity seems more suggestive of Protestant bodies with an episcopacy. Is this a polity of confusion or one that binds together in a rich synthesis the best elements of Protestantism, Catholicism and the Eastern traditions?

*Presbyterian Polity

Of course this polity is identified with the Presbyterian Church. Essentially it is a kind of representative democracy. The congregations and other bodies in the Church elect representatives, and then these representatives (the Presbyters) meet in Presbyteries and Assembles to take actions that will be binding on the congregations. Bishops are not part of this polity, for there has been much corruption associated with that office and also references to Bishops in the New Testament simply make clear, it is argued, that the power of all ministries described in the New Testament are equal (Second Helvetic Confession, II, XVII). Appeal is made to Luke 22:26. And more support for a Presbytery is said to be provided in 1 Timothy 4:14.

The similarities between this model and the American political system are not accidental. James Madison, primary author of The Constitution in his role as Secretary of the Constitutional Convention was taught by Presbyterian pastor John Witherspoon whose writings opted not just for a representative democracy, but also with an appreciation of Augustine's view of Sin opted for a check-and-balance system of government like the one his students and we embrace (*Lectures On Moral Philosophy*). No argument, then, against the beneficial political implications of this polity. But is the abolition of the episcopacy justified? Perhaps it is for churches in America with the American love for democracy.

Connectional Polity

This category is a loose phrase to capture the wide variety of polities of most Protestant churches. Perhaps we should call it Denominationalism. Although it is not Presbyterian in the strict sense, in effect there is a real overlap between this polity and the one just considered. For most American denominations, whether they opt for Bishops or just have Presidential polities, defer to the establishment of a Synod or Assembly, which is comprised of congregational representatives, and contend that this is the highest authority in the denomination (even more than the Bishops, other church administrators, or even of congregations). This kind of representative democratic model seems just right for the United States, which probably explains its popularity in American Christianity. (The European equivalent of it is the **State Church System**, patterned on Constantine's Establishment of Christianity in the late Roman Empire. In this polity the government is a kind of protector of the visible church, ensuring it is supported financially and adequately staffed. But of course there are strings attached in making church leaders employees of the state.) The question to be raised with the Connectional Polity is whether it too closely identifies denominations with the ways of American culture (as most of these denominations run their day-to-day operations in national offices with administrative and interpersonal models a lot like the models of American business). And if that becomes the popular perception of Christianity, that it is enmeshed in American ways, then the Gospel loses its status of being counter-cultural in the eyes of the public. Is that a problem today and is this polity one of the reasons?

Congregational Polity

In Baptist, Mennonite, some Reformed congregations (especially The United Church of Christ), and in Non-Denominational churches, another alternative is to be found. The Biblical model for polity should prevail, it is argued, and in the minds of theologians opting for this alternative, this means that the Church is local, in particular places, as evidenced by the fact that Paul and other Epistle writers found the Church in particular towns and regions (Rome, Galatia, Corinth, etc.). This cashes out into a model for church life that locates the authority for church life in the local congregation. Congregations can best discern God's Will in their setting. The rulings of Bishops or representative Assemblies cannot impose their views on the congregation. Of course there is no place for Bishops with this polity (though some Baptists are beginning to adopt this title for Pastors in the largest churches).

For Baptists and Mennonites this polity is closely linked to the doctrine of the Church As Community of the Faithful, which we have observed. Even other proponents of such Congregationalism typically affirm a Third Use of the Law. Consequently, because so much is riding on the local congregation with this polity, it is important to keep it pure, and so often churches with a Congregational Polity will have membership expectations.

In assessing the strengths of this model, its claim to be Biblical and to assert local control as well as local responsibility, it should be noted that challenges can be raised about what it makes of Biblical references to the Bishops. The solution to that matter offered above in the Presbyterian model seems relevant. But it might also be asked if Congregationalism really takes seriously the catholicity of the Church and Biblical references to the Body of Christ (see the 2nd paragraph of Chapter Tem for references). Another matter: It is interesting that most churches with a Congregational Polity belong to fellowships which (at least in the case of UCC's and Southern Baptists) exhibit all the characteristics of the Connectional Polity which dominates in American Christianity. Is this an indication that the Congregational Model does not work in practice?

Adiaphora

Perhaps due to its accidental, "make-it-up-as you-go" character, the Lutheran Church has been very flexible about its polity. One can find some Lutheran churches which are Congregational, others with an episcopal polity, and others with a Connectional Polity (with the highest authority residing in the Conventions or Assemblies of the church). Although each Lutheran denomination prefers it own polity, the way in which we organize the Church, or even the way in which we worship to some extent is not deemed divisive. For church structure, how we run the church as an institution, is *adiaphora* (indifferent) (*Formula of Concord* SD, X).

In other words, this position is that it does not matter how you structure the Church unless you violate the Gospel with what you are doing (recall for Chapter One that Lutherans stress a distinction between Law and Gospel). Church polity is a matter of whatever works best in furthering the Gospel is the model you should use. Is this a valid perspective on structuring ministry, or should we look to the Bible for guidance? How about opting for the oldest post-Biblical option, the Threefold View of Ministry? (It should be noted that though Luther himself did not succeed in creating a church with an Episcopal polity, he and his colleagues were open to continuing an Episcopal polity [*An Example of How To Consecrate a Christian Bishop*, in *Weimar Ausgabe*, Vol. 53, pp. 231–260; cf. Philip Melanchthon, The Augsburg Confession, XXCIII].)

NATURE OF PASTORAL AUTHORITY

The Pastor is set apart from the laity. But why? For what purpose? And what is the relationship between Pastor and the laity. We examine the historic options for answering these questions, for determining what sort of authority the Pastor has.

Clergy Set Apart To Lead By Exercising Authority Over Laity

This model presupposes that God has made clergy ontologically different in Ordination, for Ordination is indelible. Set aside by God with Apostolicity, this implies that those ordained should exercise authority over the Church, and so over the laity. This is the position of the Catholic Church (*Catechism of the Catholic Church*, 1582, 1536) and the Eastern Orthodox churches (John Karmiris, "Concerning the Sacraments," in *Eastern Orthodox Theology*, p. 30). In line with his Catholicism, Augustine spoke of the authority Apostolic Succession confers on the clergy (*Epistles*, XLIV.III.5). But this affirmation is still mixed by some proponents with an affirmation of the Priesthood of All Believers (Tertullian, *Exhortation to Chastity*, VII; Augustine, *City of God*, XVII.5; Augustine, *Expositions On the Book of Psalms*, LXXCII [LXXVIII].35; for Vatican II references, see the discussion of the Threefold View of Ministry, above).

We have already observed the Biblical references for this model (see the section on how the Church is built on the foundation of an Apostolically-ordained Ministry in the previous chapter). Exercising authority is not a very popular viewpoint for leadership in our "anything goes" ethos. But for that reason, do we not need it today, especially to the extent that this leadership style still relates itself to the Priesthood of All Believers? On the other hand, maybe what we need is more facilitating by clergy and less exercise of authority?

Clergy Set Apart To Do a Special Job

This model has a lot in common with the preceding one, but is unwilling to embrace Apostolic Succession and the idea that Ordination makes you different in your being. No, Ordination sets you apart to do a special job. That is the basis for the distinction between clergy and laity. This is the position of the denominations springing from Martin Luther and John Calvin. Both agree along with Baptists that the special job that sets the Pastor apart is the preaching of the

Word (Second London Confession, XXVI.10). Lutherans and Calvin add administering the Sacraments (Philip Melanchthon, The Augsburg Confession, V; *Institutes*, IV.3.6). Calvin also adds discipline as a special duty for the Pastor sometimes. Even a Liberal Theologian like Friedrich Schleiermacher noted the Pastor's authority only pertains to the Word of God, not to administrative matters in the Church (*The Christian Faith*, 145). Martin Luther King focused on another special job for the Pastor to do, one to which he dedicated his life— Prophecy (*Stride Toward Freedom*, Ch.11).

Paul's many references to preaching the Word and the fact that the Disciples often administered the Sacraments (especially Baptism) provide the Biblical support for this vision. This is a viewpoint that focuses Pastors on the important priorities, and also has the advantage of limiting their authority to specific realms, still allowing for lay leadership in church functions not directly related to Word and Sacrament. But does it limit unrealistically the Pastor's leadership to just certain realms and also undermine the miraculous character of Ordination? Another question is whether this model of Ministry in asserting the Pastor's authority undermines the kind of collaboration that the next model affords.

Set Apart To Lead or Facilitate the Flock

Traditions that stress the **Priesthood of All Believers** (the idea that all baptized Christians are priests in virtue of the lifestyle Baptism launches them into of dying to sin as a sacrifice to God [see 3rd paragraph of the chapter for Biblical references]) also tend to stress this model of Pastoral Authority. Luther and Calvin (*Institutes*, IV.I.12; IV.XIX.28) also sometimes opt for this model, as well as Tertullian (see above) and Ambrose (*Commentaries On Twelve of David's Psalms*, 4.1) It is also characteristic of most of Protestantism, for example in Pietism (Philip Spener, *Pia Desideria*, III) and so Methodism (John Wesley, "Letter To John Mather" [1777]; *A Farther Appeal To Men of Reason and Religion*, 11ff., advocating lay preachers), the Baptist heritage (E. Y. Mullins, *The Axioms of Religion*, pp. 68ff., on "soul competency [1 Corinthians 10:29]; Southern Baptist Convention, "Resolution On The Priesthood of All Believers"), Quakers (*Faith and Practice*, II.II), and much modern Pastoral Theology (Thomas Sweetser and Carol W. Holden, *Leadership in a Successful Parish*).

We have already noted the strengths of this Ministerial vision. It is all about participation, getting the Pastor off the pedestal. This seems in line with the Participatory Management Techniques of modern Business Management Theory. But is this what we need in our present context in light of the crisis of leadership and erosion of confidence in leaders?

Martin Luther, John Calvin, Augustine, the Catholic heritage, the African-American church raise another question: Must we make a choice? Is the answer that sometimes one must exercise authority (especially when the Gospel is at stake), but other times facilitation of the laity is the way to proceed—to pluck both strings, each at the right times. Or should we be more consistent, deciding on just one of the preceding options or one of the ones that follow?

Set apart as an Example of Christian Living

A number of traditions contend that what sets the clergy apart is the example thy set. As early as the late fifth century in Africa, Fulgentius was insisting on life-style roles for the clergy (Ferrandus, *The Life of the Blessed Bishop Fulgentius*, Pro.). More recently, representatives of this model include Pietism (at least Philip Spener [*Pia Desideria*, Pt. I]) many Baptists (Second London Confessions, XXVI.6, 9, insists on being gifted), and Quakers ("Ministers," in *Faith and Practice*) embody this position. Friedrich Schleiermacher (*The Christian Faith*, 133.1) even distinguished clergy from the laity on grounds of the former's strength in grasping truth. Perhaps the Gnostics (The Gospel of Truth, 42, in The Nag Hammadi Library) and Father Divine ("As a Man Thinketh In His Heart So Is He And as You Visualize Act from That Angle...") in claiming that God is in themselves as well as in all believers qualify as examples of this viewpoint as well. In that case, then, perhaps we would also need to consider all those who believe in a Second Incarnation exemplified in their founders as embodying this viewpoint (several African Independent Churches noted in Chapter Three).

Certainly there is some Biblical support for expecting more of clergy regarding behavior (1 Timothy 3:2-7; Titus 1:7). For those interested in emphasizing Sanctification, this vision for Ministry makes sense. The Pastor is an *example*. But for those emphasizing the importance of grace, the idea of the Pastor as a model for Christian life seems to lapse into a legalism, perhaps even leading to Donatism (see below), overlooking that the Pastor is as much a sinner as any other Christian.

Donatism

All of the preceding models in some sense take a stand against this model, the heresy of Donatism—a heresy that is still very much alive in the pew today. It had its origins in fourth-century North Africa after the persecution initiated by the Roman emperor Diocletain ended. Apparently some priests had collaborated with the persecutors or even renounced Christ. Rigorists in the Church contended that these lapsed priests were no longer to be considered priests, and so no longer had a valid ministry. The movement was resisted notably by Augustine, and finally condemned as a heresy by the First Synod of Arles.

The heresy continues unofficially today when Christians flee congregations because they don't "like" the Pastor, do not find the pastor a true child of God. This is a function of a sense that the Pastor has not lived up to the lifestyle standards expected (see texts cited for the preceding model of Ministry). Some may be attracted to this way of thinking because of a desire that pastors truly be examples of faith. But if a Pastor no longer has a valid Ministry because of who he or she is, then the focus is more on the human than on God's grace. And if Donatism is correct, then we can never really be sure of the validity of the Sacraments administered or of the preaching we hear, because just suppose those pastoral acts were performed by someone who does not measure up in her/his spirituality to our standards. Keep this in mind the next time you feel repelled by the personal characteristic of Pastors. Can God still use them?

CONCLUDING REFLECTIONS

In developing one's thinking about Ministry, a number of key questions must be considered: (1) Are you and your church inclined to believe more in congregational autonomy or in the authority of the wider church over your congregation (a Connectional Polity)? Why or why not? (2) If the latter, where do you and your congregation stand on Bishops? (3) If you are favorable towards an episcopal polity, why do you favor or reject Apostolic Succession? (4) What are your reasons for or against Bishops in view of this being the oldest polity, and if the historical roots of this polity are not convincing, what is the most efficient alternative and why? Finally remains the issues related to Pastoral Authority": Should clergy have authority over the congregation or are they just facilitators (part of the Priesthood of All Believers)? If they have authority, what sort of authority do they have? The first set of questions is about the institutional church. The ones pertaining to Pastoral Authority are questions that will demand answers from every Theologian and Pastor.

I2

SACRAMENTS/ORDINANCNES

Almost since the beginning of the Church, the faithful have participated in at least two, if not more, ceremonies—commemorations of things Jesus did or things He directed be performed. He Himself had been baptized (Mark 1:9–11; Matthew 3;13–17; Luke 3:21–22). He seems to have called on His followers to baptize new converts (Matthew 28:19). His first followers continued this practice (Acts 2:38; Romans 6). Likewise, Jesus Himself instituted a kind of sacred meal or love feast (Mark 14:12–25; Matthew 26:17–29; Luke 22:7–13). This ceremony continued as a common meal among the first churches (1 Corinthians 11:17–34; Jude 12). But despite the widespread endorsement of this data by Christians virtually throughout history, few doctrines have been as contentious as the Sacraments and Ordinances. Let's review the options.

WHAT THEY ARE AND HOW MANY

The first debate is over what to call these rites—Sacraments or Ordinances. But perhaps even more prior is the question posed to all other Christians by the Quaker tradition, whether these rites actually nurture faith or might be a barrier to our spirituality.

The Value of Celebration

The position of ecumenical consensus is that these rites do have value for spirituality. This commitment is rooted in both the Biblical precedents cited above (see below for authorization for the additional 5 Sacraments) and the Church's Traditional practice. Another argument in favor of Sacraments is that the logic of Christian faith entails that God works through visible, physical means. Christianity is an Incarnational religion, it is argued. God is revealed in the earthly, physical Body of Jesus. Thus it makes sense that God would continue to reveal Himself through physical means like water, bread, and wine. (The same argument is used by those traditions [especially Roman Catholicism, the Eastern churches, Lutheranism, and the Anglican heritage] to justify the use of icons [physical objects which are believed to mediate grace] [Second Council of Nicaea, I; *Catechism of the Catholic Church*, 1160–1161, 2141; (Lutheran) Apology of The Augsburg Confession, VII–VIII.32].) On the other hand, it could be argued (as it is by critics) that celebrating these rites gets our focus off spirituality and on the physical, makes worship mere ritual.

No Sacramental Dimension

The Salvation Army does not practice formal sacraments for a variety of reasons, including a belief that it is better to concentrate on the reality behind the symbols; however, it does not forbid its members from receiving sacraments in other denominations (Handbook of Doctrine, pp. 269ff.). And as we have noted, the Quakers (Society of Friends) also do not practice formal sacraments (Declaration of Faith). They believe that all activities should be considered holy. Rather, they argue, we should focus on an inward transformation of one's whole life. Some Quakers use the words "Baptism" and "Communion" to describe the experience of Christ's presence and his ministry in worship. In short, Baptism and Communion are not abolished. They are spiritual experiences whose essence happens when we experience regeneration (new birth) and fellowship with the faithful (Declaration of the Faith). But the question that may be posed to this position is whether the Incarnational character of Christian faith and the traditional practice of the Church do not warrant more attention. The issue at stake in this dispute is whether our focus should be more on spirituality as distinct from physical signs or whether God works through the physical.

Call Them Sacraments

In most traditions the rites we examine are called Sacraments. This is not a Biblical term, but one conferred on these rites in the first centuries of the Church's life. It is derived from the Latin term *sacramentum* referring to holiness—a holy rite in the sense that the rite's visible means convey grace. In Eastern churches the Greek word *Musterion* [Mystery] is employed to characterize these rites (*The Holy Catechism of Nicolas Bulgaris*, p. 2). The use of the term has Biblical precedent. The difference seems to be one of emphasis. The East stresses the transcendent character of God, the inexplicable character of God making

Himself Present to us in the elements of the holy rites. By contrast, those referring to Sacraments seem more concerned to highlight that God's Promises, that grace, have been made incarnate in the rite.

Keep in mind the point you want to make about these rites with the term you use to describe them. Do you want to stress God's grace and His Promises? Then the language of *Sacrament* is just right. But if a priority on God's Majesty, God's incomprehensibility, is the point you want to make, then calling these rites *Mysteries* may be more in line with your thinking and piety.

Ordinances

Some Protestants (notably Baptists) reject the term Sacrament to designate these rites, preferring instead the term *Ordinances* (Church of God in Christ, *Official Manual*, pp. 75ff.; American Baptist Association, Doctrinal Statement, 18; Karen Bullock, in *Baptist News Global* [April 22, 2010]). This is a Biblical term [*dikaioma* or *chuqqah*], while Sacrament is not. The term is intended to make clear, in contrast to the Sacramental interpretation, that these rites are not necessary for salvation. Proponents of this designation are typically unwilling to regard the elements of these rites as conveying grace.

Want to emphasize that grace or Christ is Present in the elements of the Sacraments? Then the term "Sacrament" is right for you. But if you are more concerned about using Biblical language and maintaining a distinction between the spiritual Christ and earthly elements, then the language of Ordinances may be preferable. We move next to the issue of the number of these rites, not matter if we call them Sacraments, Mysteries, or Ordinances.

7 Sacraments/Mysteries

The Roman Catholic and Eastern churches as well as The Cherubim and Seraphim Church located in Nigeria have designated not just Baptism and The Lord's Supper as Sacraments (see Biblical authorization for these rites above). One rite that holds Sacramental status in these churches is **Confession**—a structured opportunity to confess one's sin and receive forgiveness in the Name of Christ from a Priest. The rite is founded on the Biblical notion of The Power of the Keys (Matthew 16:19; 18:18; John 21:23; cf. Matthew 3:6). Others include **Confirmation**, the confirming of one's faith given in Baptism, usually accompanied by the laying of hands or anointing with oil, a sign of a further outpouring of the Holy Spirit (Acts 8:14–17). Proponents of these Sacraments also regard **Ordination** (the setting apart of a Minister through the laying on of hands) in this way. Biblical precedents for this Sacrament include 1 Timothy 4:14 and Acts 13:3. **Marriage** is likewise deemed a Sacrament, based on Ephesians 5:31–34; it is said to be a "great mystery" (and recall this term, in *musterion* in Greek is translated Sacrament). Finally **Extreme Unction** is said to be a Sacrament. Based on James 5:14, Acts 28:8, and Mark 16:17, this rite involves the anointing the sick and dying, providing the gift of the Spirit and intercessions for accompanying the sick and dying in their journey, a sort of spiritual healing.

2 Sacraments/Ordinances

Most Protestants only designate Baptism and The Lord's Supper as Sacraments or Ordinances. We have already noted the Biblical authorization for this designation. Typically proponents of this position rule out the additional five Sacraments on grounds that they are not Biblically based. (Some Holiness and Pentecostal churches teach only 2 Sacraments/Ordinances, but also practice Healing Services.) But as noted above these additional rites do in fact have Biblical basis. Of course, proponents of designating just Baptism and The Lord's Supper in this category may counter that only these two were actually authorized by Christ. Readers are invited to study the Biblical texts cited above and make their own judgments. Another factor to consider in making these judgments is whether one's Theological Method includes attention to Tradition and traditional practice.

3 Sacraments/Ordinances

Just a few Protestants, notably some Lutherans, Baptists, or Pentecostals, and African Independent Churches add a third rite to Sacramental status. Martin Luther on several occasions designated **Confession** as a Sacrament (see Biblical authorization for this rite's Sacramental status, above). The third Sacrament for some African Independent Churches like the Celestial Church of Christ located mostly in Nigeria (Doctrine and Services) and the Harrist Church of the Ivory Coast is **Marriage**. In the case of some Baptists, Church of the Brethren, and Pentecostals, the third Sacrament/Ordinance is **Feet-Washing**, a rite symbolizing practice of Christian humility (Church of God in Christ, *Official Manual*, p. 77, but also practices Healing Services; United Brethren, Confession of Faith;

George Hammon Syons, *Redemption and Original Sin Vindicated*, pp. 9–10). The Biblical basis for this rite is provided by Luke 7:36–50, John 13:1–7, and 1 Timothy 5:10.

Before sorting out the number of Sacraments it is wise to determine what one makes of the Sacraments of Baptism and The Lord's Supper, for once you have determined Christ's relationship to these two Sacraments/Ordinances, then one can better judge if these additional rites do the same thing—in which case they perhaps should be deemed Sacraments. Perhaps, though, there is wisdom in a comment on this subject in one of the official Lutheran Confessions of faith, The Apology of The Augsburg Confession (XIII.17), which asserts that "no intelligent person will argue much about the number [of Sacraments]."

BAPTISM

There are a lot of areas of ecumenical agreement about Baptism: (1) Its outward sign—the pouring or immersing in water; (2) The sign's meaning—that we are born again or washed clear from our sin (Romans 6:3; Titus 3:5); (3) The Sacrament's eschatological character (it provides a radically new manner of life); and (4) It is regarded as a Work of God (see Titus 3:5). But in addition to disagreements about whether we should immerse in water, as the New Testament baptisms of and by Jesus seem to have been performed, or if sprinkling with water is sufficient, disagreements emerge over: (1) Who is to be baptized; (2) Whether Baptism actually gives grace or merely symbolizes some inner spiritual transformation.

Immersion and Believer's Baptism

Of course immersion was the practice of John the Baptist and the Church prior to the invention of Baptismal fonts. The question is whether this is the only valid means of administering the Sacrament. If one follows that Bible's precedent the answer seems to be that this is the only valid approach. But such a position overlooks the ancient practice of the Church, which had been allowing sprinkling since the late first century (the *Didache*). As Martin Luther once asked the Anabaptist proponents of immersion in Baptism, does it not entail that the bulk of Christians (many devout ones) who were not baptized as believers and through immersion are not really Christian after all (The Large Catechism, IV.49)?

Similarly, there is no doubt that John the Baptist's baptisms and at least the bulk of other baptisms reported in the New Testament were of believers. Luther's challenge above pertains to this claim. But on the other hand, another strength of insisting on believers' baptism is that infants are not capable of committing themselves to their Baptism, so infant baptism seems to reduce the sacrament to magic. Only believers' baptism, it appears, can maintain the individual's responsibility to accept the gift of faith. Of course this practice presumes that we are accountable for our sins only when reaching the age of being responsible for our sin (see the discussion in Chapter Six).

Infant Baptism and Sprinkling

In the preceding discussion we have already cited ancient precedent for baptizing merely by sprinkling, merely pouring water on the baptized. But the argument might still be made that this represents an appeal to Tradition, not Scripture, to authorize this position. It may be harder to make that argument against infant baptism. Some of its proponents not only argue along with Martin Luther that denying infant baptism would call into question the Christianity of some of the Church's greatest saints who were baptized as infants. To update the point, would we dare challenge the faith of Mother Teresa who was baptized as an infant? But some proponents of this view also appeal to Biblical precedent—not just to Jesus' blessing of little children (Matthew 19:13–15; Mark 10:13–16; Luke 18:15–17), but also to reports of the baptisms of entire households (Acts 16:15, 33; 1 Corinthians 1:16). The argument is then made that these households surely included infants.

Critics of this position are likely to contend that this is a weak Biblical argument. And it is certainly true that the practice of infant baptism did not become widespread in the Church until well into the fifth century, after the development of the doctrine of Original Sin by Augustine. Given the belief in Original Sin (see Chapter Six), infant baptism makes sense, since on grounds of that belief even babies are sinners (filled with concupiscence). But if you believe infants are innocent until they reach the age of accountability, then infant baptism is an unbiblical, unnecessary practice.

Another weakness of infant baptism seems to be that it makes salvation or adoption by God automatic, not something we have chosen or for which we have assumed responsibility. But just like the difference between salvation by faith and salvation by grace (see Chapter 8), if you seek confidence in your salvation and do not want it to depend in any sense on our response, then infant baptism is clearly the best position to endorse. It makes clear that salvation does not depend on the quality of our faith, but on the working of God's grace.

Born Again in Baptism

Roman Catholic, Eastern, Lutheran, and sometimes Episcopal Christians and John Wesley regard Baptism as a born-again experience, believe that we are regenerated in Baptism (*Catechism of the Catholic Church*, 978; John Karmiris, in *Eastern Orthodox Theology*, 24; Luther, The Small Catechism. IV.3; The Thirty Articles, XXVIII, if one reads the Sacrament's status as an "instrument" as connoting regeneration; Wesley, *Treatise On Baptism*, II.4). Based on Romans 6:2b–11, Titus 3:5, and John 3:5, proponents of this view teach that as our sins are drowned in Baptism, wiped clean, so this is the way we are now—brand-new creatures who spend their lives living the life of Baptism, dying to sin and rising with Christ. It is not that the water is holy in and of itself, but that when accompanied by God's Word, the Holy Spirit uses the water of Baptism to affect this new birth.

Roman Catholics speak of how this regeneration inevitably happens, that it can never be negated, by referring to the Sacrament's work by working, just by being performed (*ex opera operato*). This is why Baptism need never be repeated. Protestant and Eastern proponents of Baptismal regeneration are more cautious, but do not negate this idea. Once born again you do not ever stop being regenerated, and it cannot and need not be repeated. However, as Lutherans and to some extent Eastern Orthodox Christians put it, Baptism works apart from faith but is only effective with faith. You are born again in the Sacrament, but it does you no good without faith. Even modern Catholics seem somewhat open to that qualification (*Catechism of the Catholic Church*, 1128).

An analogy might be helpful in explaining this position. The new birth in Baptism has parallels to a physical birth (let's say the birth of a good athlete). Just as the infant does not choose to be born or to have natural athletic ability, so we are baptized and born again. It just happens to us, and is never repeated. But just as the natural-born athlete may or may not develop into a great athlete, so it is with the born-again Christian. She/he has the disposition to live the baptismal lifestyle of self-denial, love, and service, but it only happens when it is embraced in faith (see the discussion of the spontaneity of good works in Chapter Nine), just as good natural talent needs to be exercised in order to do the budding athlete any good. Yet (and here the analogy breaks down), the ability to live holy is never lost, just like you are the child of your parents even if estranged from them.

This viewpoint not only seems supported by Scripture, but provides strong assurance about those in doubt about their salvation and worth. On the other hand, critics may point out its association with infant baptism and so challenge whether such a belief would be an impediment to encouraging the practice of the Christian life. And the idea that ordinary water, even if working with God's Word, can play a role in bringing about such a startling new spiritual reality seems far-fetched to some. Of course proponents this position might simply refer to this Baptismal vision as another example of Christianity's Incarnational character (God working through physical means).

As Seal of Election

Another option for understanding what transpires in Baptism was articulated most clearly by John Calvin and the theological heirs of his tradition (*Institutes*, 4.17.16–18, 26, 31). Some contend that this view has roots in Augustine (at times). It is also suggested in the Anglican 39 Articles (XXVII) and so reflects in the Methodist Articles of Religion (17), though the Anglican document could also be read as opting for baptismal regeneration. Proponents of this view of Baptism as a seal or sign tend to cite the same Biblical texts noted by the previous option, though they read these texts differently, not literally but as referring to the Sacrament's role in sealing election or as a sign of it, as per references to certain rites functioning as signs (Romans 4:11; 15:19; 2 Corinthians 1:21–22; 12:12; Ephesians 4:30).

Essentially this model argues that the born-again experience happens outside Baptism. In the case of Calvin and his tradition this happens in eternity when God predestines us. But others of the Wesleyan traditions might simply say that Baptism is a work of prevenient grace, which entails that there is a sense in which the fruits of Baptism (regeneration) have transpired before the Baptismal ceremony, just as Israel was an elect nation prior to the practice of circumcision. In accord with the analogies to circumcision, which was administered to infants and because the elect are elected prior to their birth, proponents of this model typically opt for infant baptism.

Another analogy may be useful in illustrating this position (one even used to some extent by Calvin [*Institutes*, IV.XV.5]). The idea of Baptism as a seal might be compared with a government seal on a document, the ceremony that makes the document and its contents official and public. So we might say hypothetically that just as the will of my rich Norwegian uncle and his death made me a rich man, yet the wealth is not mine until the Norwegian money heading my way clears customs (certified by a government seal), so the elect and/or reborn Christian does not have full possession of the gift until the divine seal of Baptism has been put on her/him.

Strengths of this model: As the discussion of the next model will make clear, this image of Baptism as a seal seems to be a nice middle ground between options, combining all the strengths and overcoming their weaknesses. If we allow for the Biblical texts authorizing the first model to be read in light of the additional texts about signs and seal cited by this model, it seems to have Biblical authorization. The downside might be that this is perhaps the most difficult of the models to explain and understand, and proponents of the first model would critique it for not sufficiently asserting the Incarnational character of the faith. And its association with infant baptism would be problematic (on Biblical grounds) for proponents of the next (symbolic) view of the rite.

As Symbol of Regeneration

The dominant Protestant image, dating back to the Reformer Ulrich Zwingli (*On True and False Religion*) and Anabaptists like the Mennonites (The Waterland Confession, XXX–XXXI), regards Baptism as a mere symbol of a prior experience of regeneration and cleansing. One must first be born again or elect, these theologians argue, in order to be ready for Baptism. What Baptism does is merely afford opportunity for a public testimony to one's faith.

As such it is a mere symbol of what has already happened to the one baptized. A distinction is posited between the spiritual baptism one has already had (or will have in the case of infants) and water baptism (as in the case of Matthew 3:11; Luke 3:16; Acts 8:14–17; 11:16).

This is a model for depicting Baptism that certainly makes sense. Water cannot give life, it could be argued. The emphasis on faith, that Baptism means nothing apart from our faith or understanding of its symbolism, gives more attention to Christian responsibility rather than ritual. (Of course proponents of the other models could argue that they give more credence to the miraculous work of God.) Given these strengths (the model's rationality and the premium it places on individual responsibility) its impact on American Protestantism is not surprising. But if you are looking for more emphasis on the mystery of the divine ways and on security of salvation then other models might be more in line with your piety. The symbolic view is more dualistic; like Greek philosophy it distinguishes the physical and spiritual. Yet if you are more inclined to side with the holism of Hebraic thinking, not separating the body and the things of God (see Chapter 5), then the Born Again in Baptism model should have a stronger hold on your thinking.

THE LORD'S SUPPER

There are also many areas of agreement about The Lord's Supper, often called the Eucharist, from the Greek word *eucharistia*, which literally means "thanksgiving." It is celebrated as a common meal, whose origins lie with Christ's celebration of the Seder Meal (commemorating the Hebrews' escape from Egypt at Passover) the last week of His life. Rooted in this Jewish Festival's celebration of freedom, it should embody that theme for Christians as well. Bread and wine are commonly regarded as the elements (though many Protestants employ grape juice rather than wine and The Kimbanguist Church founded in Zaire employs a cake of potatoes and eggs with honey water in place of the Jewish staple). Disagreements surface on the status of the consecrated elements which in turn have implications for how to portray the communal elements of the rite, and under what circumstances the Sacrament works are in evidence. Thus the historic options on these issues now need to be considered.

Transubstantiation

The Roman Catholic position is committed to believing that Jesus Christ is Really Present in the bread and wine of the Sacrament. The argument is that the Words of Institution of Jesus (Matthew 26:26–28), when pronounced by a duly-ordained priest, by the Work of the Holy Spirit do *transform* the elements into the Body and Blood of Christ. The elements are no longer bread and wine; their substance has been changed, *transformed* into Christ's Body and Blood. The elements may still look like bread and wine, yet that is just an accident (a non-essential quality). The new substance created in the consecration is really, *substantially* Christ's Body and Blood. This transformation of the elements into the Body and Blood of Christ happens with the Words of Institution regardless of the faith of the recipient (*Catechism of the Catholic Church*, 1373–1377). Even unbelievers receive Christ in the Sacrament (a belief called *manducatio impiorum*). It works by working (*ex opera operato*) (1128).

Two other implications follow from this understanding of the Sacrament. If the faithful are actually receiving Christ when they eat and drink what appears to be bread and wine, they actually receive Christ Bodily; they swallow Him (*manducatio oralis*—eating Christ through the mouth). Another implication is that an Alexandrian Christology is presupposed (see Chapter Three). In order for Christ's Body to be Present everywhere at all the Catholic celebrations of the Mass held all over the world at 11:00 AM Sundays evening Mass in Eastern Europe and early morning Mass West of us, Christ must be omnipresent. But strictly speaking a human body cannot be omnipresent; this is only true of God. No problem, though, if what is said of Jesus' divine nature can be attributed to His human nature. The Omnipresence of His divinity can then be attributed to His humanity (His Body and Blood as well). You need such an Alexandrian Christology in order to teach that Christ is in the consecrated elements.

The miraculous character of Christ's Presence is certainly affirmed by this option, as well as fidelity to The Words of Institution, as Jesus says that "This *is* My Body and that this *is* My Blood." Confidence in Christ's intervention in our lives is affirmed, for no matter what my level of faith Christ comes to me and encounters me on grounds of this teaching. On the down side, this conception seems to undermine the importance of Christian responsibility, for it posits that God comes to me no matter what. Transubstantiation also seems harder to believe; the consecrated elements do not look like Jesus, but more like bread and wine. Of course the resemblance of the consecrated elements to bread and wine are just appearances or accidents, for they are substantially the Body and Blood of Christ according to its proponents (who trade on Aristotle's distinction between substance and accidents). But that concept is not readily understood. Likewise, the idea of the bread and wine actually changing substances is a relatively new idea, not even formally taught in the Catholic Church until the Middle Ages.

Consubstantiation

Another view dating from the Middle Ages (often confused with, but not actually the view of Martin Luther) was this second version of affirming Christ's Real Bodily Presence in The Lord's Supper. Condemned as a heresy it was taught by late Medieval scholar John Duns Scotus (*Opus Oxoniense*) and some by Lollard followers of Pre-Reformer John Wycliffe (The Lollard Conclusions, though the language may be more suggestive of the Heavenly Ascent, see below).

This alternative agrees with Transubstantiation, including all its strengths, except that it does not contend that the bread and wine change substances. Rather, the consecrated element is said to be substantially *both* bread or wine *and* Christ (but not his earthly body). It is like they are half bread or wine and half Christ.

At one level this formula seems to overcome the difficulties associated with Transubstantiation. This model explains how the bread and wine still look like bread and wine. But these consecrated elements seem now to be half bread and wine and half Christ. In short, the elements become hybrid substances. Because the hybrid substance is only half Christ, He is not *fully* Present. This is the main difficulty with this model. The failure of this model to gain acceptance by the Church is also problematic for its credibility.

Real Presence

An older model of understanding the Sacrament and Christ's Real Bodily Presence in the elements of bread and wine was endorsed by most of the theologians of the Church after the era of the Apostolic Fathers in the first and early second centuries (Ignatius of Antioch, Letter To the Smyrneans, 7; Justin Martyr, *First Apology*, 66; Irenaues, *Against Heresies*, 4.XVIIII.4–5). It was the model that even prevailed in the Catholic Church prior to its endorsement of Transubstantiation in the Fourth Lateran Council of the Middle Ages. It continues to be affirmed by all the Eastern Orthodox churches (*The Holy Catechism of Nicolas Bulgaris*, p. 3), and was the view of Martin Luther and still some strands of The Episcopal Church (those segments of the Anglican Communion with a more Anglo-Catholic, High Church orientation). This vision has a lot in common with Consubstantiation (with which it is often confused). But the consecrated bread and wine are not part of a hybrid substance on these grounds. They are fully bread and wine. But Christ is fully *in* them ("in, with, and under").

The Presence of Christ in the elements as posited by this model, as well as in the first two raises interesting possibilities for depicting the communal character of the Sacrament. As Martin Luther articulated it, in The Lord's Supper we receive the Body of Christ, but His Body must also be understood in terms of the Church. In receiving Christ we receive all His Body's members. In short the cares and joys of all Christians become mine when I receive Christ's Body. And in turn, as He takes on my despair and anxiety to comfort me, they are now also borne by all the members of the Body. On such grounds, The Lord's Supper is a rite of mutual support in addition to being strengthened by encountering Christ.

This Real Presence position exhibits the strengths of Transubstantiation and Consubstantiation regarding a literal reading of The Words of Institution and the comfort one has that Christ is Really Present with us regardless of how weak our faith might be. It entails like Transubstantiation an Alexandrian Christology (see the discussion above). It also teaches the *manducatio oralis* and the *manducatio impiorum* (that even the unfaithful receive Christ). But unlike the next two positions, proponents of this view teach that without faith we receive Christ only to our judgment or detriment (1 Corinthians 11:29) ([Lutheran] Formula of Concord, SD VII. 16ff.). In that sense this model seems to embrace the Transubstantiation model's confidence in Christ's intervention in our lives, for no matter what my level of faith Christ comes to me and encounters me. And both of these also attend to the dimension of Christian responsibility, insofar as its proponents contend that those who receive the Sacrament without faith or feeling a need for it receive Christ to their detriment, as judgment. But they are still receiving Christ. Readers need to determine if this is sufficient sensitivity to encouraging practice of the Christian life.

Another problem (or could it be a strength) of this model is that it seems difficult to understand, even defies common sense. How can the consecrated element be two things at once? The alternatives already considered and the Symbolic view that follows seem to make much more sense. The Eastern Orthodox response to such a critique is to appeal to the mystery of faith, those matters we cannot explain highlight that we are dealing with matters of faith (Hebrews 11:1). The Lutheran response is that the very nature of the Incarnation entails that Two can be One—the Person of Jesus is both divine and human at the same time. Sometimes two things can be one in everyday life, like a physical embrace also has love in and with the embrace.

Symbol

As in the case of Baptism, a symbolic view of The Lord's Supper dominates in Protestantism, to some extent for the same reasons (Southern Baptist Convention, Baptist Faith and Message, VII; Church of God in Christ, *Official Manual*, p. 76; Black Methodism tends to interpret The Articles of Religion, XVIII, in a symbolic manner). The bread and wine are said to be symbols of Christ's Body and Blood. Of course this view of the rite makes sense. The consecrated elements look and taste like bread and wine—they must still be bread and wine. And so they symbolize Christ, "remind" us of Him. Paul recalls Jesus' words about the character of the Meal as a "remembrance" (1 Corinthians 11:24). Christ is Present, but only in a spiritual, not a physical way.

The prime advantage of this view is obvious. It is more intellectually credible. Furthermore, since one gets nothing out of the Communion without faith (the *manducatio impiorum* is rejected), emphasis on the role of faith in the Sacrament is affirmed. Without faith, one receives nothing in consuming the elements but bread and wine. Christ is only Present in remembering Him.

The communal character of the Lord's Supper is preserved in this model, but in a different manner than noted in the other Real Presence models. The meal itself is seen as a community experience. For since it is bread and wine (often grape juice since Christians ought not drink many Protestants teach) we eat and drink, this is a meal. And people eat meals together.

An Antiochene Christology is affirmed by this model (see Chapter Three), and the idea of eating Christ through the mouth (*manducatio oralis*] is rejected. These commitments could be deemed either strengths or weaknesses. Again these positions seem more intellectually tenable.

The idea of eating Christ seems cannibalistic and an Antiochene Christology in refusing to designate Mary the Mother of God seems more intellectually palatable. But on the other side, it could be argued that both of these affirmations trade on a dualism indebted to Greek philosophy. Not receiving Christ physically appears to trade on a distinction between the spiritual and the physical, that the finite cannot contain the infinite (*finitum non capax infiniti*]. There seems to be New Testament roots for this commitment (John 3:6; Romans 8:4-6; Galatians 5:16-19). But it could also be argued that such dualism is not in line with Hebraic thinking, which posits a unity of body and spirit and so makes it quite logical to refer to the finite containing the infinite. And likewise this view is characterized by the same strengths and weaknesses pertaining to Antiochene Christology we noted previously in Chapter Three.

Other questions about the Symbolic view include the apparent compromise of the objectivity of grace. We receive nothing unless we believe. But of course, it can be argued that this emphasis on Christian responsibility is a strength. Challenges may also be issued to the way in which Paul's words about remembering Jesus are construed by Protestants (1 Corinthians 11:24).

In Greek thinking, when you remember someone or something, they are not present, but in your mind. Not so in the Hebraic sense of the term (*zakar*). When someone or something is remembered (when stories about them are told), they are present. We see this in Joshua 24 as the people of Israel remember Yahweh and then proceed to engage Him in covenant, in which case He must have been Present in the remembrance. Critics of this view might argue that since Jesus and Paul were Jews, this is what was meant by the reference to remember Jesus, as Promise that He would be Present in the Sacrament. After all, Jesus claims in the Words of Institution that the bread and wine *are* His Body and Blood; nothing is said of them merely *symbolizing* Him. But the American common-sense understanding of the term "remember" seems to favor Symbolic thinking. A Christ Who is spiritually present is easier for the mind to accept than believing that He is Bodily Present.

Seal: The Heavenly Ascent

The same theologians and churches that regarded Baptism as a seal also make this affirmation with regard to the Lord's Supper. It seems like a mediating position between the Symbolic and Real Presence proposals. Unlike the former, this position asserts that Christ is Really Present in the Sacrament. (Its proponents term the rite in this way.)

In contrast to the Real Presence, Transubstantiation, or Consubstantiation models, though, proponents of this view do not believe that Christ is Present Physically in the Communion elements. In this regard this model shares some of the rational credibility associated with the Symbolic vision.

This raises the question of how Christ can be Present in the Sacrament if not in the elements. The image used by John Calvin and which seems presupposed by other proponents of this view is called the "heavenly ascent" (*Institutes*, 4.17.18, 31; this view could be reflected in The Thirty-Nine Articles, XVIII and in The [Methodist] Articles of Religion, 18). The elements when received in faith provide us with access to an ascent to heaven where our souls encounter the heavenly Christ. It is in that context that He is Present. But unlike the first options considered, instead of Christ coming to us on earth in the Communion elements, this model posits that through a miracle of the Holy Spirit we go to Christ.

There is no *manducatio oralis* in this view. The faithful do not receive Christ through their mouths. This view shares with the Symbolic vision an Antiochene Christology. No need to assert that Christ's Body is omnipresent, for He remains in one place, in heaven. And likewise *manducatio impiorum* is not maintained, for if you eat the bread and wine without faith all you get is bread and wine.

THE EUCHARIST
TO SACRIFICE OR NOT TO SACRIFICE?

There are essentially two options on this question, a topic that has historically divided Christians. It is plausible to argue that the idea of The Lord's Supper as a Sacrifice only became a Christian understanding after the ritualizing of Christianity and the development of a priesthood late in the first century (the period of the Apostolic Fathers). But proponents of this view invoke 1 Corinthians 10:18–21 and Malachi 1:11 as authorization for their understanding.

Although allegations have been made that this image of Sacrifice entails that Jesus' Sacrifice on the Cross has not been sufficient, this is not affirmed by the Roman Catholic and Eastern Orthodox Christians traditions. Rather, they argue that the rite is a Sacrifice because Christ, the One true Sacrifice, is Present. However, for Catholics this Sacrifice is also associated with the sacrifice of praise, a sacrifice of the Church (*Catechism of the Catholic Church*, 1368). The risk of this for Protestants is that it could imply that we must add something to Christ's Sacrifice on The Cross.

The typical Protestant response, then, has been a complete rejection of attributing the language of Sacrifice to The Lord's Supper. Hebrews 9:24–27 might be cited in support. This makes sense for proponents of the symbolic view, since on their grounds the one true Sacrifice, Christ, is not Really Present. However Real Presence traditions seem open to speaking with Catholics in describing the Supper as a Sacrifice in the sense that He is Present and that a sacrifice of praise is offered by the faithful (Hebrews 13:15; Apology of The Augsburg Confession, XXIV.126; The Heidelberg Catechism, Q.43).

The position one takes on this question is clearly related to how inclined one is to assert the Real Presence of Christ in the rite. The issue for those who believe the one true Sacrifice is really Present in The Lord's Supper is how convincing arguments for the Biblical roots of the language of Sacrifice in connection with the Supper are and how concerned one is to protect possible threats to the uniqueness of Christ's Sacrifice.

CONFESSION

The primary disagreement about this Sacrament or rite is between Roman Catholicism, the Eastern churches, and those Protestant bodies that practice it. The disagreement is over what is involved in the rite.

Catholic View

Four elements constitute this Sacrament for Roman Catholics—Contrition, Confession, Absolution, and Penance or Satisfaction (*Catechism of the Catholic Church*, 1451–1460). If any are missing, the rite is not valid. First, one must feel remorse about one's sin. Without this, more must be done in order to obtain forgiveness. The second element involves Confession of all sins, even enumerating how many times mortal sins (see Chapter 6) have been committed. Next is Absolution—the Priest's proclamation of forgiveness on God's behalf. Finally Satisfaction is to be offered by the penitent. This is an attempt to remedy the disorders of sin, recovering full spiritual health by making amends for sin, undertaking spiritual tasks assigned by the priest. This fits the Roman Catholic understanding of Justification, which posits a role for works inspired by grace in saving us (see Chapter 8).

Eastern View

In the Eastern Orthodox tradition, all but the first element of the Catholic approach (Contrition) is practiced. But even in the second element, Confession of sins is modified, in the sense that the enumeration of sins is not demanded. Both the Good News of forgiveness (Absolution) and Satisfaction (Ecclesiastical

Discipline, the assigning and executing of tasks to conquer sin) remain in place. This fits the Eastern churches' commitment to understanding salvation as deification, which also includes a role for works in saving us (see Chapter 8).

Lutheran View

Most Protestants have not continued Confession, and never privately with an openness to its Sacramental character, except the Lutheran tradition and to a lesser extent The Episcopal Church. Confession of sins in all Protestant bodies, if done, happens corporately in a general confession.

We focus on the Lutheran version since this tradition alone, among Protestants has, sometimes expressed a willingness to consider this rite a Sacrament. The first and last elements of the Catholic Sacrament are not practiced. Confession in this tradition includes only confession of sins (without enumeration) and Absolution (The Small Catechism, IV.IV.16). This approach eliminates doubts over whether one's Confession is adequate and deserving of Absolution. For the sincerity of one's repentance is not an issue. It is not marred by failure to mention some sins that could otherwise be overlooked. And the Absolution is unconditional, without the need to be supplemented by our response.

These commitments fit the Lutheran and broader Protestant commitment to Justification By Grace Apart from Works of the Law. But on the down side, one could challenge this model of the Sacrament for not taking Christian responsibility seriously enough. There is no place for Satisfaction, which charts a new way of living (in line with the Lutheran teaching of the Spontaneity of Good Works, see Chapter Nine). And not naming all one's sins could be taken as not providing opportunities for penitents truly to "own" their sins (a critique that could also be leveled against the Eastern Orthodox model).

CLOSING THOUGHTS
HOW IMPORTANT IS THE VISIBILITY OF GRACE?

Besides determining which viewpoints have the most Biblical background or roots in the Tradition, what is at stake in the position taken on these rites is linked to the question of the Christology you hold (review again Chapter Three on the difference between Alexandrian Christology and Antiochene Christology). But even more essential in guiding one's conclusion is whether what makes rational sense should guide your thinking (certainly the Symbolic view is strongest on this matter), if you want to stress God's incomprehensibility (in which case deeming the Sacraments as Mysteries and/or as Signs would be your best option), or if you yearn for grace's visibility, want to be assured of God's love, to have it be something you can touch, taste, have in your gut (in which case the Real Presence or Transubstantiation options are the way to go). Sorting out one's position on these issues will go a long way towards sorting out the option/s/ one finds most amenable on this range of issues, and also give insight about what priorities readers' denominations set in ministry.

13

ESCHATOLOGY

The doctrine of Eschatology is concerned with the "last things." It refers to matters related to Christ's Second Coming, when the Kingdom of God will be fully realized. Questions about the status of humans after death also belong to the doctrine.

Some New Testament scholars have argued that Eschatology is the heart of the early Church's Message. It is certainly true that Jesus proclaimed an Eschatological Message (Matthew 4:17). On the basis of His preaching, His earliest followers may have expected the imminent *parousia* (the belief in Christ's immediate Second Coming). When He did not Return immediately it became necessary to establish institutions and ceremonies which would keep this hope alive. The Church, as we have noted, always understood itself as an eschatological community. However, this reconstruction of the history of the early Church, all dimensions of the Christian life, including the Sacraments, spiritual gifts, and life itself must be deemed as conveying the Eschatological expectation.

These beliefs refer to future realities, and may be termed *Future Eschatology*. However another dimension of this doctrine is the belief that the Eschaton has been realized (at least in part)—termed *Realized Eschatology*. This seems to have been more in line with the New Testament witness (see Mark 1:15). We turn to both senses of Eschatology now, distinguishing different options under each.

FUTURE ESCHATOLOGY

This approach to the doctrine interprets references to the Kingdom of God as a reality to come. But differences exist on when and how the Kingdom will come, and what it looks like.

Apocalyptic

To hold this position entails believing that Christ's Second Coming is imminent, and will transpire as a cataclysmic event. It often manifests itself in predictions about the date of *Parousia*. Jesus would have believers to be always ready (Mark 1:15). Among the most famous believers in this commitment have included the founder of the Jehovah's Witnesses, Charles Russell who predicted the End of the World in 1914. Earlier theologians endorsing this viewpoint include Anabaptist Melchior Hofmann, who predicted an end in 1533 after he was imprisoned, and ancient North African theologian Julius Africanus thought the End would come in 800. More recently Jerry Falwell and others predicted the End would come on Jan.1, 2000. Obviously everyone was wrong, but who knows whether some future user of this book might live to experience fulfillment of this prophecy?

Rapture

This eschatological option is closely related to the Apocalypse. It is the belief that the faithful will be returned to heaven without tasting death, as a prelude to Christ's Second Coming. Biblical texts suggesting this concept include Matthew 24:36–44, Luke 17:34–37, Genesis 5:22–24, 1 Thessalonians 4:15–17, and 2 Kings 2:11. Among numerous advocates of this belief include the Assemblies of God (Statement of Fundamental Truths, 14), another Pentecostal church, the Church of God (Cleveland, Tennessee) (Declaration of Faith, 13), and the General Association of Regular Baptists (Articles of Faith, XIX, XVIII). Earlier it had been taught by nineteenth-century American theologian John Nelson Darby, the founder of the Plymouth Brethren ("The Hope of the Church of God," in *Collected Writings*, Vol. 2, p. 563). In view of the Biblical texts noted, it is no surprise that theologically conservative American Fundamentalists gravitate towards this conviction. But even in these circles there may be problems with the belief if one thinks that catastrophic tribulations on earth will not occur prior to the creation of Christ's Millennial Kingdom (see Postmillennialism below), and so there is no need for the faithful to be raptured away from this chaos.

More typically in mainline Protestant, Catholic, and Eastern positions, the Rapture is dismissed as speculation, based on too flimsy Biblical evidence. In addition, insofar as the New Testament speaks of death as the way to life (1 John 3:14; 2 Corinthians 4:11–12; John 5:24), the Rapture appears to conflict with

Biblical testimony. One who is raptured, it seems, has not fully died to sin. Theologians need to decide which set of arguments is most persuasive.

Millennial Speculation

This model related to the belief that at the End of Time there will be a 1000 year period of blessing during which Christ will reign prior to the End of the World. This belief in its different genres is based on a literal reading of Revelation 20. It has ancient theological roots, affirmed in the second century by Justin Martyr (*Dialogue With Trypho*, LXXX). The disagreements on this are over whether to believe in a Millennium or not, and then among the faithful when the Millennium will happen. We turn first to that debate.

Premillennialism

The most influential of all the positions on those believing in the Millennium contends that the Second Coming of Christ will occur *before* His thousand-year reign, a period when peace, justice, and plenty will prevail on earth. This entails that there must be a cataclysm that precedes Christ's Coming. Texts cited in support include Revelation 20; 2 Timothy 3:1; 2 Thessalonians 2:1–8; and Mark 13:3ff. Historically on the American scene this position was related to Dispensationalism (see Chapter One). Some Bible texts refer to the present Dispensation and the evils of our time, others to the Dispensation of works, and others to the Millennial Kingdom to come. Some of the best known proponents include the great American Revivalist Dwight Moody ("The Second Coming of Christ," in *The Best of D. L. Moody*, pp. 193–195), the Assemblies of God (Statement of Fundamental Truths, 14), and the Church of God in Christ (*Official Manual*, pp. 63–64), the General Association of Regular Baptists (Articles of Faith, XIX, XVIII), and most Fundamentalists. This position seems affirmed by the early North African theologian Lactantius (*The Epitome of the Divine Institutes*, LXXII) and could be suggested by his predecessor Tertullian (*Against Marcion*, III.XXV).

The first question regarding this viewpoint is whether its Biblical backing is strong enough and whether it has not exceeded the bounds of speculation. On the other hand, it has captured some Biblical themes and its realism about how things are getting bad and must get worse before Christ comes is a pessimism that may speak to the modern and post-modern world. Premillennialism was in many respects a reaction against the optimism of the next option.

Postmillennialism

This alternative to Premillennialism has a more optimistic outlook. It asserts that Christ's Second Coming will be preceded by the Millennium, and so the more progress we can make in culture, bringing the world to Christ, the sooner the Millennium will be established. There is more optimism and hope in what we can accomplish for Christ with this model in comparison to the resignation about evil times associated with Premillennialism. This model cites Psalm 110 and Isaiah 2:1–4; 10 along with Revelation 20 to make its points. The first Pietist Philip Spener championed something like this view (*Theologische Bedenken*, Vol. 3, pp. 965–966; *Von der Hoffnung zůkunftiger besserer Zeiten*) as well as the nineteenth-century Revivalist Charles G. Finney (*The Oberlin Evangelist* 1 [Aug. 28, 1839]: 147). The early Holiness Movement endorsed this viewpoint and it may have contributed to the support of Abolition in America (A.M. Hills, *Fundamental Christian Theology*, Vol. 2, pp. 339ff.), and to this day one finds a number of Holiness theologians still opting for it, though the Movement as a whole was linked to the typical Fundamentalist and Evangelical Pretmillennialsim.

Once again we must ask whether this viewpoint has satisfactory Biblical backing and whether it has not exceeded the bounds of speculation. The activism that this vision encourages (working to help bring about the Millennium) is certainly commendable. The question to be asked, especially in view of its association with those teaching Perfection, is whether it takes sin seriously enough.

Amillennialism

The majority of mainline Protestant churches (see Philip Melanchthon, The Augsburg Confession, XCII) as well as the Catholic and Eastern traditions reject the idea of a Millennium on grounds of its flimsy evidence. Either they completely ignore the issue as unseemly speculations, or based on a collective reading of Matthew 7:21–23, Luke 17:20–21, and Romans 14:7, they conclude that as the promises made to Israel are realized spiritually or refer to the state of blessedness in eternity so we should understand the Biblical texts cited above spiritually or refer to the state of blessedness in eternity. The unwillingness to engage in speculation about these matters is clearly appealing to some and is perhaps more responsive to the actual intention of the Biblical authors. But for those seeking all the answers, and in view of the Biblical texts cited in support of Millennialism, perhaps this viewpoint falls short.

Soul Sleep at Death until Christ Returns

This model goes against the grain of what a majority of Christians, steeped in a Greek philosophical anthropology, believe. The soul is not really detached from the body as the following options suggest. Because of this unified sense of human beings, it would be problematic to think of a soul separated from the body in death. A glance at the significant number of Biblical texts which refer to death as sleep supports this position (2 Samuel 7:12; 1 Kings 2:10; 11:43; 15:38; 16:20; Luke 8:52; John 11:12). Primary proponents of this view are Martin Luther (most the time, *Lectures On Genesis*, in *Luther's Works*, Vol. 7, p. 296; Vol. 4, p. 313), Reformation-era Anabaptist Michael Servetus, and also the Seventh-Day Adventists.

There is some sound Biblical evidence for this position. But it is not clear how it can address Biblical texts suggesting the dead have an active life in heaven (Luke 16:22ff; Revelation 4–5). The Reformer responds that in the sleep of death the soul experiences visions and discourses of God. The soul sleeps in the bosom of Christ, and He acts as a Mother bringing the infant to a crib. The time flies in this sleep, just as an evening passes in an instant as we sleep soundly (*Lectures On Genesis*, in *Luther's Works*, Vol. 4, p. 313).

Is this a satisfactory alternative to our usual vision of death and how the faithful are swept off to heaven in death? The comfort of the dead living in heaven seems threatened by this model. But is sleeping in the arms of a loved one so bad? We turn now to options that believe the soul is eternal and meets with God in death.

*The Dead Are Judged/Rewarded Based on Works Done with Grace

This model presupposes the view of **Justification by Grace and Works**. This entails, then, that faith will not be alone to ensure salvation. Our works count too, and so this is why a judgment by God must be rendered in or to determine our eternal fate. There are plenty of Biblical texts that seem to support this position (Revelation 6:10; 20:12; Hebrews 10:29–30; 2 Timothy 4:1). Examples of this position are evidenced in all the theological options listed under the Justification By Grace and Works, By Works and Faith, and the Pelagianism options. One of these is the historic Roman Catholic position whose complete commitments are sketched in the next option.

This position opens the door to God making discriminations in heaven. Thus Clement of Alexandria taught that the grades or offices in the Church are imitations of heavenly glory, determined by the worth of one's belief (*Stromata*, VI.XVIII.XIV, see Matthew 19:28, Luke 22:30, and Revelation 3:21 for Biblical authorization). And ancient monk Macarius the Egyptian taught that there are different levels for the faithful in heaven (*The Spiritual Homilies*, 40.3, 6; 17.5–6).

The same strengths and weaknesses stated about the associated positions of Justification of these theologians pertain to this model. Certainly the thought that I might be judged by my works may stimulate Christian responsibility. But on the other hand, if I have to worry about doing works in order to be saved (even if these works are first inspired by grace), then I am not sure about my salvation, and so anxiety can result.

Most Dead Christians Dwell In Purgatory:
Intercession of Saints

This is the model characteristic of the Roman Catholic Church since Pope Gregory I (*Dialogues*, IV.XXXIX; *Catechism of the Catholic Church*, 1030–1032; Ancient African theologian Tertullian (*A Treatise On the Soul*, LV, LVI, LVIII), had earlier spoken of a reality termed "lower regions" which seems similar to Purgatory. Because we are judged by works as well as faith, on Catholic grounds only saints have overcome sin and are qualified for heaven. Texts cited in support of Purgatory include Matthew 12:32, 1 Corinthians 3:15, and 2 Maccabees 12:43–45.

Purgatory is a place only for Christians requiring more purification. It is a place of purifying fire. And through Eucharistic sacrifices, prayers for the dead, requesting the intercession of Mary and the Saints as well as through Indulgences, the process of purification and consolation for the dead and dying can be aided (Matthew 25:21; 2 Kings 2:9; also see *Catechism of the Catholic Church*, 2673–2679, 2682–2684, 2692; John Chrysostom, *Homilies on 1 Corinthians*, 41.5). It should be noted that although the Eastern Orthodox churches do not endorse Purgatory they are open to the deceased in hell being released through such prayers of others (Confession of Dositheus, Ch. 6, Decree 18).

The issue for Protestants and the Eastern churches is that there is not suffi-cient Biblical support for Purgatory. Is that the case? The other problem for Protestants (though not for the Eastern churches) is they are teaching Justifica-tion By Grace or by faith, which entails that all sin is forgiven already through the Word of Christ. Problems and strengths noted in the previous model pertain to this set of beliefs as well.

Those With Faith Are Saved

This is the belief that those with faith are assured of salvation and that in death their souls go to heaven, to be reunited with the body when Christ comes again. It is the view characteristic of most Protestants, as they teach Justification By Grace Through Faith. There is no judgment because on grounds of this mod-el, the Judge is our Savior. Among texts supporting this position seem to be Luke 23:42–43, Romans 5:10; 10:13, 1 Corinthians 1:18, Hebrews 9:27–28, and 1 John 4:17. This mode for Eschatology has all the strengths and weaknesses of those teaching Justification By Grace and By Faith noted in Chapter Eight.

Of course those opting for Soul Sleep At Death Until Christ Comes Again challenge the belief of this model that the souls of the dead who are saved in heaven are alert and have an active life. (See the Biblical texts cited above in the section for this rival model). Readers must determine whether the strengths of the Soul Sleep model outweigh our usual thinking about the active life of souls in heaven, and if so why?

Openness To Salvation To All

This model takes two forms, either unqualified universal salvation or the possibility that all that even the unfaithful may get a second chance to be saved after death. Biblical references to this commitment are provided in Chapter 7 in the "Actuality of Salvation" section as well as in Chapter 8 in the "Single Predes-tination" and "Universal Salvation" section. Also see 1 Peter 3:19 and the passag-es cited above on how prayer requesting the saints to intercede. Since we have already dealt with those who teach all will be saved in Chapter 8 (the *apokatasta-sis*), and those who opted for it will have already addressed the position they want to take on the issues at stake in this chapter, we focus here only on those who believe in a second chance after death.

We have already noted above that the Eastern Orthodox Church is open to the idea that those in hell may be liberated through the intercession of the Church. But based on the 1 Peter text cited above, the idea that the Creed's reference to Christ's Descent into hell indicates that Jesus preached to the dead in hell, gave them another chance, has been taught by Clement of Alexandria (*Stromata*, VI.VI) and by the Catholic Church (*Catechism of the Catholic Church*, 632–635, fitting the idea we noticed in Chapter 1 that practitioners of other religions might still be saved). Martin Luther was a little more vague on this point (*Sermons On the First Epistle of Saint Peter*, in *Luther's Works*, Vol. 30, pp. 114, 113). But he clearly affirmed the hope that God might impart faith to some after death (Letter To Hans von Rechenberg, in *Luther's Works*, Vol. 43, p. 54).

Those emphasizing grace and God's love may find these options most appealing. But is there sufficient Biblical support for them, and do they cheapen the importance of faith and Christian responsibility? How one addresses this matter will say a lot about the overall emphases and tone of one's theology.

REALIZED ESCHATOLOGY

In contrast to considering the Eschaton as only a future reality, this construal interprets the Kingdom of God as a reality at least to some extent Present, and so we are already in the End Times. We have already noted how Mark 1:15 supports this belief. Also consider Matthew 3:2; 4:17; 10:17 and 1 Peter 4:7. Martin Luther and his tradition have been leaders in this affirmation. The first Reformer once claimed that the End is present wherever there is faith or good works are done (The Small Catechism, III.2). Fellow Lutheran Dietrich Bonhoeffer takes this position, claiming the future is present in the sense that who we are is related to how Christ will act on us (*Act and Being*, p. 182). And Rudolf Bultmann also affirmed this (*Jesus Christ and Mythology*, pp. 32ff.). A Realized Eschatology seems to have played an important role in the Black church heritage. Father Divine taught it ("We Shall Have a Righteous Government") and it seems evidenced in Martin Luther King's famed speech in Washington (for his Dream is eschatological) as well as in James Cone (*For My People*, pp. 302ff.) and James Evans (*We Have Been Believers*, pp. 152–153) claiming that the eschatological vision of liberation moves the Black church to ethical action.

Most proponents of this view do not deny Future Eschatology, though Bultmann leaves the question open. One need not choose between this option and Future Eschatology. But the question is whether theologians want us to live with the sense of urgency and a social-ethical imperative that characterizes the belief that we are in the End Times, that the Kingdom of God is at hand.

FINAL REFLECTIONS ON THE END OF TIME

In wrapping up your thinking about Eschatology, the first issue to address is what to make of Realized Eschatology, whether we live in the End Times or not. If we do, what do you make of this commitment? What are its implications for daily life? How important is this insight for your theology as a whole? Would you join the Theology of Hope in interpreting all the doctrines of Christian faith in light of their future, to the point that even Jesus' Resurrection is a future event? If not, why not?

Next consider Future Eschatology: The questions to consider are first, whether you believe in Christ's Second Coming and if so what it will be like. Then consider: (1) Do you believe in eternal life, and if so, how many receive it? (2) Is eternal life only for Christians, and if not, how do unbelievers receive it? (3) Finally, when does eternal life begin? When you die, or later?

Sometimes Christianity is accused of being "other worldly." Keep that accusation in mind in addressing all these issues. We now turn to the "this worldly" side of Christianity—Social Ethics.

14

SOCIAL ETHICS

Because the Church was founded in a colonial context (among people conquered by or at least subject to the Roman Empire), there is little in the New Testament directly related to how the Church should conduct itself in relation to governing authorities. Romans 13:1–7 as well as 1 Peter 2:13–17 and their collective call for Christians to subject themselves to governing authorities come to mind. We also think of Jesus' recorded comments in Mark 12:17 (cf. Matthew 22:21) regarding rendering to Caesar what is his. And then we are reminded of the New Testament's willingness to tolerate slavery (Philemon; 1 Peter 2:18; Ephesians 6:5–8; Colossians 3:22–25) as well as the Pauline and Deutero-Pauline subordination of women to men (1 Corinthians 11:3, 5–6, 8–9.12; 14:34–36; 1 Timothy 2:11–15).

This is not to say that the first Christians were devoid of a social concern. Passion for the poor seems to typify the Church from its origins (Romans 15:25–27; Galatians 2:10; 2 Corinthians 8; James 2:2–6). And this concern for the poor has roots in the Hebraic heritage Christians inherited (Isaiah 58:6–10; Leviticus 25:35–38; Exodus 22:21–23).

Old Testament precedents are also relevant for sorting out Christian attitudes towards government. There are certainly references to the role of faith in God and a just government in the Prophetic admonitions to Israel's rulers. And likewise, we need to keep in mind that all the New Testament Christians were rebels of a sort, defying the Roman Empire in their own way.

The diversity in the Biblical witness on Social Ethics has manifested in a rich diversity among Christian theologians on the relationship between church and state as well as on various social issues to be considered in this chapter. We need to start with church-state relations, because the position a theologian takes on that matter has implications for the social ethical norm with which he or she works in making social ethical judgments.

CHURCH-STATE RELATIONS

Five distinct models have appeared on this issue. We begin with two options that entail the least amount of visible engagement with the state.

Absolute Separation of Church and State

One strand of the Reformation-era Anabaptist Movement (especially Mennonites and Amish) rejects all involvement in the affairs of state. This position tends to emerge from the commitment of these heritages to following the New Testament paradigm as the basis for church life in the present as well as to their pacifism. This entails first of all that just as the New Testament church received no state support, so Christians today should not receive government support. But also since Christians are to be pacifists, not wielding the sword, they must separate from the world and from government, which uses force and coercion to support itself. (Consider how governments defend themselves militarily [with violence] and coerce obedience [force us to pay taxes].) This is not the Christian way (Menno Simons, *Foundations of Christian Doctrine*, II.G; cf. The Dordrecht Confession, XIII–XV).

Jesus' word on rendering to Caesar what is Caesar's (cited above) might offer Biblical justification for this position, as well as the fact that there is no evidence of the first Christians holding political positions. But it could be argued in response that people of God in the Old Testament were Kings. Proponents of this position counter with the claim that we live in a new covenantal era, and that the Old Testament has been superseded.

Critics of this absolute separation of church and state might also reject this model for essentially abdicating the Christian's responsibility to government, which some would consider one of God's good creations. Perhaps that is true, and it could be argued that many segments of American Christianity have de facto opted for this model in joining churches that under the guise of church-state separation do nothing about society's ills. Some proponents of this model do offer as a response that when Christians separate themselves from government dynamics they provide a counter-cultural alternative to the powers that be. The structures of government lose power when they are neglected, and as these structures become increasingly impotent, morality and not coercion may then begin to prevail in the world (John H. Yoder, *The Politics of Jesus*, pp. 151–153, 247–250;

Jim Wallis, *Post-American* [Aug.–Sept., 1975]: 4). But ultimately and realistically, will this model just perpetuate the evils of the status quo? In this connection it is interesting to note that Mennonites influenced American Quakers to condemn slavery—the first American religious body to do so.

Spirituality of the Church

This model has much in common with the preceding viewpoint, but it claims to have more in common with John Calvin's and Martin Luther's views (see below). Again based on Jesus' words about giving Caesar what is Caesar's, proponents of this vision teach that the Church is about spiritual matters and the state about the physical and temporal. As a result, Presbyterians like the forerunner of American Fundamentalism Charles Hodge ("Response To the Spring Resolution," in the 1861 General Assembly of The Presbyterian Church in the USA), Billy Graham's father-in-law L. Nelson Bell (*The Southern Presbyterian Journal* [March 1944]), and Old School Southern Presbyterianism in general maintain that the Church should keep out of politics. Another representative of this position has been the Dutch Reformed Church (South Africa) during the apartheid era (*Human Relations and the South African Scene*). Likewise German Christians who supported Hitler's policies during World War II seem to have opted for something like this viewpoint.

Obviously a problem with this model, like the first, is that it removes Christian involvement in society. And most of its proponents have been very conservative, even reactionary in their politics, even to the point of taking positions that allow for slavery, segregation, and oppression.

Church and State in Paradoxical Tension

This model is subtly distinct but very different from the preceding model, insofar as it more closely relates church and state. It has been called the **Two-Kingdom Ethic** (Martin Luther, *On Temporal Authority*, in *Luther's Works*, Vol. 45) or the **Two Cites Model** (Augustine, *City of God*). At times Martin Luther King opted for this approach ("Letter From a Birmingham Jail"). This view takes very seriously Romans 13, but it can also be combined with previously cited texts such as Isaiah 58:6–10 and James 2:26.

Scripture is not deemed relevant for social ethical decision-making on grounds of this model. But this is not to say that God has not ordained secular government on grounds of this model. God is said to have established the state as part of the created order. And Creation is construed as reflecting the natural law, that it is structured according to the principles of the second part of The Ten Commandments. Consequently, at their best, the institutions built into the created order (marriage, government, economics, and the like) must operate according to the principles of the Law.

The task of the Christian, then, is to ensure that government and other institutions are ruled by the principles of the second half of The Ten Commandments. Where government is unjust it is the Christian's duty to ensure that that justice is served. Christian commitments and the Gospel may motivate Christian engagement in society, but do not provide direct or governing input on government policies. At its best this model leads to an activist Social Ethic. But the politics undertaken is not done in the name of the Gospel or according to Christian principles. To do that would confuse Law and Gospel, and if that happens the Gospel would be compromised. For as we sought to legislate the Gospel it would become a Law, something citizens had to do, thereby compromising the Gospel's character as free and unconditional love.

One way of illustrating this model might be to draw two concentric/overlapping circles: One on the left labeled Kingdom on the Left, Law, or state; the other labeled Kingdom/City of God, Gospel, or Church. The circles are distinct, but not separate (like they would be in the models previously considered). The area in which they overlap might be labeled Christian existence, for a Christian belongs to both realms/circles.

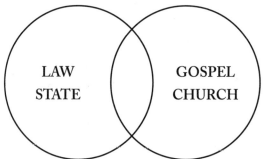

LAW STATE — GOSPEL CHURCH

The last point seems a commendable strength in this model. And it seems compatible with American Constitutional thinking, especially when we consider the links between the Founders' realism about human nature and institutions leading to the separation of powers (*Notes of Debates in the Federal Convention of*

1787, pp. 322–323, 311–312, 233–234, 76–77) which is related to the strong doctrine of human egocentricity in Martin Luther King, Luther, and Augustine (see references in Chapter Six to Sin as Concupiscence). Because government is presided over by sinful, selfish people, we dare not trust it and its policies too much. It will never approximate the Kingdom of God on earth. The best we can do it to try to achieve approximations of justice, never thinking that even the best laws embody perfect justice. This model keeps Christians and all citizens a little cynical and so never satisfied with present politics (lest the policies of the day only be good for those in charge).

Like the American system, this model does not make someone less able to discern political goods because they are not Christian. Of course, it must be noted that the links to the American separation of church and state are not precise. Neither Luther (*Temporal Authority* in *Luther's Works*, Vol. 45, p. 91) nor Augustine (*City of God*, IV.34) regarded government as secular, for in their view it was still under the Rule of God (ruling by the Law).

This vision has been criticized for separating church and state and leading to a reactionary politic, as witnessed by the Lutherans in Germany who caved in to Hitler before and during World War II. However, these Lutherans and some contemporary Lutherans misinterpret the two realms, acting as though they were separate, so that Christians should not engage the political realm like the second model advocates. Is this model, then, able to overcome this abuse and truly engage society inclusively (Christians joining with non-Christians who on these grounds also know the natural law and so what justice is) in seeking justice? A related approach advocated by nineteenth-century Dutch Reformed theologian Abraham Kuyper might rectify this concern. He spoke of "common grace," distinct from "saving grace." Common grace is said to make civil righteousness possible by non-Christians as well as by Christians. Kuyper made this claim in the spirit of the next option of not radically distinguishing church and state, yet insisting on the independence of government in its own sphere (*Common Grace*; *Lectures On Calvinism*, 3).

Christianizing Society

Probably the dominant model in the History of Christian Thought has been the belief that the Gospel and Christian values should dominate in society, that society and the political sphere should be in some sense at least "Christianized."

Among its many advocates include Augustine (sometimes, as we note that he, like Luther and Wesley and Martin Luther King, opted for different positions in different contexts), the Civil Rights Movement at times (also present in Martin Luther King, "The Rising Tide of Racial Consciousness") at times, James Cone (in *Journal of the American Academy of Religion* [December 1985]: 755–756). Others operating in this way include Medieval Scholastic Theology (Thomas Aquinas, *De Regimine Principum*, I.14, though typical of Catholicism, sometimes mixed with appeal to the natural law [see his *Summa Theologica*, I/II.91.3; I/II.95.2]; compare *Unam Sanctam* and Vatican II, *Lumen Gentium*, 36), John Wesley (at times, as in *Thoughts Upon Slavery*, IV.4–5, but he also sometimes appeals to the natural law for his Social Ethic, see his *Of Former Times*, 20), John Calvin and the Reformed heritage (*Institutes.* 4.11.3–4), and the Baptist heritage (Southern Baptist Convention, Baptist Faith and Message, XV, XVII). This model also operates in the liberation perspectives of much Womanist Theology (Delores Williams, *Sisters in the Wilderness*, pp. 164–165, 176–177) and to some extent in Feminist Theology circles (Rosemary R. Ruether, *Sexism and God-Talk*, pp. 18–19).

This model could be illustrated with two circles, this time with a smaller one inside a larger circle, labeling the larger circle Church and Gospel and the smaller circle State and Law.

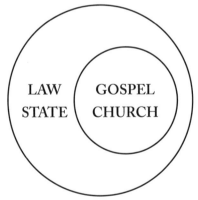

The many Biblical texts cited in the second paragraph of the chapter regarding justice along with the Exodus narrative might be cited in support of this model. Also noteworthy is the theocratic orientation of the ancient Kingdom of Israel. This is a model that seems to assure Christian engagement in society. There is an idealism associated with the model as it endeavors to establish laws that accord with the Kingdom of God and love. On the negative side, this model can be exclusive insofar as it pre-supposes that Christians have better insight than non-Christians about what is good for society, for Christians alone have access to the Gospel by which the state is to be normed. In addition this model also seems to overlook the fact that the first New Testament Christians were not engaged in holding political office. And the model also must address Jesus' words in Mark 12:17.

Identifying Church and State

This model has some similarities to the preceding model, especially when churches are state churches, the official denomination of a geographical region receiving state support as is typical still of some European nations. But while all the previous models are typically Western, this model is characteristic of Eastern Christianity. In the Eastern traditions, church and state are identified. To refer to the diagrams above, it is like there was just one circle with this model, both church and state. This has important implications for how Social Ethics is done.

This way of doing Social Ethics is rooted in a famed early church theologian and Eastern Bishop, John Chrysostom. He reneged on the idea that Christians could or should protest decisions of political authorities. This heritage largely continues to the present, as Eastern churches in Eastern Europe, Asia, and North Africa did not protest against the state in Communist or Muslim states. The Church's job is seen to be as influencing the body like the soul affects the body, sanctifying the community (see Russian Orthodox Church Department for External Relations, III.1, 3; Alexander Schmemann, in *Eastern Orthodox Theology*, pp. 198–199).

Given the fact that both John Chrysostom and the Eastern theological commitment to teaching deification entails that Justification is by both grace and works, it is not surprising that a diversity of norms for Social Ethics appears in this tradition. Most of the time, because church and state are in unity, the primary appeal for political deliberation is the Gospel, for it is seen by many modern Eastern theologians that what Western society most needs is a human link with God like deification affords (Nikolai Berdyaev, *Freedom & the Spirit*; Ecumenical Patriarch, Dimitrios, *Message patriarcal à l'occasion de Noël*). But on the other hand, sometimes this appeal to the Gospel can be combined with an appeal to

Creation and the Law (Ecumenical Patriarch, Dimitrios, *Message patriarcal à l'occasion de Noël*).

The Biblical backing for this model is established by the theocratic orientation of the ancient Kingdom of Israel. But the same potential weaknesses noted in the Christianizing Society model seem to pertain. In addition the patience and occasional passivity resulting from this confidence in the transforming character of deifying grace entails that a lot of suffering and coping with the oppression of the status quo may need to be endured. Is this willingness to cope with the status quo a strength or a weakness of this characteristically Eastern model?

Each of these models for doing Social Ethics is applicable for understanding and addressing pressing social issues today. Keep them in mind as we examine various options that have evolved in some of the pressing social issues of today.

CHRISTIANITY AND RACISM/SLAVERY (AND OTHER FORMS OF OPPRESSION)

What to make of oppression of others by race or ethnicity is certainly an issue that especially continues to plague American and Western society in general, if not worldwide. We consider the two logical options.

Supports Oppression of Ethnic Minorities

The Church has a sad record at points in dealing with oppression of minorities. Employing the models of Christianizing Society and the Spirituality of the Church it has been argued by some that the Gospel entails the censure of Jews and Muslims or that slavery is God's Will. Among proponents of this way of thinking include early Church theologians Ignatius of Antioch who effectively disinherited the Jews in the sense of asserting that Judaism is based on Christianity (*Letter To the Magnesians*, 10.3). Justin Martyr advocated censure of Jews (*First Apology*, 63).

Fourth-century Bishop Ambrose rejected the Roman Emperor's efforts financially to help Jews to rebuild a burned synagogue (*Epistles*, 40.14). Persecution of the Jewish community continued in the Middle Ages by the Catholic Church in the Fourth Lateran Council and then again Martin Luther, angered by his sense of betrayal of earlier advocacy of their civil rights (*That Jesus Christ Was Born a Jew*, in *Luther's Works*, Vol. 45, pp. 199ff.) called for extermination of

Jews (*On the Jews and Their Lies*, in *Luther's Works*, Vol. 47, pp. 137, 174–176, 268–274). Many of Luther's twentieth-century German followers, The so-called German Christians, supported Hitler's policies.

Regarding slavery and later the people of Africa, there are plenty of other instances of oppression. In the early Church Ignatius of Antioch urged that slaves not be set free at public expense (*Letter To Polycarp*, 4.3). (Apparently some Christians in the first century were setting slaves free.) John Chrysostom defended slavery on grounds that the slave is already free (*Homilies On 1 Corinthians*, XIX.5–6) and though Augustine criticized the institution he was willing to allow it to remain in place (*City of God*, XIX.15–16). The Catholic Church sanctioned the practice of African slavery in the Middle Ages as occasioning opportunities to save the lost (Pope Nicholas V, *Dum Diversas* [1452]) as did much of Southern Protestantism prior to the Civil War (see the Spirituality of the Church Model, above, for details). These churches similarly affirmed racial segregation as well as the Dutch Reformed Church (South Africa). Also worthy of note is that John Calvin did not condemn slavery, on grounds that the Bible did not condemn it (*Commentary On Genesis*, 12:5). (But he clearly did not espouse white superiority, as he also states in *Institutes* [4.6.16] that Westerners are less sharp and quick of wit than Asians and Africans.)

Rejection of Islam and Muslims also has roots as early as the eighth century. One finds it in John of Damascus (*Fount of Knowledge*, II), in the Middle Ages in Pope Pius II ("Letter To Mehmed II"), and in modern times in the reflections of Southern Baptist Convention seminary president Albert Mohler (in *Baptist Press* [Oct. 2001]) as well as Jerry Falwell. All these theological reflections teach us a lesson: If you focus on certain Biblical texts reflecting the Biblical era's cultural context, read the New Testament without appreciation of its Jewish roots, and construe the created order in terms of a diversity that is not reconciled, then the theological outcome is likely to favor the oppression of non-Christians and those without a European background.

Rejects Oppression

On the side of justice, the Church has sometimes appealed to the priority of the Gospel and in other cases appeals to the natural law (reason) in order to condemn oppression, and has even worked to end it and establish justice. Gregory of Nyssa is an example of such a theologian rejecting slavery in the early Church

(*Homilies On Ecclesiastes*, 4). St. Patrick took a similar position in the next century, advocating that those servants baptized should be set free (The Letter to Coroticus, 7). In the Middle Ages the Third Lateran Council rejected slavery to the extent that the Bishops taught that baptized slaves must be set free, a position that would cause problems for the slave-owning establishment in America (leading to hesitancy in baptizing slaves). Others working to undermine slavery include Catholic missionary to colonial Latin America Pedro Claver, John Wesley (*Thoughts On Slavery*), and late eighteenth- and early nineteenth-century Anglican Evangelical William Wilberforce. On the American scene early opponents of slavery were the Society of Friends (1688 Germantown Quaker Petition Against Slavery) and the Holiness Movement (Orange Scott, *The Grounds of Secession from the M. E. Church*; Luther Lee, *The Evangelical Pulpit*, 1854–1864).

Of course the African-American church including Martin Luther King ("I Have A Dream"), Father Divine (in *The New Day* [July 9, 1936]: 16), and other leaders like Richard Allen (*The Life Experience and Gospel Labors*) as well as Jermain Loguen (*As Slave and As a Freeman*, pp. 391–394) worked to end segregation and racial injustice. Black Theology has also championed this cause (James Cone, in *Cross Currents* [Summer, 1977]: 150–156). On the international scene champions against racism and injustice have included the Anti-Apartheid Movement (The Belhar Confession; World Alliance of Reformed Churches, Racism in South Africa), crusader for social justice in the Kougo Simon Kimbangu, and even the Roman Catholic Church (Vatican II, *Nostra Aetate*, 5).

Jewish rights were admirably defended by the World War II-era Barmen Declaration. Dietrich Bonhoeffer died while opposing Hitler, and the Norwegian Lutheran Einvind Berggrav staged similar resistance against Hitler and his policies. It is interesting to note that, though critical of Islamic teachings, Martin Luther praised Islamic culture in (*Briefwechsel*, in *Weimaer Ausgabe Briefwechsel*, Vol. 10, p. 162, and *Sermon Against the Turks*, in *Weimar Ausgabe*, Vol. 30[II], p. 189). Regarding slavery he argued that slaves should be encouraged to escape and that a just government will protect the freedmen's life and livelihood (*Lectures On Deuteronomy*, in *Luther's Works*, Vol. 9, pp. 232–233). Though it is uncertain whether his concern for the slaves was actually for African slaves, it is noteworthy that Luther had high praise for ancient African culture (*Lectures On Genesis*, in *Luther's Works*, Vol. 2, p. 305, the kind of praise sometimes though not always offered by John Wesley [*Thoughts Upon Slavery*, II.8–11]. A similar concern for the welfare of freedmen was evidenced in the establishments of schools for the freedmen by Toribio de Mogrovejo a Bishop in colonial South America and the Third Lima Council he convened.

There is a diversity of Social Ethical models employed by these champions of liberation and justice. Some appealed to the Christianizing Society Model. Others relied on the Church and State in Paradoxical Tension. This is a reminder that theologians committed to liberation need to spend a lot of time either on whether their view of Justification entails social engagement and a freedom perspective. And those appealing to the natural law or reason for guiding Social Ethics need to be sure they are thinking about the created order and construing it in such a way that it entails that all human beings are equal and intertwined, that human beings and nature and inextricably linked.

CHRISTIANITY AND ECONOMICS

We now turn to the issue of what Christians make of economics, which systems and policies have been historically endorsed by Christian theologians. We begin with the oldest Christian option.

Share All Property

There is no doubt that collective ownership was practiced in the New Testament church (Acts 4:32–37) and property seems to have been regarded as communal in Hebrew culture (Deuteronomy 24:19–22). Although this viewpoint seems to have waned even in the Biblical era there are some heirs of this position. Sixteenth-century Anabaptist Jacob Hutter and his spiritual heirs, the Hutterian Brethren, still practice community property. Theologians influenced by Karl Marx, notably most Latin American Liberation Theologians (Rubem Alves, *A Theology of Human Hope*, p. 153) and the Presbyterian-Reformed Church in Cuba, Confession of Faith, 3/A, C) reject private property. For some, this image of sharing all resources will suggest an appealing eschatological image of what life should be like. Most of its adherents authorize the position by appeal to Christological and Gospel principles. But the hard question is that if this economic system is God's Will, why did the Church abandon it? Is this a vision that is too idealistic for those living on this side of the Fall into sin? And what is to be made of the Biblical texts seeming to support capitalism, cited below in the Prosperity Gospel section. In addition, all critics of capitalism must deal with the hard fact that wherever in history capitalism has been established as the prevailing economic system, a higher standard of living has flourished.

Preferential Option for the Poor

A somewhat less radical, though clearly counter-cultural model is articulated by those theologians who are critical of capitalism and argue that it is the Will of God that His People, as He has, identify with the poor. Many, but not all who support this position are influenced by or at least attracted to Socialism (an economic system that does not abolish private property like Communism does, but which still would have the means of production owned by society/the workers, coupled with generous safety nets for the poor). Biblical texts that seem to support this position (along with those cited for the previous model) include Exodus 22:21–23, Isaiah 1:10–17, Amos 5:21–24, and Micah 6:8. Among contemporary options affirming this preferential option include Liberation Theology (Gustavo Gutiérrez, in *Frontiers of Theology in Latin America*, pp. 1–4) and Black Theology (James Cone, in *The Christian Century* [Feb. 18, 1981], p. 166).

It should be noted that these theologians do not precisely fit this model since Liberation Theology is more oriented towards Marxism than Socialism and Cone did not clearly break with capitalism. Older options more in line with Socialism or something like it include AME Bishop and social activist Reverdy Ransom ("The Negro and Socialism", in *AME Church Review* [1896-1897]), Walter Rauschenbusch and the Social Gospel (*Theology for the Social Gospel*, pp. 41–42, 142–145), as well as Reinhold Niebuhr ("Liberals and the Marxist Heresy," in *The New Republic* [June 23, 1970]). The Roman Catholic Church since the nineteenth century has aligned with these commitments, especially with organized labor (Leo XIII, *Rerum novarum*). Martin Luther King, Jr, was also an advocate of something like European Socialism (*Where Do We Go From Here: Chaos or Community?*, Ch.5).

Older options include classical Pietism including John Wesley (*Letters*, CCLXX; CCLCCI; *Journal*, 1/4/1785; 6/11/1747) and the Norwegian Pietist Hans-Nielsen Hauge, were concerned with a safety-net for the poor. In fact, Hauge wanted the people, not just the rich, to own the means of production. Also addressing poverty and calling for the redistribution of wealth in the early church included John Chrysostom (*Homilies On the Gospel of Matthew*, 66.3) and Clement of Alexandria (*Instructor*, 2.13).

Challenges posed to the Share All Property Model may pertain to this vision, so consider them. But could it be argued that the Socialist economic related to this model is the golden mean between the first option and the support of capitalism? Besides, is not God on the side of the poor, as He was and is the God of Israel, that community of former slaves?

Identify With the Poor

A less radical position has been taken especially by a number of Catholic monks and nuns who practice poverty, who identify with the poor much like proponents of the previous Model, but who do not necessarily seek to change the structures of society. Jesus' living among the poor seems to justify this Social Ethic (Matthew 11:5; Luke 4:18; 7:22). Some of the first African monks and nuns, notably St. Anthony seem to embody this model. Mendicant Orders (monks and nuns who live by begging) begun in Europe in the Middle Ages (Franciscans and Dominicans) also endorse this model. Especially noteworthy are early African monk Anthony who gave away all his fortune to the poor when taking up the monastic life (Athanasius, *The Life of St. Anthony*, 2) and Catherine of Siena who was famous for caring for the poor and risking her life ministering to the sick (*The Dialogue*, 47). Mother Teresa ("Top 110 Quotes," 47) and Clare of Assisi (*Rule of St. Clare*, VI) also embody this model.

Some may argue against this approach that Jesus does not want us to forfeit all our wealth. It is perhaps why Liberation Theologians committed to identification with the poor do not practice such poverty. We need resources to help the poor, it is argued. But the willingness to sacrifice all we have for God is a compelling ideal, challenging us to wonder whether we truly love God above all things.

Including Identification With Nature

One eminent representative of the Identify With the Poor Model, Medieval monk Francis of Assisi, adds this commitment as well. Living in poverty seems to have made intensified his appreciation of the nature that surrounded him, to love its beauty (*Canticle of Brother Sun*). Francis raises the issue of whether identifying with the poor makes you more ecologically sensitive. Some recent voices in Black Theology are taking positions in line with this thinking as they note how much waste is dumped in impoverished communities (Melanie Harris, in *Reli-*

gious Studies News [March 15, 2013]; James Cone, in *Sojourners* [July 2007]). Those theologians of the West who address ecology almost universally operate with a Church and State in Paradoxical Tension model or combine it with the Christianizing Society Model (Thomas Berry, *The Dream of the Earth*; Wolfhart Pannenberg, *Toward a Theology of Nature*, pp. 15, 134; World Council of Churches, Canberra Assembly: Come Holy Spirit; National Association of Evangelicals, *Environment and Ecology*). The lesson of the history of Christian thought is that to do ecology demands attention to the doctrine of Creation, construing it and the doctrine of human persons as intimately related.

The Compatibility of Faith and Capitalism: Prosperity Gospel

There is a history of the Church embracing capitalism. One could argue that insofar as New Testament Christians did not seek to undermine the Roman Empire and its free-market economy, there is a Biblical basis for the pro-capitalist position. In addition, several Old Testament texts suggest friendliness toward private property and the market (2 Chronicles 9:21–22; Joshua 13–21; Numbers 32:1–42; 33:54; Genesis 13:3; 17:8; Leviticus 25:13ff.). However, insofar as the first Christians were not part of the Roman establishment and the capitalist-like dynamics of its economy, the earliest clear affirmation of the compatibility of Christianity and capitalism or the belief that faith is related to material blessings, does not appear until the Pre-Augustinian North African theologian Lactantius (*The Divine Institutes*, III.XXII; VI.XVII) and in Augustine himself (*Sermones*, 239.4, 5; 86). Subsequently Jerome affirmed private property (Letter To Demetrias, CXXX). But Lactantius and Augustine clearly distanced themselves from an unambiguous endorsement of capitalism. They both condemned the charging of interest on loans, a cornerstone of such an economy.

Much changed with John Calvin. He endorsed the free market in all its aspects, even finding wealth to be a good thing (*Commentary on Exodus* 16:7; 11:2). In that sense he clearly paved the way for the full development of modern capitalism. Calvin even went so far as to describe the Christian life in terms of thrift, strictness, and moderation, commendable characteristics for the capitalist businesses of his Genevan context (*Institutes*, 3.10.1ff.). Calvinist Christians make good business owners and workers. And so the message is given that if you are a Christian you will likely prosper in the capitalist system. Faith assists you in your quest for prosperity. In view of the fact that the Reformed tradition has had the most influence on Protestantism, we can begin to appreciate the origins and what is meant by the phrase "Protestant Work Ethic" developed by sociologist Max Weber (*The Protestant Ethic and the Spirit of Capitalism*). In America and Western Europe virtually every denomination, including Roman Catholicism, embraces capitalism.

Granted Calvin represents a "compassionate capitalism," advocating that Christians share with the poor. In fact, he even claimed that the poor may be more pious than the upper class (*Institutes*, 2.8.46; *Commentary On Isaiah*, 28.14). Not every denomination follows this lead. In America such an appreciation of free-market capitalism stems from Calvin's spiritual heirs, the Puritans, through Billy Graham and earlier Revivalists, and then in the previous century there was Norman Vincent Peale and his "Power of Positive Thinking," Robert Schuller was a later heir of this thinking, that Christianity would have us focus on the positive and then good things follow with hard work. Christianity is the way to prosperity.

In African-American circles, Marcelino de Graca, "Sweet Daddy Grace," promised his followers prosperity, sowing seeds for the explosion of this way of thinking today. Others propounding this message today include Kenneth Hagin (*Godliness Is Profitable*), Kenneth Copeland (*Prosperity: The Choice Is Yours*), Joel Osteen (*Your Best Life Now*), Creflo Dollar (*No More Debt*), and T. D. Jakes (quoted in Shayne Lee, *America's New Preacher*, pp. 110–111). Being a Christian helps you prosper in life. At the very least, proponents of this Model believe Christianity and capitalism are logical partners.

When it comes to Christianity and economics, the crucial issue is first whether you approach the question more with reason and the natural law or with Jesus and the Gospel. You need to sort out which Biblical texts are most instructive, how important is the plight of the poor is for you, and whether or not you think for all its benefits capitalism exploits.

GENDER DISCRIMINATION

We should examine the Church's responses to discrimination against women. Once again there are only two logical options to take on this issue.

Preference for Male Domination: Women Not Ordained

This has been the dominant position in the history of Christian thought. From the late first century until well into the modern era (with a few exceptions) women were not ordained and the patriarchal suppositions of both Western and Eastern societies prevailed in Christian attitudes to society. In Chapter 11 we began to provide the Biblical and historical support for the position that women should not be ordained. The Apostolic Fathers (especially Ignatius of Antioch and Clement of Rome) played a major role in the Church's move in that direction. Despite Jesus' interactions with women and the word of equality in Galatians 3:28, there are many Biblical texts that seem to authorize the marginalization of women (1 Corinthians 11:3, 5–6, 8–9, 12; 14:34–36; 1 Timothy 2:11–15). To this day many theologically conservative churches, including the Southern Baptist Convention, the Church of God in Christ, and The Lutheran Church-Missouri Synod, preclude the ordination of women.

Although precluding Ordination has been largely endorsed by theologians from the time of the early Church through the twentieth century (especially proponents of the Threefold View of Ministry), several strong affirmers of this policy should be noted. They include John Chrysostom (*Of the Priesthood*, II.2; III.9; *Homilies On 1 Corinthians*, XXCI.2, 4–6). While claiming that his wife was his best beloved fellow-servant (*To His Wife*, I.1; II.1), Tertullian regarded women as the devil's gateway (*On the Apparel of Women*, I.I) and insisted they avoid ostentatious attire (*On Prayer*, XX–XXII). John Calvin claimed that women's place was in the home (*Sermon 16 on II Samuel 13:8*). Granted, other times he offered comments that could be taken as precedents for modern developments, claiming that it is merely a practical matter that women were not given ecclesiastical leadership positions or were directed to dress in certain ways (*Institutes*, 4.10.30–31; *Commentary On Mark* 16:1).

The role of Monasticism, a movement originating in ancient North Africa in response to Constantine's establishment of Christianity, has also involved women (sisters). Their leadership in the movement has been a consistent indication of the leadership role exercised by women in the Church (as we consider leaders like Catherine of Siena and Mother Teresa).

Supports Equal Rights

We have previously noted that there seems to be some Biblical precedent for women's leadership in the Church. Certainly today most mainline Protestant denominations opt for this and also for equal rights. Feminist and Womanist Theology have been champions of this commitment as well as of equal rights for women. But there are earlier historical precedents for this theological perspective.

Quakers were early champions of women's leadership and equal rights breaking with customs of male chivalry (Robert Barclay, *Chief Principles of the Christian Religion*, X). John Wesley's use of lay preachers tore down lay-clergy barriers, and some of these preachers were women. Indeed Wesley endorsed this practice in a surreptitious way (Letter To Mrs. Crosby [1761] [1769]). The first woman preacher of the African Methodist Episcopal Church Jarena Lee was certainly in line with Wesley's spirit in advocating for her ordination (*The Life and Religious Experience of Jarena Lee*).

Women were among leaders in the Pentecostal Movement (consider Aimee Semple McPherson, founder of the International Church of the Foursquare Gospel). Leader in the Women's Suffrage Movement Elizabeth Cady Stanton championed not just the woman's right to vote but also her voice in the pulpit, as well as the female perspective in interpreting the Bible (*The Woman's Bible*). Going back several centuries, among the Anabaptist Spiritualists of the sixteenth century and the Montanists of the Church's early centuries, women's ordination and leadership was also practiced.

We observed in the second chapter some ancient precedents for the Feminist and Womanist commitment to affirming the female character of God. One of those teaching this sometimes, Martin Luther, even advocated for women serving in Ministry (in emergencies) (*Concerning the Ministry*, in *Luther's Works*, Vol. 40, p. 23). But on the other hand, the first Reformer also spoke of the distinct nature of women excluding their ordination (*On the Councils and the Church*, in *Luther's Works*, Vol. 41, pp. 154–155).

In earlier centuries we can find some prominent theologians advocating for equal rights for women under the law. These voices include Bishops Basil (Letter To Amphilochius, CLXXXVIIII.9) and Gregory of Nazianzus (*On the Words of the Gospel in Matthew 19:1*, XXXVII.VI). In addition, the translator of the Bible into Latin, Jerome, argued that men had no more special privileges before God than women did (Letter To Oceanus, LXXVII.3). Despite the patriarchy of some Biblical passages, there seems to be enough precedent in the history of Christian thought to challenge Post-Christian Feminist Theologian Mary Daly's decision to give up on Christianity as an irreparably patriarchal religion.

SEXUAL PREFERENCE DISCRIMINATION

Historically there has only been one position in the Church on sexual preference—heterosexual sexual relations within the marriage relationship has been the norm (Exodus 20:14; Deuteronomy 5:18; 1 Corinthians 6:9-10). These commitments were combined, at least since the time of Augustine (*On the Good of Marriage*, 11-12,5) until the advent of romantic love, with the belief that all sexual activity must be open to procreation. (This understanding of sexual activity remains the official position of the Roman Catholic Church [*Catechism of the Catholic Church*, 2363].) We'll start with the historic position, moving to two modern options which have begun to emerge, notably not until the late 20th century.

Homosexuality Is Sinful

When considered literally the Bible seems clearly to condemn homosexuality and homosexual expressions of love (Genesis 19:1-11 [esp. v.5]; Leviticus 18:22; 20:13; Deuteronomy 23:17-18; 1 Kings 4:24; 15:12; 22:46; 2 Kings 23:7; Romans 1:23-27; 1 Corinthians 6:9-10; 1 Timothy 1:10; 2 Peter 2:6-7; Jude 7). Consequently, there is not a lot of theological reflection in the early Church on the subject, but when it does appear it is always with a negative judgment against homosexual and lesbian behavior. Indeed, there is no word in Latin for "homosexuality," though it was common to attribute effeminacy to the homosexual partner. Thus the critiques of effeminacy early in the 2nd century by Polycarp of Smyrna (Epistle To the Philippians, V) and in North Africa in the late 2nd century by Tertullian (*On Modesty*, XV), Clement of Alexandria (*The Instructor*, III.IV; *Stromata*, IV.VIII), as well as later by Cyprian of Carthage (*Treatise*, XII.III.64-66) and Irenaeus (*Against Heresies*, V.XI.1) seem to be condemnations of homosexuality. Such sexual practice was more explicitly condemned by John Chrysostom (*Homilies On Romans*, IV) and Jerome (Letters, LXIX.3). And we have already noted that Augustine rejects all sexual activity which is nonvaginal. These critical attitudes continued through the Middle Ages (Thomas Aquinas,

Summa Theologica, II-II, 154,11), and so at least at times in the writings of the early Protestant Reformers Martin Luther (*Lectures On Genesis*, in *Luther's Works*, Vol.3, p.255) and John Calvin (*Institutes*, 3.24.10) which condemned homosexuality.

The force of these precedents throughout the Church's history has resulted in condemnations of homosexual and lesbian practice by the Roman Catholic Church (*Catechism of the Catholic Church*, 2537), Eastern Orthodoxy (Greek Orthodox Archdiocese of North and South America, "Statements on Moral and Social Concerns"), the Southern Baptist Convention (Constitution, Art,III/1[1], and most Evangelical churches. Until only recently, most mainline Protestant denominations have also held this position.

The dominant theological rationale for this position has been to appeal to the Biblical texts cited above. Continuing proponents of this position typically, though not always, assume a (Dogmatic) Orthodox Method (see Chapter One). If you read these texts without using historical criticism the evidence seems to be on their side. On the other hand, there are some proponents of this position on homosexuality who apply historical criticism to these texts, noting that the New Testament texts cited could be taken as critiquing uncommitted homosexual relations and that many of the Old Testament texts cited above are Holiness Codes for Priests, not incumbent on laity. But they still condemn homosexuality either based on the natural order established by God (appealing to the Natural Law [like the North American Lutheran Church, "Confessions of Faith," The African Methodist Episcopal Church, "Stances of Faiths on LGBTQ Issues," and The Anglican Church of North America, "God's Design for Marriage"]) or at least to the Law of God and the Ten Commandments (like The United Method Church did until recently in its, *Book of Discipline*, 304.3; 806.9). After all, it is argued, given the purpose of sexuality, to propagate the species, it seems that homosexuality could not be natural or God's Will (Genesis 1:28).

Homosexuality and Lesbianism As God's Good Creation

The polar opposite to the historic position is usually articulated by proponents of the Method of Correlation or the Method of Critical Correlation (or some Orthodox Method which employs a critical perspective on Scripture). We have already noted that the Biblical evidence against homosexuality may not be as unambiguous as those condemning homosexuality contend. In response, proponents of this pro-gay position may also argue on grounds of the Christian faith (appealing to Jesus' and the early Christians' welcoming attitude [Matthew 9:9; 15:21-28; Mark 10:21; Galatians 2:10] or to Justification Apart from Works of the Law)—a Christianizing Society Model for Social Ethics. Among those taking this position include modern theologians Anglican theologian Hugh Montefiore (*Christ for Us Today*), Catholic theologian John McNeill (*The Church and the Homosexual*), and Argentinian Liberation Theologian Marcelle Althaus-Reid (*The Queer God*).

Another aspect of this position is that it may challenge the conservative position by citing the American Psychiatric Association's claim in 1968 that homosexuality is not abnormal. More recently researchers have observed that the brains of homosexuals differ from heterosexual brains, having a smaller hypothalamus or possessing a distinct chromosone (Simon LeVay, "A difference in hypothalamic structure between heterosexual and homosexual men," *Science* [30. Aug. 1991]: 1034-1037; Dean Hamer, "A linkage between DNA markers on the X chromosone and male sexual orientation," *Science* [July 16, 1993]: 321-327). Such findings seem to verify the testimony of a number of gays and lesbians contending they were born that way. And so with the Metropolitan Community Churches in the lead, most mainline Protestant denominations have concluded that homosexuality is part of God's good creation.

Supports Equal Rights

A third, middle-ground position insists on the full equality of the homosexual, lesbian, and so calls for equal treatment of all sexual preferences under the law, including full recognition of gay marriage and no discrimination by sexual preference. This is in line with the previous position. However proponents of this option stop short of affirming the "naturalness" or divine sanction of the practice of homosexuality.

How is such a position viable? If seems a contradiction. However, proponents of this viewpoint can do so by opting to do Social Ethics with the Church and State in Paradoxical Tension Model, along with healthy doses of Augustinian realism about our fallen condition.

Thus proponents, following the models that several American mainline Protestant denominations held prior to the gay revolution, could assert that the natural law demands equality for all citizens. (Also see modern American Lutheran Carl Braaten, *The Ten Commandments for Jews, Christians, and Others*; *The Apostolic Imperative*.) In the spirit of Martin Luther, proponents of this view may contend that Biblical injunctions of homosexuality need not apply to the laws of the land (*On Marriage Matters*, in *Luther's Works*, Vol.46, p.291).

But then if homosexuality is not natural, not God's Will (like the Homosexuality Is Sinful alternative), why should sinful behavior be countenanced in society? If you endorse the Augustinian view of Sin As Concupiscence, that we sin in all we do, then the sin of gay sex is no more or less sinful than the sexual intimacy of a happily married heterosexual couple. And so the gay relationship and its parties warrant the same protection as parties to a heterosexual marriage.

This line of thought seems to entail that homosexuality is natural and God's Will, like the previously considered approach. But it would be possible for proponents of the Equal Rights alternative to note with some Scientists, whose basic findings are compatible with the results gleaned by the Human Genome Project, that behavior and sexual dispositions are as much a matter of environment as genetic disposition (Andrea Ganna, Shengru Guo, Brendan Zietsch, et al, "Large-scale GWAS reveals insights into the genetic architecture of same-sex sexual behavior," *Science* [30 Aug 2019]; Francis Collins, *The Language of God*, p.260). Such a position does not negate the claims of some homosexuals and lesbians who contend they always felt gay. Environmental factors are sometimes overwhelming, precluding choice.

But even if these arguments are negated, proponents of the Equal Rights position can argue that just because something is natural it is not necessarily the will of God on this side of the Fall into Sin. This point might be strengthened by appeal to the Biblical accounts which seem to condemn homosexuality. And since environment is such a factor in shaping thought and behavior it can be argued that it is important not to regularize homosexuality in the Church. If we do, the Church might unwittingly nurture those with the genetic homosexual disposition/characteristics to practice homosexuality, when in an environment which norms heterosexual behavior the brain connections in their youth might rearrange the role and impact of the homosexual dispositions in their genetic make-up.

Is this position the perfect middle ground in the debate? Or is it too disorganized, not firm enough in fidelity to Scripture, or not sensitive enough to the gay experience and the Gospel Word of freedom?

CHRISTIANITY AND WAR

Finally we examine the theological options on war and peace, whether Christians can or should participate in military actions.

Advocates Revolution

Despite Jesus' call for peace, there have been Christian theologians advocating revolution and the use of violence to achieve justice. The Revolutionary Anabaptists of the sixteenth century embody these commitments. The Latin American [Catholic] Bishops' Medellín Conference (Justice, Peace and Poverty, Peace, II.19) along with El Salvadoran Catholic Ignacio Ellacuria (*Veinte años de historia en El Salvador*, p. 169) advocate the use of violence in revolution against oppression. Nat Turner, leader of a slave rebellion, and those Black Theologians critiquing the King strategy of nonviolence have taken this position (James Cone, *Black Theology and Black Power*, p. 143). Despite Biblical calls to peace noted below, we see David initiating a revolution against Saul with God's blessing (1 Samuel 21ff.). And from an African-American or Latin American perspective the use of violence is just self-defense, since many in these communities contend that institutional violence is always being perpetrated by the oppressor on the oppressed. A Freedom From the Law, Situational Ethic perspective has not typically been employed by proponents of this Model, but it seems that such an appeal could nicely complement this approach to Social Ethics. Certainly a critical perspective on the Biblical texts cited in support of the next options would be required.

Just War

Augustine and Ambrose were two of the first theologians to embrace this widely-held option (*City of God*, XIX.7; IV.15; *On the Duties of the Clergy*, 1.27, 129, 176). However, there was some precedent even earlier for Christian participation in military actions, as such a position was endorsed by Cyprian of Carthage (*On the Address To Demetrianus*, 20) and Athanasius (*Epistles*, XLVIII). Historian of the Constantinian era, Eusebius of Caesarea, comes even closer to the concept (*Life of Constantine*, 4.56.3). Subsequently Thomas Aquinas further elaborated on the concept in the Middle Ages (*Summa Theologica*, II/II, Q.40). The vast majority of denominations and theologians since Augustine have embraced this concept. There are references in the Old Testament that seem to authorize the faithful's involvement in war (Numbers 31:7; Deuteronomy 25:19; 1 Samuel 15:1–3, 7; 2 Samuel 5:19; 1 Chronicles 14:10; Psalms 144:1).

The concept of the Just War requires some elaboration, as it has been distorted by past American political leaders. The Just War is a war that is not fought for mere purposes of territorial expansion, but is fought only for defensive purposes, only for purposes of peace and not for self-gain (a stipulation added by Aquinas). An individual can never use violence on his or her own behest, just as no nation may use it for the probability of enhancing "national interests." In some modern literature, the Probability of Success and Proportionality have been added as criteria for a Just War. Have the wars America has fought always been just by these standards? They may be useful in addressing today's political realities.

Granted there is some Biblical authorization for this Model, but note the texts advocating Pacifism below. Generally speaking the theologians we have noted address this by appealing to the natural law more than the Gospel and distinct Christian principles. This pattern largely continues for churches today opting for this concept. To be expected, the Church of Norway (a Lutheran body) takes a Church and State in Paradoxical Tension approach (*Kirken og freden*) as did a predecessor of the today's Evangelical Lutheran Church in America (The American Lutheran Church, War, Peace, and Freedom). Even bodies more inclined to a Gospel orientation for authorizing Social Ethics like The United Methodist Church make their point about the justness of some wars by appeal to natural law (Social Principles, VI). Those Christians who make this case from a Christocentric viewpoint, employing distinct Christian themes (like the All Africa Conference of Churches, The Gospel of Reconciliation, and the Christian Reformed Church, Guidelines for Ethical Decisions about War) need to develop these doctrines in such a way as to permit force and violence (perhaps by linking Gospel and Law together) so that there is an element of discipline or coercion associated with God's love (see the discussion of the distinction between Law and Gospel in the first chapter). Besides needing to come to terms with these critiques, its adherents must address whether there is really a significant difference between themselves and the Revolution Model in view of the fact that the oppressed understand themselves as under attack and just defending themselves.

Pacifism

The final option contradicts all of the previous models, arguing for the complete rejection of all war and violence. The use of violence is not Jesus' way or in line with Biblical teaching. Biblical texts cited include Matthew 26:52, John 18:36, 2 Corinthians 10:3–6, and Ephesians 6:12. Of course the historic Peace Churches subscribe to this Model—Amish, Hutterian Brethren, Mennonite Church (The Dordrecht Confession, XIV), Church of the Brethren (Justice and Nonviolence), Seventh-Day Adventists, and the Society of Friends (Declaration of Faith). Among famous modern theologians taking this position include John Howard Yoder (*The Politics of Jesus*, pp. 90ff.) and Stanley Hauerwas (*War and The American Difference*). Certainly there is an attractiveness to this viewpoint in its apparent Biblical fidelity and idealism. But does it work, given the realities of our sinful world? Do we need to defend ourselves and take deliberate action against oppression?

Non-Violence To Coerce Justice

A variation of the preceding model has been maintained by at least two eminent modern theologians who were not passivists in the strict sense, but persuaded that non-violence was always preferable to revolutionary means in achieving domestic agendas. Martin Luther King and his Civil Rights heritage (in *New South* [March, 1958]: 9ff.) as well as Walter Rauschenbusch and the Social Gospel participation in Labor Union strikes (*Christianity and the Social Crisis*, especially p. 287) clearly embodied this perspective. The protests or work stoppages get attention of the establishment and the power brokers and coerce them to change. This is not a pacifism in the sense of being passive, but an active aggressive action.

Perhaps the Pacifist option noted above can have the same effect as this model aims to achieve. But most of its adherents are less politically engaged. And neither King nor Rauschenbusch were philosophically opposed to military actions (though King did not support the Vietnam War). Is this a model that addresses the strengths of the preceding options? Or is it merely a softer, more compromising version of strict pacifism?

CLOSING THOUGHTS

When addressing Social Ethics, the first thing to do is to clarify how church and state are to be related, whether social issues are the business of the Church to address, and if so, the norms to be used in making socio-political judgments (whether the Gospel and distinct Christian teachings or if reason and the natural law should guide deliberations and actions). Then approach the social issue, no matter what it is, with your warrants. If you opt for a Method of Correlation or if employing the natural law and/or reason as your norm, learn all you can about the issue from a scientific and/or social scientific viewpoint. For example if homosexuality or Affirmative Action is the issue, take what you have learned about whether homosexuality is natural, determined by genes, what you have learned about the role of race in educational outcomes and employment statistics as well as social scientific theories as to what determines these outcomes, and then apply those insights to the various pertinent doctrines. Perhaps the doctrinal formulation with which you were already working has insights and guidance for the issue at hand. With that kind of critical thinking, you are ready to do Social Ethics.

CONCLUSION

CONSTRUCTING YOUR OWN THEOLOGY

Having worked through the previous chapters, readers are now ready to formulate their own constructive positions. A careful consideration of each chapter by readers in dialogue with what he/she believes should have been a review for all readers of their own formation in the Church, helped them review what they church has taught them to believe prior to engaging in theological education or reflection. Now with this additional information and exposure to fresh options, the process of formation should have risen to the next level. Now it is time to put it all together, to try to articulate your own theological position. How do the various things you believe on each doctrine relate to each other? What follows are a few suggestions to make this task, formulating our own theology, a little easier.

First, determine if you want to be systematic in your theology. If you do, and operate with a Method of Correlation or Method of Critical Correlation, the philosophy or worldview employed can help you organize your positions on the various doctrines, to help you articulate the various elements of theology in a common conceptuality. If you are more Orthodox in your approach you can still find a way to establish coherence in your faith statement. One option in that connection would be to note your overall concern in Ministry (perhaps something like liberation, Christology, striving for perfection, love, Sanctification, Justification By Grace, Restoring New Testament Practices, appreciating the catholic character of faith). Liberation Theologians, Karl Barth, many Methodists like Kenneth Grider, Lutherans like Regin Prenter, Carl Henry, or John Henry Newman can be cited as examples of each of these options respectively.

If this is an appealing approach, the first thing to do is to review what you have written about each doctrine, seeking a consistent thread, perhaps bringing everything together around the overall emphasis discerned. For example, one who stresses with Martin Luther and Prenter that Justification By Grace is the central doctrine of the faith will seek to ensure that Sanctification is portrayed as God's Work and likewise that the Church is a Work of God. Likely there will no role for a Third Use of the Law in such a theology. In addition a strong doctrine of Sin (perhaps with Sin As Concupiscence) fits this line of thought. Conceptual moves in one's Hermeneutic would need to be made (either with the Law-Gospel distinction or a critical approach to Scripture) in order to deal with Biblical texts teaching or exhorting behavior.

In a similar manner, one who finds the theme of Sanctification central will emphasize that doctrine, perhaps with more emphasis on our responsibility to live the Christian life, and so a Third Use of the Law is likely to be affirmed. Logically there might be a role for works posited in Justification, and if not, certainly less of a strong sense of Sin. Those with a characteristically Baptist concern to restore New Testament practices in their theology will not have an episcopacy in their polity, probably will have a view of the Church as Community of the Faithful along with Believers' Baptism.

Another option for theologians is not to be so concerned with consistency in one's statement of faith. If so, you need to justify this. Is the lack of systematization in your theology a function of the mysterious character of the faith (rather like for Eastern churches there is no particular order of grace and works, but that both must be affirmed)? But if so, how do you know that faith must be a mystery?

Other alternatives for explaining why theology may not be systematically organized include appreciating its dialectical/paradoxical character. Certain readings of Martin Luther, Søren Kierkegaard, and the young Karl Barth exemplify this approach. On these grounds, it is argued that because faith defies reason, polar tensions are held together without resolution—tensions like reason and faith, Scripture and God's Word, history and salvation-history, Law and Gospel, faith and works, or church and state. Another possible reason for not being systematic in your Theology relates to a desire to be pastorally sensitive. This argument is rooted in the supposition that there are numerous situations in Ministry that demand different responses. For this reason you need a theology flexible enough to address these different contexts—one that can comfort the afflicted (by stressing God's love and grace) and also trouble the pompous and the narcissist (by offering a portrait of God as Just [and loving], a strong view of Sin and Providence, and perhaps a Third Use of the Law). Some of my previous books suggest that we can understand Augustine, Martin Luther, and perhaps John Wesley that way (see *The Richness of Augustine*; *Martin Luther's Legacy*; for Wesley, see *The Asbury Theological Journal* [Spring/Fall, 2004]).

One other possible model for handing theological diversity in your thought (which could, but need not necessarily be integrated with the preceding) is the Narrative way. On these grounds, it is noted that the characters in a narrative seem inconsistent but have a unity. Consider how in your life-story you have been both loving and harsh, both bright and dumb at times, and yet there is a narrative consistency in your life. So likewise in the Biblical accounts God has been loving and just, it is proclaimed that we have been saved by grace, but also that we need faith and works, are instructed to rely on both natural law and Christian assumptions in our politics (see my *A Common Sense Theology*, pp. 224–229, for an elaboration of this option).

I close with an invitation. As you construct or formulate your own theology, don't be content to let it just be yours. Theology is indeed a formation process that involves making what belongs to the Church, the formation dynamics it works on her flock, your own. Yes, be creative in your theologizing. But consider the possibility that even the theology you articulate may not be yours after all, that if what you say and write is true, it really belongs to Another, to Christ and His Church. Keeping that insight in mind, remembering that theology is about Christian formation, will keep you more on your toes, committed to doing your best in the preaching, teaching, theological studies, and Christian living that you do.

APPENDIX

DOCTRINAL CHARTS

THEOLOGICAL METHOD

Method of Correlation (employing)

-Greek Philosophy

Justin Martyr

Clement of Alexandria

Origen   Tatian (with qualifications)

Gregory of Nyssa

*Aristotelian Philosophy

Thomas Aquinas

-Romantic Philosophy

Friedrich Schleiermacher

-Existentialism

Paul Tillich   Rudolf Bultmann

Søren Kierkegaard (as interpreted by

Liberal Theology)

-Process Philosophy

John Cobb   Daniel D. Williams

-Psychology or Experience

Georgia Harkness

John Wesley or Pietism

(as interpreted by Liberal Theology)

Boston Personalism

Ruel Howe

-Indigenous Cultures

Accommodationists

Kwame Bediako

African Independent Churches

*Other Religions or Reason Can Lead to Salvation   John Mbiti

Justin Martyr

-Morality

Immanuel Kant   John Locke

Albrecht Ritschl   Adolf von Harnack

Wilhelm Hermann

-Marxism

Latin American Liberation Theologians

-Black Power

James Cone and much Black Theology

*Back Experience

Martin Luther King (as

interpreted by Cone)

-Feminist Ideology

Rosemary Ruether and

most Feminist Theologians

-Womanism

Womanist Theology

-DeConstruction

Post-Colonial Interpreters

-Evolutionary Science

Philip Hefner

Ian Barbour

Ted Peters

Orthodox Method

Dogmatic Orthodoxy   Typically affirms total inerrancy   Clement of Rome and Other

	of Scripture	Apostolic Fathers
		Tertullian
		Fulgentius
		Anselm
		Bonaventure
		Catholic Orthodox Theology (esp. Council of Trent)
		Protestant Orthodox Theology
		Fundamentalism B. B. Warfield
-Limited Inerrancy/ Infallibility	Bible only authoritative on faith and morals. It may contain errors on other issues.	Chicago Statement on Biblical Inerrancy
		Carl Henry
-Presuppositionalism	Theology operates with the presupposition that God exists and infallibly reveals himself.	Abraham Kuyper
		Carl Henry
		Francis Schaeffer
		Lutheran Church-Missouri Synod
-Bible as Culture-Creating Literature, not an historical/scientific text		Biblical Narrative Theology
		John Polkinghorne
-Letter/Spirit distinction (or canon within the canon)	Bible the dead letter until it becomes Word of God by the Spirit and/or is known in faith.	Augustine
		Athanasius
		Martin Luther
		John Calvin
		Philip Spener
		Black Bible-believers
	Affirm that the Bible is a special salvation-history not accessible without faith.	Erlangen Theology
		Karl Barth and Neo-Orthodoxy
		Dietrich Bonhoeffer (interpreted as a Barthian)
	Bible is true even if challenged, based on the internal certainty the faithful have of its truth	John Wesley
-Method of Indirect/ Communication/Theology of the Cross	Reason and Faith in tension.	Letter To Diognetus
		Patrick
		Martin Luther
		Søren Kierkegaard
	Move people through various modes of existence to faith.	
Method of Critical	The Word of God and our	Horace Bushnell
		Story Theology
Correlation	experience/philosophy mutually	Paul Ricoeur

	criticize each other	Gerhard Ebeling
		Karl Rahner
		Bernard Lonergan
		David Tracy
		Constructive Theology
		James Cone
-Theology of Hope	Interpret faith in light of Eschatology	JürgenMoltmann
		Wolfhart Pannenberg
Rationalism or Empiricism	Methods of Correlation which	Justin Martyr
	posit that reason or experience fully	John Mbiti
	reveal Christian truth	Rene Descartes
		John Locke
		G. W. F. Hegel
-Anonymous Christianity		Vatican II
-Secular Christianity		Dietrich Bonhoeffer
		(as interpreted in a liberal way)
God Is Dead		Thomas Altizer

SOURCES OF AUTHORITY

Council of Hippo and Council of Carthage determining Books of the Bible

Scripture and Tradition	Catholic and Eastern churches
(with Apochrypha)	Most Pre-Reformation theologians
	Martin Luther (on occasion)
	Anglo-Catholics
Tradition As	
*Authoritative When in Agreement	Martin Luther
With Scripture	Anglican heritage
	Methodism
*Indefectible When Received by the	Eastern Orthodox Churches
Church Over Time	
(consensus fidelium)	
*Infallible In Conciliar Decisions	Roman Catholic Church
Scripture Alone	Most Protestants
(without Apochrypha)	
Scripture and Reason	Rationalism
	Empiricism
	Unitarian Universalist Church
Experience and Scripture	Montanus

		Thomas Muntzer
		Andreas von Karlstadt
		Sebastian Franck
		Nat Turner
	Inner Light	Quakers
	Dreams and Visions	The African Church of the Holy Spirit
		The Cherubim and Seraphim Church
Quadrilateral	Scripture, Tradition, Reason, Experience	Methodism

HERMENEUTICAL TOOLS OF INTERPRETATION

Dispensationalism	Dividing Scripture into distinct historical eras/covenants	Westminster Confession
		Friedrich Lampe
		John Nelson Darby
		Plymouth Brethren
		Scofield Reference Bible
		Independent Fundamental Churches of America
-Covenant Theology	Dividing Scripture into distinct covenants	Westminster Confession
		Heinrich Bullinger
		Princeton Theology
Law and Gospel	Distinguishing texts in Scripture between demands (Law) and assurances of God's love (Gospel	
-Posit Their Essential Harmony		Most theologians
-Radical Distinction of Law and Gospel		Martin Luther and Lutheran theologians

Uses of the Law

-Three	Political Use (as norm for governing institutions)	Most theologians
	Theological Use (to condemn sin)	
	Third Use (to guide Christian in how to live)	
-Two	Rejects Third Use	Martin Luther and some Lutheran theologians

PROOFS OF GOD'S EXISTENCE

Cosmological Argument	Creation demands conclusion that God exists	Thomas Aquinas
		Tatian
		Basil
		Macrina
Moral Argument	Morality presupposes God a law-giver	Immanuel Kant
		John Henry Newman
		C. S. Lewis
Teleological Argument	Creation must have a purpose, and the purpose must have a source.	Isaac Newton
		Alvin Plantinga
		Intelligent Design Theology
Ontological Argument	Nature of God entails His existence	Anselm
		Bonaventure (along with Cosmological Argument)
		Karl Barth

GOD

RELATION TO THE WORLD

*Transcendent	God not of the world, existing in a dimension beyond space and time	John Calvin Karl Barth
*Immanent	God resides in the world	Paul Tillich Pierre de Chardin
-Pantheism	God identified with world	Baruch Spinoza
*Panentheism	God both transcends the world, but is also identified with it (one with it)	Marius Victorinus Martin Luther Charles Hartshorne Process Theology Wolfhart Pannenberg Augustine
	God a vast ocean and the universe but a sponge dropped into it. The world is in God.	Jürgen Moltmann

NATURE OF GOD

*Just	God will condemn and will strike down the sinner; His justice must be placated if we are to be forgiven	Catholic Scholastics Protestant Orthodoxy Apostolic Fathers John Calvin and Reformed churches Most theologians teaching Satisfaction Theory of Atonement Martin Luther
*Love	God's actions characterized by forgiving love; even wrath serves love	
	Wrath a misperception of God's love	Friedrich Schleiermacher Paul Tillich

GENDER/ ETHNICITY OF GOD

*Father		John Calvin and most theologians

*Mother	Earliest proponents of this model refer to God in both genders	Julian of Norwich Martin Luther Martin Luther King Mary Daly and Feminist Theology Womanist Theology
*Spirit		Origen Christian Science Friedrich Schleiermacher Paul Tillich
*Black		James Cone Henry M. Turner

TRINITY
Council of Nicea; Synod of Alexandria; Council of Constantinople

Affirm Filioque	Tertullian Ambrose Protestant and Catholic churches
Reject Filioque	Council of Constantinople Eastern and Oriental Churches
*Like a three-link chain, each link distinct but indivisible	Basil
*Like different forms of water (a river, its source, its ocean outlet)	Tertullian Athanasius Augustine
*Father and Son relate to each other like the sun to its rays	Tertullian Athanasius Martin Luther
-Like three suns and one light *Like fire passed among three torches	Gregory of Nazianzus Gregory of Nyssa
*God is Three for He acts in Three Ways, yet since these Three actions are in harmony God is One. (God is what He does.)	Karl Barth Gregory of Nyssa Gregory of Nazianzus
*Resembles the three-fold structure of the human mind – the mind, begetting self-knowledge, from which self-love proceeds	Augustine

*Father loves the Son and Holy Spirit the love Who makes
  Them One

                                            Augustine
        Athenagoras
        Catherine of Siena
        Jonathan Edwards

*Father as Mind, Son as Intellect, Spirit Will of God   Augustine
        Martin Luther

*Like tree, comprised of root, trunk, and branches   Augustine

*Father is the Fountain, Son is the Wisdom, and the Spirit   John Calvin
  is the Power of God

*Father, Son, and Spirit are temporary manifestations of   Sabellius/Modalism
  the One God   G. T. Haywood and
        Pentecostal Assemblies
          of the World

-Father, Son, and Spirit symbolize different   Paul Tillich
 responses God makes to three different questions

*The Son is the greatest of all God's creatures, begotten of   Arius
  The Father   Jehovah's Witnesses

*Unitarian   Michael Servetus
        Faustus Socinus
        Unitarian Universalist Church

279

CHRISTOLOGY

Council of Chalcedon

*Alexandrian	Whatever is said of one of Jesus' Natures can be attributed to the other. As Jesus suffers, so does God.	Cyril of Alexandria Origen Athanasius Gregory of Nyssa Martin Luther
*Antiochene	Each attribute of Jesus belongs either to His divine nature or to His humanity. God did not suffer when Jesus did.	Theodore of Mopsuestia John Chrysostom Most Protestants
*Monophysite	Jesus had just One Nature -The One Nature is a compound Substance. -In the One Nature Jesus' humanity Is overcome by His divinity	Clement of Alexandria Eutyches Oriental Orthodoxy (Ethiopian, Coptic, Armenian Jacobite churches) Caspar Schwenkfeld Sons of Grace Sons of Unction
*Nestorianism	The Two Natures of Jesus are united like partners in a good marriage	Nestorius Assyrian Church
*Apollinarianism	Jesus has a human body and a divine soul	
*Docetism	Jesus is divine, but only appears to be human	
*Monothelitism	Jesus has a human body and a divine will	Sergius of Constantinople Maronite Church

*A Great Human Being	A leader in morality	Michael Servetus
		Faustus Socinus
		Immanuel Kant
		John Locke
		Unitarian Universalists
	Superior God-consciousness	Friedrich Schleiermacher
		Paul Tillich

DESCRIBING THE HYPOSTATIC UNION

| * United like body and soul are one | Augustine |
| | Martin Luther |

*Two Natures united like a glowing iron or burning coal	Martin Luther
	Lutheran Formula
A	of Concord
	Origen

| *United like sugar in water | Martin Luther |

| *Jesus is what He does; divine because He does what only God can do, and human because He does what humans do | Karl Barth |

OFFICES OF CHRIST

| Priest | Christ is the Sacrifice for our sin (Proponents often affirm other Offices) | Protestant Orthodox and Catholic Orthodox Theology (and others teaching Satisfaction Theory of Atonement) |

| Prophet | Christ is Critic of our present condition | Martin Luther King Liberation Theology / Black Theology |

| King | Christ is Cosmic Lord, His Being reflects in the structures of existence and so He is giver of all good things. or Rules the cosmos. | Justin Martyr F. Schleiermacher Robert Hood and some African cultures |
| | or Whoever liberates is Jesus Christ | Early Southern U.S. Black Christianity |

or

All that exists concerning God and the
world is revealed in Christ

          Karl Barth

or

As Ruler, all the world needed to return
it to its true allegiance was a visit from
Christ

          Athanasius

CREATION AND PROVIDENCE

*Creation in 7 Days	Literal reading of the Genesis accounts. In modern forms entails total a total denial of Evolution	Ambrose Westminster Confession Second London Confession Protestant Orthodoxy Fundamentalism
	The seven days are not interpreted as 24-hour days	Augustine Martin Luther Francis Schaeffer Carl Henry
*Creation an ongoing Process	Do not read the Creation story literally. In modern forms, interpret Evolution as driven by God; creation still continuing in the daily events of life	Tertullian Origen Martin Luther Process Theology
Gap Creationism	There is a gap between a first creation In Gen 1:1 and the 6 days of creation that follows	Thomas Chalmers Scofield Ref Bible
*Out of Nothing		Most theologians since Clement of Alexandria
*The Result of Rebelliousness in God		Origen
-The Result of The Fall into Sin		Paul Tillich
*Made From Pre-Existent Evil Substances		Marcion Gnosticism
*Essentially Moral	Presuppose the concept of natural law	Augustine Ambrose Scholastic Theology Martin Luther Vatican II Boston Personalism Martin Luther King

Providence: God's Involvement in Everyday Events

*Weak View of Providence	Free will affirmed; God said to be not involved directly in any daily events for we have freedom	Apostolic Fathers Apologists Philip Melanchthon Faustus Socinus 39 Articles John Wesley and Pietism Deism Liberal Theology Georgia Harkness Open Theism

	-Free will and destiny in in tension
	    -God is said to foreknow
	        events
		Kwesi Dickson
		Origen
		Augustine
		Ambrose
		[Mennonite]
		Waterland Confession
		John Smyth

*Sovereign God	All events of life determined by God
	-God compels us to do His bidding
	-God works through our wills
	-God's act and our acts are
	    simultaneous
		John Calvin
		   and
		Reformed churches
		Anselm
		Martin Luther
		(sometimes)
		Daniel Payne
		Gayraud Wilmore
		Jonathan Edwards

	-God permits some evils	Augustine
		  (sometimes)
		John Wesley
		  (sometimes)

*God as Band Leader	Like a band-leader and movie producer, composer, God determines the plot and lures us to behavior, but sometimes mistakes (and evil) mars the way to the outcome	Athanasius Dionysius of Alexandria ProcessTheology Arthur Peacocke
	-God in a struggle with Evil	Martin Luther (sometimes)
*God as Parent Letting Children Play		Francis Collins

HUMAN NATURE

*Employ Greek Philosophy (usually Plato) and its body-soul dualism	Nearly all theologians
-Image of God construed as reason	Christian Science
-Use Aristotle	Thomas Aquinas
*Regard the flesh as evil, so that only the spirit is good, even contending that some do not have soul.	Gnosticism Pre-Civil War Southern Protestantism
*Maintain the dualism with a more relational understanding of the image of God (that we are constituted for fellowship with God or with each other), that we are what we do.	Clement of Alexandria Martin Luther Martin Luther King and Black church traditions Boston Personalism Karl Barth Dietrich Bonhoeffer
-Uses Phenomenology to make these points	Paul Ricoeur Langdon Gilkey
*Human beings as priests of a divine temple, as spectators of God's Work	Lactantius
*Employ Romantic Philosophy	Friedrich Schleirmacher
*Employ Existentialist Philosophy	Rudolf Bultmann Paul Tillich
*Employ Process Philosophy	Process Theology
*Construe God and human beings with a more wholistic and relational understanding in accord with Hebraic and African models of human nature	Karl Barth Dietrich Bonhoeffer John Mbiti Theology of Hope

SIN

Totally Sinful in Everything
We Do, Feel, or Say

Sin usually depicted as a condition of
of selfishness or concupiscence. We
are in bondage to sin; all sins are
equally heinous.

Augustine
Martin Luther
John Calvin

*Structures of Society Mired in Sin

Augustine
Mennonites
Reinhold Niebuhr
Martin Luther King
Liberation Theology

*We Are Inclined To Sin

We are disposed to sin in all we do.
(Concupiscence disposes us to sin,
 is the "tinder" of sin.)
But sometimes it can be avoided as we
make progress in the Christian life.

-Sin Can Only Be
  Avoided With the Help of Grace

Catholic Theology
Southern Baptists
    and most other
Protestant churches

-We Can Choose To Avoid Sin

Clement of Rome
The Didache
Epistle of Barnabas
        John Chrysostom
Athanasius
Quakers

-Temptations Are Not Sin
(at least not as serious as acting on them)

Polycarp
Origen

*Spiritual Sickness
(which diminishes divine likeness)

Eastern churches

*Sin Is a Choice

Pelagius

*The Result of Creation
*Difference in the
Character of Sins

Actualizing potential creates alienation
Distinguish Mortal and Venial Sins

Paul Tillich
Jerome and
Catholic Theology
Nicolas Bulgaris
and some Eastern churches

ATONEMENT

*Classic View	Jesus defeats evil, death, the devil, and sin in the Passion-event	Irenaeus Athanasius Early monks and nuns Martin Luther
*Moral Influence Theory	Jesus' life an example which saves by providing a model to emulate.	Clement of Rome Schleiremacher Immanuel Kant John Locke
-Ministerial Vision	More emphasis on Jesus as an example for right relationships.	Delores Williams
*Satisfaction Theory	Jesus dies to take away the punishment for sin which we deserve (esp. to satisfy God's wrath)	Anselm Thomas Aquinas
-Penal Substitution	More stress placed on a judicial framework to emphasize that Christ paid the penalty for sin.	Reformed churches Augustine (on occasion) Martin Luther (on occasion) Most Protestant churches
*Governmental Theory	Jesus' Passion restores the created order which sin had disrupted; it is not God Who demands punishment of the sinner, but the created order making this demand, contrary to God's Will.	Holiness churches Martin Luther (sometimes)
*Black Easter	The Body and Blood of Christ are assimilated with body and blood of Simon of Cyrene, manifesting God's alliance with Africa.	The Harrist Chruch

What Christ's Saving Work Accomplishes

*Possibility for Salvation	Christ's Work makes it *possible* to be saved, if we accept the offer of salvation.	Apostolic Fathers Pietism Medieval Scholastic and Modern Catholicism
*Actuality of Salvation	Christ's Work puts us in a new situation in which our salvation is assured	Augustine (sometimes) Karl Barth

JUSTIFICATION/ SALVATION

Council of Carthage; Synod of Orange

HOW IT HAPPENS

*By Grace	Salvation is entirely God's work; even faith is a Work of God	Letter To Diognetus
		Augustine
		Catherine of Siena
		Martin Luther
		John Calvin and
		  Reformed churches
		Jansenism/
		Blaise Pascal
		  Particular Baptists
		Karl Barth

*By Faith	You must believe to be saved. (If the Holy Spirit is never given credit as the source of faith, Pelagianism is implied as faith is turned into a work.)	John Wesley Most Pietists Liberal Theology Paul Tillich General Baptists Vatican II

*By Grace and Works	No particular order; they may function simultaneously	Apostolic Fathers
		Most every
		  Pre-Augustinian
		    Theologian
		Advocates of Deification
		  (see below)

A

or

God does His part first (prevenient (grace); you then do yours (earning merits by your works)	Roman Catholic
	  Theology
	Thomas Aquinas
	Augustine (as per
	  Pope Gregory I)
	Ambrose

or

If you do your part (if you tithe, repent, etc.), God will bless you. (If the human response is portrayed as something we do without God's aid,	William Ockham Gabriel Biel Semi-Pelagianism

	Pelagianism is again implied.)	Keswick Movement
*By Works and Faith	Faith saves you, but you must do something with it to be saved.	Synergism Prosperity Gospel
*Pelagianism	We can only be saved if we live righteously/morally, etc.	

WHAT HAPPENS
(What It Means To Be Born Again)

*Forensic Justification	God doesn't regard us as sinners anymore	Letter to Diognetus
(Declared Righteous)	(even though we still are)	Augustine (sometimes) Martin Luther (sometimes) John Calvin and Most Protestants
*Made Righteous (Given New Qualities of Holiness)	We are not the same since being redeemed/ justified (no longer sinners)	Thomas Aquinas Council of Trent Quakers
*Deification/ Theosis	We have been made God-like; references made to the God in you	Clement of Alexandria Irenaeus Origen Athanasius Macrina Gregory of Nyssa Gregory of Nazianzus Nikolai Berdyaev Eastern churches
*Intimate Union (Conformity to Christ)	We are now part of Christ, like the spouse of a beloved husband. We share Jesus' legacy like happily married couples share community property.	Tatian Augustine Catherine of Siena Most Mystics Martin Luther (sometimes)
-God In Us; We Are God		Father Divine Gnosticism

SANCTIFICATION/ CHRISTIAN LIFE

(As Distinct From Being Required for Justification)

*Good Works Spontaneous	Sanctification begins in Justification; good works transpire freely without exhortation. Usually combined with a situational ethic.	Augustine (sometimes) Martin Luther Dietrich Bonhoeffer (sometimes) Some Lutheran churches
-Simultaneously Saint and Sinner	Since we remain in sin in all we do, even our good deeds (for which the Holy Spirit gets all the credit), there is no growth in the Christian life	Lutherans
*Good Works Must Be Exhorted	We must be taught what good works to do (or exhorted to do them) usually with instruction from the Ten Commandments of other Biblical laws	Pre-Augustinians Catholic Church Eastern churches Most Protestants (except Lutherans) Pietists Dietrich Bonhoeffer (sometimes)
-Growth in Grace	Though we are sinners, we can advance in the Christian life by enhanced obedience to the Commandments	Every theologian except Lutherans
Perseverance As Sign of Election		John Calvin and Reformed churches
-Perfection	We may grow in grace to the point of being gifted with perfection (no longer wanting to sin). For some such perfection is a process. For others it is an event which follows salvation/justification and holiness/ sanctification.	Gregory of Nyssa Macarius the Egyptian Hans Denck Philip Spener John Wesley Methodist churches Society of Friends
-As an event		Holiness churches Church of God in Christ

PREDESTINATION/ELECTION/FREE WILL

*Pelagianism	Free will to choose to believe	
*Possibility of Salvation	God offers salvation to all. In believing we are aided by the Holy Spirit.	Apostolic Fathers Pietism Medieval Scholastic and Modern Catholicism

*Arminianism
 	
    -Reprobation by
      divine permission
	God elects people to salvation or damnation based on divine foreknowledge or whether they will come to believe or not	Jacob Arminius
		General Baptists
		Gottschalk of Orbais
		(sometimes)
		Bonaventure

*Double Predestination	God unconditionally gives faith to some, but not to all This gift is given by the Holy Spirit either in violation of the human will or or through the structures of the will.	Augustine (sometimes) Ulrich Zwingli John Calvin Reformed churches Particular Baptists
*Single Predestination	All are elect, but some throw away the gift of faith and salvation (which is already in the hands of everyone)	Lutherans Moravians Anglican 39 Articles National Baptist Convention
*Universal Salvation	All *are* (not just will be) saved	Origen Macrina Gregory of Nyssa John Scotus Erigena Martin Luther (sometimes) Paul Tillich Unitarian Universalists

GRACE AND THE HUMAN WILL
(Work of the Holy Spirit)

*Heteronomy   Grace dominates the will, forcing the will to do what
it must do

*Autonomy   The human will is totally free to do what it
               wishes with grace

*Theonomy   Grace prevails over human autonomy, but works
though the dynamics of the human will
Refers to the position as Theurgy   Radical Orthodoxy
All events are simultaneous for God   Augustine
                                           Martin Luther
                                           John Calvin

MANIFESTATIONS OF THE HOLY SPIRIT

No Tongues   Most Western
                                             Christians

Inner Light   Quakers

Mysticism   The Spirit establishes a direct, unmediated   Francis of Assisi
intimacy with Jesus which is akin to but not   Catherine of Siena
    limited to a marital union.   Bernard
                                              of Clairvaux
                                         Theologia Germanica
                                         Howard Thurman

Montanism   The experience of the Spirit outweighs the   Vita Kimpa
    authority of Scripture and Tradition or at least   Father Divine
    offers new revelatory insights   Josiah Ositelu

Two-Step   Speaking in tongues (Baptism of the Holy Spirit)   Most Charismatics
happens after Justification and Sanctification   Assemblies of God
                                           Church of the
                                         Foursquare Gospel

Three–Step   Justification considered the first work of grace,   Church of God
                                           in Christ
    followed later by entire Sanctification   Church of God
    (perfection). Followed by Baptism of the Holy   (Cleveland, TN)
    Spirit

CHURCH

God's Work, created through Word and Sacrament	Church's holiness not dependent on the holiness of its members	Lutheran churches
		Reformed churches
		Methodist churches
-Also marked by discipline		John Calvin
		John Wesley
-A Sacrament	Also said to be the single goal of humanity	Henri de Lubac
		Cyprian of Carthage
		Vatican II
-Built on the Foundations of an Apostolically-Ordained Ministry	Church's holiness not dependent on the holiness of its members	Ignatius of Antioch
		Cyprian of Carthage
		Roman Catholics
		Eastern churches
		Anglican churches
*Openness to Protestants as separated brethren		Vatican II
*On this foundation, Church is infallible		Roman Catholic Church
*On this foundation, Church is indefectible		Eastern churches
		Martin Luther (sometimes)
*Spirit Unites the Faithful		Church of God in Christ
*Body of the Predestined		John Wycliffe
		Ulrich Zwingli
*House of God with a Lamp-light		Didymus the Blind
*Mother of All Christians	Entails no one is a Christian apart from the Church	Clement of Alexandria
		Cyprian of Carthage
		Augustine
		Martin Luther
		John Calvin
*Culture	Shapes and nurtures Christians like like cultures impose their mores on their citizens	Dietrich Bonhoeffer
		George Lindbeck
		Ethnic churches in cultures in which members are a minority (eg. The Invisible Institution)

*Hospital for Sinners	Entails the Church is only for sinners	Martin Luther
*Exodus Church	A community to pioneer the future of	Theology of Hope
Community for the Future	the world	Edward Schillebeeckx
		Johannes Metz
		Liberation Theology
		Martin Luther King
		and the Black Church
*Community of the Faithful	A fellowship of the born again, community	Menno Simons
	with discipline exercised on the members in	Baptist churches
	order to keep them active and holy	Holiness churches
		Assemblies of God
		Friedrich Schleiermacher
	Membership restricted to those who remain	Novatian
	holy.	Hippolytus
		Amish

POLITY/ MINISTRY

*Threefold View of Ministry	Ministry in the form of Bishops, Priests,and Deacons	Apostolic Fathers Roman Catholic Church Eastern churches To some extent, reflected in every church with Bishops
Apostolic Succession		Roman Catholic Church Eastern churches Anglican churches
Collegiality of the Bishops		Jerome Vatican II
One Bishop the First Among Equals		Eastern churches (designating Bishop of Constantinople in this role) Coptic Church (designating Bishop of Alexandria in this role)
Papal Primacy *Infallible when speaking ex cathedra		Roman Catholic Church Vatican I
Reformed Papacy *Bishop of Rome the Head of the Church by human rite		Lutheran Confessions

Primacy of High Priest		The African Church of the Holy Spirit
Primacy of The Head of the Church		The Kimbanguist Church

*Five-Fold Ministry
  -Pastors/Bishops/Elders; Deacons; Apostles; Prophets; Evangelists — Church of God in Christ / Some in Assemblies of God
  -Pastors; Prophets; Evangelists; Shepherds; Teachers — Celestial Church of Christ / The Cherubim and Seraphim
Church
  -Bishops; Pastors; Disciples; Apostles; Primate — The Church of the Lord (Aladura) Worldwide

*Presbyterian Polity — Presbyters elected to represent the congregations — Presbyterian churches

*Connectional — Congregations subordinate autonomy to a denominational authority whose (somewhat representative) Assembly — Most Protestant churches (even those maintaining an episcopacy)

*Congregational — The congregation has the primary authority in denomination — Baptist churches / Non-denominational churches

*Adiaphora — No polity model has Biblical authorization. The model employed should be the one that works best in furthering the Gospel. — Lutheran churches

NATURE OF PASTORAL AUTHORITY

*Clergy Set Apart To Lead By Exercising Authority Over Laity — Churches employing Apostolic Succession noted above

*Set Apart To Do a Special Job (preaching God's Word or administering the Sacraments while affirming the model that follows) -Prophesy — Martin Luther / John Calvin / Martin Luther King, Jr.

*Set Apart To Lead or facilitate the Flock
  Priesthood of All Believers — Tertullian (with first model) / Ambrose (with first model) / Philip Spener / John Wesley and Pietism / Baptist churches / Society of Friends

Much modern Pastoral Theology
Vatican II (with first model)

*Set Apart As an Example of Christian Living or Due
  To Special Charisma or Secret Knowledge
Confession

Philip Spener
[Baptist] Second London
Society of Friends
Gnostics
Father Divine

*Donatism   Only pure clergy who have not lapsed
                     have a valid Ministry.

SACRAMENTS/ ORDINANCES

HOW MANY

*Seven

| Baptism, The Lord's Supper, Confession, Confirmation, Ordination, Marriage, Extreme Unction | Roman Catholic Church Eastern churches The Cherubim and Seraphim Church |

*One

| Baptism only | The African Church of the Holy Spirit |

*Two

| Baptism, The Lord's Supper | Most Protestant churches |

*Three

Baptism, The Lord's Supper, Confession	Martin Luther
Baptism, The Lord's Supper. Marriage	Harrist Church
	Celestial Church of Christ
Baptism, The Lord's Supper, Feet Washing	Anabaptists
	Some Baptists
	Church of God in Christ

*Four

| | The Kimbanguist Church |
| Baptism, Eucharist, Marriage, Ordination | |

*None

| (though taught as symbolizing events in spiritual life) | Sebastian Franck Quakers |

BAPTISM
Who Is It For

*Anyone

| Even infants may be baptized | Most theologians from Augustine until 16th Century. Most denominations |

*Believers Only

| Administered only to those who have first confessed their faith | Most Pre-Augustinian theologians Anabaptists; Baptists Pentecostals; Holiness churches |

<table>
<tr><td></td><td style="text-align:center">How Administered</td><td></td></tr>
</table>

*Immersion		Anabaptists
		Baptists
		Pentecostals
		Some Holiness churches
*Sprinkling		Other denominations
		(though open to immersion)

What It Accomplishes

*Baptismal Regeneration	Actually born again in Baptism	Pre-Reformation theologians
		Catholic, Eastern, and Lutheran churches
		Anglo-Catholics
*Symbol	The born-again experience transpires independent of (often prior to) Baptism which merely symbolizes this experience.	Anabaptists Most Protestants not listed above and below the African Church of The Holy Spirit
*Seal of Election	Baptism is like a government seal making declaration official. God's eternal electing love for the baptized is made official and visible in Baptism.	John Calvin Anglican/ Reformed churches

THE LORD'S SUPPER

*Symbol	Christ is spiritually Present, but not in the Elements. Like the next two options, rejects the idea of the rite as a Sacrifice.	The Didache Ulrich Zwingli Menno Simons Most Protestants
*Seal	Christ is not in the elements, but is Really Present in the Sacrament. The recipient is brought by the Holy Spirit to Christ Who is in heaven for this encounter with His Presence.	John Calvin Reformed churches Anglican Evangelicals Some Methodists
*Real Presence	Christ is *in* the bread and wine, though the elements remain bread and wine. Recipients actually receive Christ bodily through their mouths. Under some circumstances and qualifications will deem this Sacrament a Sacrifice	Theologians prior to Middle Ages Eastern churches Oriental churches Lutheran churches Anglo-Catholics

	-Celebrated with cake of potato and honey water	The Kimbanguist Church
*Consubstantiation	Christ is in the bread and wine, but after consecration the Communion elements are half bread and half Christ's Body.	Berengarius (incorrectly said to be Luther's view)
*Transubstantiation	Christ is in the bread and wine, but after. consecration they are no longer bread and wine (as their substance has been changed). Also teaches that recipients receive Christ bodily through their mouths and deems the Sacrament a Sacrifice.	Catholic Church

CONFESSION

*Catholic Model	The Sacrament consists of four elements: (1) Contrition; (2) Confession (including enumeration); (3) Absolution; and (4) Satisfaction
*Eastern Model	Consists of only first three elements as necessary, but Confession is without enumeration and Satisfaction or Ecclesiastical Discipline as merely therapeutic.
*Protestant Model	Consists of two elements: (1) General Confession (without enumeration); and (2) Absolution

ESCHATOLOGY

*Future Eschatology	Interpret references to Kingdom of God as a reality to come	
-Apocalyptic	Talk about Christ's Return as a cataclysmic event	

-Rapture	Believe the faithful will be returned to heaven without tasting death as a prelude to the Christ's Second Coming	Assemblies of God
		Church of God
		  (Cleveland, TN)
		General Association of
		  Regular Baptists

-Millennial Speculation		

*Premillennialism	Christ will return prior to a 1000 year period of blessedness during which God will reign on earth	Dwight Moody
		Assemblies of God
		Church of God in Christ
		Church of God
		  (Cleveland, TN)
		Plymouth Brethren
		General Association
		  of Regular Baptists
		Most Fundamentalists

*Postmillennialism	Christ will return after God establishes His 1000 year reign of blessedness prior to the End of time.	Philip Spener Charles Finney Early Holiness Movement
*Amillennialism	Rejection of the teaching of a Millennium	Lutheranism and most mainline churches
-Soul Sleep at death until Christ Returns		Martin Luther Michael Servetus Seventh-Day Adventists
-Soul is eternal and meets God in death		
*The dead are judged (rewarded) judged (rewarded) based on works done with grace		See relevant entries in Justification Charts
*Most dead Christians dwell in Purgatory where remaining sins are purged; Indulgences and the intercession of saints may assist this process		Pope Gregory I Catholic Church
*Those with faith are saved		Most Protestants
*Some openness to salvation of all or that salvation of all or that unfaithful		Martin Luther Clement of Alexandria

	might have a second chance after death	Eastern Orthodoxy See relevant entry in the Justification Charts
*Realized Eschatology	Interpret Kingdom of God as reality at least to some extent present, so that we are already in the End Times. (An urgency about the present and decisions to be made in the present, an appreciation that we are no longer bound by our pasts, characterize this commitment.)	Martin Luther Father Divine Rudolf Bultmann M. L. King James Cone

SOCIAL ETHICS

CHURCH-STATE RELATIONS

*Absolute Separation of Church and State	The Church and Christians need to stay out of politics	Mennonites Amish
*Identification of Church and State	The Church takes no active stands against the state.	John Chrysostom Eastern Christianity
*Spirituality of the Church	The Church has no role in society	Southern Presbyterianism (before the Civil War) Dutch Reformed Church (South Africa)
*Church and State in Paradoxical Tension	We need to get common values (right and wrong) reflected in the laws of the land, not to legislate distinct Christian principles	Martin Luther Augustine
-Appeal To Natural Law To Make Political Judgments		(as interpreted by Luther) Martin Luther King
-Common Grace	More said about independence of the state than paradox.	Abraham Kuyper
*Christianizing Society	This is a Christian nation, and we need to get Christian values legislated	Pope Gregory I Augustine (as interpreted by Catholics) Medieval Scholastics and John Wesley (along with appeal to natural law) John Calvin Reformed churches Martin Luther King Baptist churches Wesleyan/Holiness churches

CHRISTIANITY AND RACISM/SLAVERY
(AND OTHER FORMS OF ETHNIC OPPRESSION)

*Supports Oppression of Ethnic Minorities

Ignatius of Antioch (Judaism said to be
    based on Christianity
Justin Martyr (would censure Jews)
Ambrose (opposed government support of
    Jews)
Martin Luther (late in life)
Catholic Church as well as Southern
        Protestantism in US (supported
        slavery until 19th century)
German Christians (in World War II)
Dutch Reformed Church (South Africa)
Southern US Protestantism prior to 1960

*Rejects Oppression

Gregory of Nyssa
Martin Luther
Third Lima Council
The Black church (Richard Allen, etc.)
John Wesley
Pedro Claver
William Wilberforce
Society of Friends
Holiness Movement
Father Divine
The Barmen Declaration
Dietrich Bonhoeffer
Einvind Berggrav
Vatican II
Simon Kimbangu
Martin Luther King
Black Theology
Anti-Apartheid Movement

CHRISTIANITY AND ECONOMICS

*Share All Property

                                Hutterite Brethren

*Preferential Option   God favors the poor. Critical of the free   Clement of Alexandria
  for the Poor   market, tends to favor managed economies   John Chrysostom
                                                  Martin Luther

		John Wesley
		Hans. N. Hauge
		Walter Rauschenbusch and
		Social Gospel
		Reinhold Niebuhr
		Reverdy Ransom
		Martin Luther King
		Liberation Theology
		Black Theology
*Identify with the Poor		Anthony (and other
		African monks and nuns)
		Mendicant Orders
		Catherine of Siena
		Adolf von Harnack
		Mother Teresa
		Liberation Theology
		Some proponents of Black
		Theology
-Including identification with nature		Francis of Assisi
*Compatibility of Faith and Capitalism		John Calvin
		Puritanism
-Prosperity Gospel	God blesses the faithful with prosperity.	T. D. Jakes
	Presupposes the close link between faith	Joel Osteen
	and capitalism (the free market)	

GENDER DISCRIMINATION

*Preference for Male Domination;	Apostolic Fathers
Women not Ordained	John Chrysostom
	Most churches and theologians
	with a Threefold
	View of Ministry
	Southern Baptist Convention
	Lutheran Church-
	Missouri Synod
	Church of God in Christ
	Most Fundamentalist
	churches

*Supports Equal Rights	Jerome
	Gregory of Nyssa Basil

Feminist Theology
Womanist Theology
Most mainline
        Protestant churches

-Women's Ordination
John Wesley
Society of Friends
Feminist Theology
Womanist Theology
Most mainline
    Protestant churches

SEXUAL PREFERENCE

*Homosexuality As Sin
Clement of Alexandria
Polycarp of Smyrna
Irenaeus
Augustine
Martin Luther
John Calvin
Roman Catholic Church
Eastern Orthodox churches
Southern Baptist Convention
Most Evangelical and
  Fundamentalist churches
Most African churches

*Supports Equal Rights
Metropolitan Community Churches
Most Mainline Protestant churches
in USA and Western Europe

*Homosexuality As Part of God's Good Creation
Metropolitan Community Churches
Hugh Montefiore
John McNeill
Marcelle Althause-Reid
John Spong
Most Mainline Protestant churches

CHRISTIANITY AND WAR

*Advocates Revolution

Thomas Muntzer
Radical Anabaptists
Nat Turner
Catholic Medellin Conference
Ignacio Ellacuria
Black Theology (those
  critiquing nonviolence)

*Just War

Augustine
Ambrose
Most churches

*Pacifism

Mennonites
Amish
Hutterite Brethren
Church of the Brethren
Brethren in Christ Church
Old German Baptist Brethren
Quakers
Seventh-Day Adventists
Church of God (7th Day)
Christadelphian Church

-Non-Violence To Coerce
Justice

Martin Luther King and
  Civil Rights heritage
Walter Rauschenbusch

INDEX
NAMES AND SUBJECTS

Berdyaev, Nikolai, 290
Berengarius of Tours, 300
Berggrav Einvind, 250, 304
Bernard of Clairvaux, 100, 158, 293
Berry, Thomas, 253-254
Biblical Narrative Theology, 7, 24ff.,
  269, 274
Biel, Gabriel, 154, 289
Big Bang Theory, 46, 63, 64, 73-74,
  108
Black Power, 41-42, 53-54
Black Theology, 41-42, 54, 94-95, 128,
  172, 252, 253-254, 262, 282, 304,
  305, 306-307
Boff, Leonardo, 40
Bonaventure, 61, 156, 274, 292
Bonhoeffer, Dietrich, 56-57117, 122,
  168, 169, 170, 190, 238, 274, 275,
  277, 286, 291, 294, 304
Bougastos. Nikolaos, 197
Boston Personalism, 73, 110, 117, 273,
  284, 286
Braaten, Carl, 260-261
Brightman, Edgar, 37, 110, 117
Bulgaris, Nicholas, 181, 197, 212, 222,
  287
Bullinger, Heninrich, 58-59, 276
Bultmann, Rudolf, 33-34, 35, 51, 104,
  119-120, 238-239, 286, 302
Van Buren, Paul, 57
Bushnell, Horace, 53, 274
Capitalism, 254-255
Calvin, John, 21, 27, 71, 73, 83, 94,
  103, 104, 105, 106, 114, 126, 135,
  141, 146, 147, 158, 161, 171-172,
  183, 187, 189-190, 206-207, 208,
  218, 225-226, 243, 246, 249, 254-
  255, 256, 258-259, 274, 278, 280,
  285, 287, 289, 290, 291, 292, 293,
  294, 296, 300, 303, 305
Catherine of Siena, 100, 158, 173, 253,
  278, 280, 289, 290, 293, 305

Catholic Orthodox/Scholastic Theology, 94, 149, 274, 278, 282, 284, 292,
  303
Celibacy, 197
Chalmers, Thomas, 111
Chardon, Pierre Teilhard de, 63-64,
  278
Charismatic Movement, 98, 101, 102,
  104, 106, 175-177, 293
Childs, Brevard, 24-25
Christology, 9, 10, 22-23, 40, 51, 64,
  65, 66-67, 69, 77-79, 80-81, 82-83,
  85-98, 108, 122, 133-142, 152, 162-
  163, 168, 170, 179, 180, 200, 211,
  213, 221, 223, 224, 225, 226-227,
  228-229, 251, 253, 264, 267, 281-
  283
Church, 179-194, 268, 269, 294-295
Claire of Assisi, 253
Claver, Pedro, 250.304
Clement of Alexandria, 30-31, 86-87,
  108, 117, 144, 150, 164, 189, 236,
  238, 252, 258, 281, 284, 286, 294,
  301, 304, 306
Clement of Rome, 7, 20, 21, 69, 112-
  113, 129, 133-134, 140, 144, 150,
  267, 171, 256, 273, 287, 288
Cobb, John, 35-36, 75, 108, 111-112,
  114, 121, 139, 273
Coleman, Johnnie, 153
College of Cardinals, 199
Collegiality of Bishops, 198
Collins, Francis, 48, 115, 261, 285
Common Sense Realism, 17
Communicatio Idiomatum, 91, 92
Comparative Religion, 35, 38-93, 41,
  54-55, 56, 163
Complexity Theory, 47, 63
Conciliarism, 8
Cone James, 41-42, 54, 72, 95, 114,
  125-126, 128, 238, 246, 250, 252,
  253, 262, 273, 275, 279, 302

of the Holy Spirit, 174, 175, 176, 177;
of Infants, 11, 125, 183, 216-217,
218, 298
Confession, 213, 214, 227-228, 300;
Eucharist, 31-32, 91, 211, 220-227,
299-300; Ordination, 206, 207,
213-214
Saints, Cult of, 91, 178, 236
Sanctification, 31-32, 34, 37, 40, 61,
101, 103-104, 123, 154-155, 158,
165, 167-178, 187, 188, 190, 191,
192-193, 208, 228, 267, 291-293
Sanders, Cherryl, 44
Sanders, E. P., 145, 148
Sartre, Jean-Paul, 33
Scientific Method, 48, 62-64
Schaeffer, Francis, 22, 111, 274, 284
Schleiermacher, Friedrich, 7, 32-33, 36,
70, 81, 90, 95, 119, 134, 207, 273,
278, 279, 282, 286, 288, 295
Schillebeeckx., Edward, 191, 295
Schmemann, Alexander, 247
Schmidt, Friedrich, 161
Schuller, Robert, 255
Schwenkfeld, Caspar, 87, 99
Scofield Reference Bible, 111, 276
Scott, Orange, 250
Scotus John Duns, 222, 300
Semi-Pelagianism, 105, 152-153
Sergius of Constantinople, 89, 281
Servetus, Michael, 77, 90, 235, 280,
282, 301
Sexism, 255-258, 305-306
Seymour, W. J., 176
Shepherd of Hermas, 144
Simons, Menno, 148, 162, 171, 192,
295, 299
Sin60-61, 91, 109, 115, 120, 125-132,
134-135, 136, 137, 141, 143, 158,
159, 165, 169-170, 173, 216, 244-
245, 251, 261, 267-268, 287; Age
of Accountability, 129, 132, 216

Smith, Hannah W., 174
Smyth, John, 113, 285
Social Ethics, 36, 40-41, 42, 44, 61, 79,
94-95, 127-128, 145, 191-192, 234,
239, 241-265, 268, 303-307
Social Gospel, 305
Socinus, Faustus, 77, 90, 99, 112-113,
280, 282, 285
Spener, Philip, 158, 173, 207, 234, 274,
291, 296, 301
Spinoza, Benedict, 14, 74, 278
Spong, John, 306
Stanton, Elizabeth C., 257
Stavropoulos, Christoforus, 130, 140,
150, 156
Story Theology, 26, 53, 274
Stott, John, 21-22
Strauss, David, 14
String Theory, 36, 46-47, 73
Sweetser, Thomas, 207
Synergism, 290
Syrotinski, Michael, 45
Tatian, 30, 63, 112-113, 273, 277, 290
Tauler, John, 156
TeSelle, Sallie McFague, 50, 54
Tertullian, 12, 21, 29, 78, 81, 82, 99,
112, 116, 135-136, 150, 198, 258,
274, 279, 284, 296
Theodore of Mopsuestia, 92, 281
Theological Method, 4, 7-64, 103-104,
106, 145, 165, 170, 214, 259, 265,
267, 268-269, 273-277
Theology of Hope, 52-53, 122, 146-
147, 239, 275, 286, 295
Theophilus of Antioch, 110
Toland, John, 113
Thurman, Howard, 100, 293
Tillich, Paul, 34, 35, 57, 70, 72, 74, 76-
77, 90, 95, 109, 119-120, 125-126,
127, 144, 273, 278, 280, 282, 284,
286, 287, 289, 292
Timothy of Alexandria, 129

INDEX
IMPORTANT CHURCH MEETINGS

INDEX
CHURCHES

INDEX
BIBLICAL TEXTS